The Intersection between Intimate Partner Abuse, Technology, and Cybercrime

The Intersection between Intimate Partner Abuse, Technology, and Cybercrime

Examining the Virtual Enemy

Edited by

Jordana N. Navarro

Shelly Clevenger

Catherine D. Marcum

CAROLINA ACADEMIC PRESS

Durham, North Carolina

Copyright © 2016
Carolina Academic Press
All Rights Reserved

Library of Congress Cataloging-in-Publication Data

The intersection between intimate partner abuse, technology, and cybercrime : examining the virtual enemy / edited by Jordana N. Navarro, Shelly Clevenger, and Catherine D. Marcum.
    pages cm
  Includes bibliographical references and index.
  ISBN 978-1-61163-672-7 (alk. paper)
  1. Intimate partner violence. 2. Family violence. 3. Computer sex. 4. Online sexual predators. 5. Computer crimes. 6. Sex abuse crimes. I. Navarro, Jordana N., editor. II. Clevenger, Shelly, editor. III. Marcum, Catherine Davis, 1980- editor.
  HV6626.I5825 2015
  362.82'92--dc23

2015025678

CAROLINA ACADEMIC PRESS
700 Kent Street
Durham, North Carolina 27701
Telephone (919) 489-7486
Fax (919) 493-5668
www.cap-press.com

Printed in Canada

I dedicate this book to my husband, Jaret Navarro, who remains my biggest champion and source of support. I also dedicate this book to our two beautiful boys—Colton James and Jackson Nicholas. May they grow up to be men of courage who join the movement against intimate partner abuse. —J.N.

I dedicate this book to my mother, Kathleen Clevenger, who showed me how to be a strong and independent woman. I also dedicate this book to my husband Josh Apryasz and thank him for all his love and support. Finally, to my daughter Iris who is my inspiration for all things big and small. —S.C.

I dedicate this book to Deanna Walters, a survivor of intimate partner violence and champion for those who have no voice. You are an inspiration to everyone who meets you. —C.M.

Contents

Preface	xi
Acknowledgments	xiii
Editors' Biographies	xv
About the Contributors	xvii

Chapter One · The Relationship between Negative Relationships and Cybercrimes	3
Shelly Clevenger and Catherine D. Marcum	
Introduction	3
Forming Relationships Online	4
Cybercrime	8
Examining the Relationship between Cybercrime and Intimate Partner Abuse	8
References	10

Chapter Two · Exploration of Intimate Partner Abuse	13
Lindsey Blumenstein and Xavier Guadalupe-Diaz	
Introduction	13
Intimate Partner Abuse: A Historical Overview	16
Definitional Issues Surrounding Intimate Partner Abuse	18
Controversies Concerning the Definition of Intimate Partner Abuse	19
Narrow versus Broad Definitions	19
Gender Specific versus Gender Neutral	21
Attempts to Create a Uniform Definition	27
Definitions, Moving Forward	27
Summary of Controversies	28
Contemporary Issues in Intimate Partner Abuse	28
IPA in Same-Sex Relationships	29
Unique Aspects of Same-Sex IPA	30
Summary	32
References	33

Chapter Three · Relationship Formation and Maintenance via the Internet 41
Steven J. Seiler and Brad Ictech
Introduction 41
Romance in the 21st Century 41
    Romantic Relationship Formation and Maintenance in an Internet Era 42
    Romantic Relationships, Online and Connected 48
        Online-to-Offline Relationships 54
        Offline-to-Online Relationships 62
Conclusion 65
References 66

Chapter Four · Theoretical Explanations of Personal Forms of Online Victimization 75
Bradford W. Reyns, Billy Henson, and Thomas J. Holt
Introduction 75
Theories of Online Victimization 76
    The Opportunity Perspective 76
    The General Theory of Crime 78
The Theoretical Importance of Gender and the Victim-Offender Relationship 80
    Mediation Processes and Victimization 80
    Moderation Processes and Victimization 82
    Mediation and Moderation in the Cybercrime Victimization Research 84
An Example Using Original Data 86
    Results 87
Conclusion 90
References 92

Chapter Five · The Rise of the "Virtual Predator": Technology and the Expanding Reach of Intimate Partner Abuse 95
Denise N. Crisafi, Alyssa R. Mullins, and Jana L. Jasinski
Introduction 95
Changing Landscapes: How Technology Has Reinforced and Shifted Our Knowledge of Intimate Partner Abuse 97
    Defining Intimate Partner Abuse 97
    Coercive Control in an Offline Environment 99
    Coercive Control in an Online Environment 100

Exploring the Current State of Cyberabuses and Intimate Partner
   Violence Perpetration   103
   Theoretical Constructs for Understanding Online Intimate
      Partner Abuse   103
   Social Networking Sites   105
Spyware and Global Positioning Systems   108
Nonconsensual Pornography   110
Telephones and Texting   112
Online Abuse vs. Offline Abuse: Fundamental Similarities
   or Differences?   112
Conclusion   114
References   115

Chapter Six · Cyberabuse and Cyberstalking   125
Jordana N. Navarro
Introduction   125
   Abuse and Coercive Control   125
   Methods and Tactics Utilized by Perpetrators to Engage
      in Cyberabuse and Cyberstalking   127
      Low-Tech Methods   127
      High-Tech Methods   128
      Cyberabuse as a Form of Coercive Control   129
      Cyberstalking   133
Conclusion   136
References   136

**Chapter Seven · Sexting, Sextortion, and Other Internet
   Sexual Offenses**   141
Reneè D. Lamphere and Kweilin T. Pikciunas
Introduction   141
Sexting   141
   What Is Sexting?   141
   Prevalence of Youth Sexting   143
   Female vs. Male Sexting   144
   The Legal Consequences of Sexting   145
Revenge Porn   147
   History of Revenge Porn   148
      Criminalization of Revenge Porn   149
Sextortion   149
   Criminalizing Sextortion   151

Online Dating/Romance Scams ... 152
"Catfishing": The New Face of the Online Dating/Romance Scam ... 154
Conclusions ... 155
References ... 156

Chapter Eight · Policing Initiatives and Limitations ... 167
Debarati Halder and K. Jaishankar

Introduction ... 167
Profiles of Interpersonal Cybercrimes and Types of Policing ... 170
    Profile of Interpersonal Cybercrimes ... 170
What Policing May Be Offered and the Challenges Involved in It ... 175
Conclusion ... 181
References ... 182

Chapter Nine · Legislative Reactions ... 187
Thaddeus Hoffmeister

Introduction ... 187
Impersonation ... 188
Threats ... 192
Stalking ... 194
Revenge Porn ... 196
References ... 201

Chapter Ten · Future Directions ... 205
Shelly Clevenger

Prevention ... 205
    Law Enforcement ... 205
    Individuals ... 207
        Youth ... 210
    Corporate Efforts ... 211
        Offenders ... 212
Legislation ... 214
References ... 216

Conclusion ... 219
Index ... 221

Preface

In today's world, communication, socialization, and relationship formation are fostered on the multiple availabilities of technology. Texting, instant messaging, and tweeting have all but replaced the United States mail system and conversations on the telephone. Serious relationships and commitments are made between individuals who have never physically met. However, technology has also given predators additional methods of manipulation and violation, as well as allowed significant others to stalk, threaten, and harass those who are most vulnerable. Intimate partner violence has expanded from the home to a world where millions can view and participate in victimization, or silently watch and ignore the mounting evidence that someone is likely to be seriously harmed.

The purpose of this edited book is to present how technology, while beneficial in so many ways, has become a hated enemy for so many victims of intimate partner violence. Research from scholars in the academic field, as well as government studies, statutes, and other material were gathered and summarized in this text. Key concepts, statistics and legislative histories are discussed in every chapter. It is the desire of the author to educate and enlighten a wide audience, from those who are completely unfamiliar with the topic as an entirety to individuals who need more specific information on the link between technology and violation. This text should be a useful guide to students, academics, and practitioners alike.

Acknowledgments

Thank you to Beth Hall and the staff at Carolina Academic Press for their assistance and patience with the preparation of this manuscript. It was wonderful to work with a group of individuals who shared the same vision for this book. We hope it is a great success.

Editors' Biographies

Jordana N. Navarro is an assistant professor of sociology in the Department of Sociology and Political Science at Tennessee Technological University. Her research interests include cyber-victimization and domestic violence. Her current research focuses on the prevalence and underreporting of domestic violence on college campuses.

Shelly Clevenger is an assistant professor of criminal justice at Illinois State University. Her areas of research include sexual offenses, sexual victimization and victimology. She has published journal articles as well as book chapters and has forthcoming publications on the impact of sexual assault on the family.

Catherine D. Marcum is an associate professor of criminal justice at Appalachian State University, as well as the Criminal Justice Curriculum Coordinator. Her areas of research are cybercrime, correctional issues, and sexual victimization. She has published numerous articles in various criminal justice and other social science journals, as well as authored and edited multiple scholastic books.

About the Contributors

Lindsey Blumenstein is an assistant professor of justice in the Justice Center at the University of Alaska Anchorage, where she has served as a member of the Justice Center faculty since the fall of 2014. Dr. Blumenstein's current research focuses on intimate partner violence, substance abuse, consequences of domestic violence victimization, and intimate partner violence and sexual assault among college populations. Her research has been published in a number of criminology and domestic violence journals, including *Violence and Victims, Partner Abuse,* the *Journal of Drug Issues,* and *Criminal Justice Studies.*

Denise Crisafi is a doctoral student in the Department of Sociology at the University of Central Florida. Her research interests are in the areas of interpersonal violence, criminal justice responses, policies toward intimate partner violence, and prevention program design, implementation, and evaluation. Her dissertation evaluates the efficacy of state-level Stand Your Ground laws on intimate partner violence court cases.

Xavier Guadalupe-Diaz is an assistant professor of sociology in the Department of Sociology at Framingham State University. His research focuses on intimate partner violence within the lesbian, gay, bisexual, transgender, and queer (LGBTQ) community. Currently, his work is focused on identity and transgender IPV victimization.

Debarati Halder is an advocate and legal researcher. She is the managing director of the Centre for Cyber Victim Counselling (CCVC) (www.cybervictims.org), India. She received her LLB from the University of Calcutta and her master's degree in international and constitutional law from the University of Madras. She holds a PhD degree from the National Law School of India University (NLSIU), Bangalore, India. She has published many articles in peer-reviewed journals such as British Journal of Criminology and several chapters in peer-reviewed books. She has also co-authored a book titled *Cyber Crime and the Victimization of Women: Laws, Rights and Regulations* (IGI Global, 2012). She has presented her research works at many international conferences, including the Stockholm Criminology Symposium held during June 11–13, 2012.

Billy Henson is an assistant professor in the Department of Criminal Justice at Shippensburg University. His research interests include fear of crime, cybercrime victimization, interpersonal victimization, and criminology theory. He has research studies appearing in *Victims and Offenders, Criminal Justice and Behavior, Violence and Victims,* and the *Journal of Interpersonal Victimization.* He also co-authored the book *Fear of Crime in the United States: Causes, Contradictions, and Consequences* (Carolina Academic Press, 2014).

Thaddeus Hoffmeister serves as associate dean for academic affairs and professor of law at the University of Dayton School of Law (UDSL). As associate dean, he determines the curriculum and class schedule, counsels students regarding classes, and oversees the academic functions and general administration of the School of Law. As a professor of law, he teaches courses related to criminal law, technology, and the jury. He also directs the UDSL Criminal Law Clinic where his students represent indigent clients charged with criminal offenses. Prior to joining UDSL, Dean Hoffmeister worked on Capitol Hill, clerked for a federal judge, and served in the military.

Thomas J. Holt is an associate professor in the School of Criminal Justice at Michigan State University specializing in computer crime, cybercrime, and technology. His research focuses on computer hacking, malware, and the role that technology and the Internet play in facilitating all manner of crime and deviance. He has been published in various scholarly journals, including *The British Journal of Criminology, Crime and Delinquency, Deviant Behavior,* and the *Journal of Criminal Justice.*

Brad Ictech is a social psychologist interested in how social technologies affect self and society. His current research projects focus on the influence of digital cross talk on presentation of self and relationship formation through computer-mediated communication mediums. He is currently a sociology doctoral student at Louisiana State University.

K. Jaishankar is a senior assistant professor in the Department of Criminology and Criminal Justice at Manonmaniam Sundaranar University in Tirunelveli, Tamil Nadu, India. He is the founding editor-in-chief of the *International Journal of Cyber Criminology* and editor-in-chief of the *International Journal of Criminal Justice Sciences.* He is the founding president of the South Asian Society of Criminology and Victimology (SASCV) and founding executive director of the Centre for Cyber Victim Counselling (CCVC). He has published more than 101 publications, including articles, books, book chapters and editorials. He is the recipient of the prestigious "National Academy of Sciences, India (NASI)—SCOPUS Young Scientist Award 2012—Social Sciences." He was a Commonwealth Fellow (2009–2010) at the Centre for Criminal Justice Studies, School of Law, University of Leeds, UK. He pioneered the development of the new field of cyber criminology and is the proponent of the space transition theory of cyber crimes. His areas of academic competence are cyber criminology, victimology, crime mapping, GIS, communal violence, policing, and crime prevention.

Jana L. Jasinski is a professor of sociology and associate dean in the College of Graduate Studies at the University of Central Florida. Her research interests are in the areas of lethal and non-lethal interpersonal violence with an emphasis on intimate partner violence, substance abuse, and institutional responses to violence.

Reneè D. Lamphere is an assistant professor of criminal justice in the Department of Sociology and Criminal Justice at the University of North Carolina at Pembroke. Her areas of academic interest include corrections, juvenile delinquency, digital media crime, and mixed-methods research.

Alyssa Mullins is a doctoral student in the Department of Sociology at the University of Central Florida. Her research interests include intimate relationships, family life, and media and consumer culture. Her current research focuses on the use of technology for personal safety on college campuses, and experiences of voluntary childlessness in social arenas.

Kweilin Pikciunas is a doctoral candidate in the Department of Criminology and Criminal Justice at Indiana University of Pennsylvania. Her research interests include cyber-victimization, media crimes, and female offenders. Her current research focuses on the prevalence of cyber-bullying on college campuses.

Brad Reyns is an assistant professor in the Department of Criminal Justice at Weber State University. His research interests span the field of victimology, but his recent research has focused on victimological theory, stalking victimization, and cybercrime victimization.

Steven J. Seiler is an assistant professor of sociology in the Department of Sociology and Political Science at Tennessee Technological University. As a social psychologist, his research focuses primarily on the impact of the Internet and mobile phones on social life, generally, and on the self, identities, and personal relationships, specifically.

The Intersection between Intimate Partner Abuse, Technology, and Cybercrime

Chapter One

The Relationship between Negative Relationships and Cybercrimes

Shelly Clevenger and Catherine D. Marcum

Introduction

The Internet is a place of limitless opportunity and lightning-fast efficiency. Communication that may have taken days or had a hefty price tag now occurs within seconds for free. The majority of American homes have Internet access, generally in multiple forms, and it is prevalent around the world. However, while difficult for us to imagine a life without the ability to look up information online within seconds, it has only been a mainstay in American homes since the early 1990s.

J.C.R. Licklider, employee of the Massachusetts Institute of Technology (MIT), developed an idea of a "Galactic Network" in 1962 (Licklider & Clark, 1962, as cited in Leiner et al., 2003). Essentially, Licklider envisioned an internationally connected group of computers that could trade information. Fellow MIT colleague, Leonard Kleinrock, convinced Lawrence Roberts and colleagues at the Defense Advanced Research Projects Agency (DARPA) to use packets in networking to increase communication efficiency. After multiple tests with a dial-up telephone, the need for packet switching was confirmed and the ARPANET was developed. After continued improvements and the addition of Transmission Control Protocol/Internet Protocol (TCP/IP), the Internet became a mainstay in businesses and homes worldwide (Kleinrock, 1964; Leiner et al., 2003).

Today's Internet allows users to conduct business, deposit a paycheck, research dinosaurs and, possibly most importantly, communicate online. Further, online communication can occur in multiple ways. Chat rooms allow friends and strangers to participate in conversations simultaneously, generally about a shared topic of interest. Instant messaging is a conversation between two or three individuals in a private chat box. Email, a method of communication used in professional, academic, and social settings, is essentially letters and messages sent electronically rather than waiting for the United States Postal Service to take days or weeks.

However, potentially one of the most popular methods of communication, especially for today's youth, is the social networking website. Originating in 1978 from the idea of an IBM employee to transform a pushpin bulletin board to an electronic system, the social network slowly developed from ideas of better information exchange. Electronic bulletin boards evolved into public forums, such as GeoCities and Beverly Hills Internet. However, popularity boomed with the creation of Classmates.com, which allowed individuals to rekindle relationships from the past (Strickland, 2009). The ability to not only communicate, but also find individuals quickly and for free, was extremely appealing for the online nation.

The transition continued with the creation of Friendster.com, which actually termed the concept of "friend" as a verb, and then MySpace. MySpace was a place of self-expression and complete user control but still enabled the user to find and reconnect with past relationships. Further, it was free membership, as MySpace obtained revenue through advertisements rather than registration fees (Stenovec, 2011). Yet the popularity of MySpace faded, and the new king of social networking, Facebook, emerged as a result of Mark Zuckerberg's brain child—the Harvard-based student rating website, "Hot or Not." Now, Facebook is a social networking website that allows users to reconnect with old and new friends, post information and pictures, and consistently stay informed on world news. In September 2012, it celebrated its one-billionth user, and it continues to gain membership daily.

Forming Relationships Online

Forming and maintaining relationships through writing is not a new phenomenon. In the past, people wrote letters to one another when separated and sustained long-distance relationships through the written word. However, the change that is seen today with online relationship formation is that the relationship is often limited to solely corresponding online, with the individuals never meeting in person, or the initial contact between two people is made online and not in person. In the past, it was a rarity to have a relationship with an individual solely through writing or with someone that you didn't first meet in person. But today this has become commonplace, as social interaction has become one of the main uses of the home computer (Moore, 2000). It is the first time in the history of human communication that relationships are initially forming and continuing without any physical contact (Ben-Ze'ev, 2005).

The Internet has allowed people to meet others online that they would never ordinarily meet in their daily lives. It enables individuals to branch out and meet others with similar interests regardless of geographic location, age, sex, race, religion or background, and to form relationships with them. Individuals are able to meet others easily online due to the large number of individuals on the Internet. As indicated by statistics for 2013, 39% of the world's population is online, with 84% of the population of North America accessing the Internet (Internet World Stats, 2014). This large number of people online allows many individuals to form friendships and support networks through the Internet. The Internet is always "on," and individuals can access it whenever they desire to find people to talk to and connect with. A major change that has been seen in online relationships is that the Internet has become a leading way that individuals meet to form romantic relationships. Cacioppo, Gonzaga, Ogburn and VanderWeele (2013) found in their research that 45 percent of couples meet through online dating sites, and 35 percent of marriages were originally online relationships. Individuals may use the Internet to form romantic relationships, as opposed to meeting people offline.

Initially, online relationships, whether they are platonic or romantic, usually begin with an interaction through a public site or chat surrounding a common interest. This gives the individuals a starting point of conversation. From there, people can enter a private chat or begin corresponding via email. However, they can also begin in other ways online such as through a dating website or social media sites (Boyd, 2014). While people have the ability to be anyone online, most are more honest online in communications with others than they are offline when forming relationships (Baym, 2010). The nature of exchanges online provides for greater anonymity and ease in the ability for self-disclosure of thoughts and feelings which are associated with intimacy (Hale, Lundy, & Mongeau, 1989). This is similar to the "strangers on a train" phenomena, which is the notion that people share deeply personal information with their seatmates on a train who are strangers because they have no ties to that person and there is little to no risk in divulging secrets (Rubin, 1975). People feel free to open up online as the people they are interacting with do not have access to their social circle or family. There is also less risk of rejection or ridicule from friends or family which people can face when sharing intimate details about their behaviors or preferences to people in their life (Pennebaker, 1989; Derlega, Metts, Petronio, & Margulis, 1993). As a result, intimacy that would often take months or years to build in person can be achieved in days or weeks online. Many people feel that they can show their true selves on the Internet (McKenna & Seidman, 2005), and the exchange of "hyperpersonal communication," in which people exchange very intimate details about themselves or their life online, often leads to increased closeness and intimacy between people (Baym, 2010). Another component for increased intimacy for online relationships is that contact between individuals can take place anytime and anywhere, often frequently, and it can include large amounts of information being shared on a daily basis. A person can instantly correspond with people online with little to no effort as they have easy access, which is not the case with physical relationships that are often constrained with other obligations (Ben-Ze'ev, 2005).

The Internet can serve as a place for individuals with limited social skills or who have trouble meeting people and maintaining relationships in person, to make connections with other human beings and form relationships (McKenna, Green, & Gleason, 2002). Online relationships can also serve as an outlet for preferences or desires that a person cannot freely express or live out in real life. This is often takes the form of sexual desires, interests or fetishes. A person can find others with similar interests to live out these fantasies with online if they are unable to find a partner offline willing to participate (Ben-Ze'ev, 2004). Online relationships can also be used to partake in infidelity and cheat on one's real-life spouse. Many individuals form Internet relationships and engage in chats, cybersex and intimate disclosure of personal details, and they do not consider it to be cheating because it is not happening in person. Some individuals actually view their cyber romances as a way to prevent physical in-person affairs, as it is a way for their sexual or emotional needs to be met without being involved physically with another person (Ben-Ze'ev, 2004).

In addition to the online relationships formed between adults, there is particular concern related to the formation of online relationships that occur between youth and adults, with the potential danger for children being preyed upon. Boyd (2014) argues that this fear is our new moral panic, which has replaced the moral panic of the past, in which we as a society were panicked over child abductions by strangers. While this is often a point of great concern for parents and society, research has revealed that being preyed upon online for sex or trafficking is a rare occurrence. Minors are using the Internet to communicate with people, but they are not experiencing sexual solicitation or using it to engage in romantic and/or sexual contact with adults to the extent in which people may think. While sex crimes committed against minors has decreased overall since 1992, and sexual solicitation on the Internet is rare, there may be incidents of manipulation, harassment or coercion that youth face online from adults (Boyd, 2014). The formation of online relationships with youth started in similar ways as it did with adults. Youth, or in some cases adults and youth, often meet each other on a website in which they share a similar interest and begin talking, and then may progress to personal communication (Wolak, Mitchell, & Finkelhor, 2002).

Early research from the 1st Youth Internet Safety Study conducted by Wolak et al. (2002) in 2000 has indicated that 14 percent of youth had a relationship online with a stranger, 7 percent met face-to-face with people whom they first met online, and 2 percent had romances with someone they met online. Of the relationships that formed online, 70 percent were with peers of the same-age, 70 percent were with individuals of the opposite genders, and 74 percent of the online relationships of the youth were known to parents. However, 15 percent of the online relationships were with adults, and 12 percent met face-to-face with them. The most current research using the 3rd Youth Internet Safety Survey revealed that 10 percent of youth had one close online friendship, with 28 percent having two, and 34 percent having three to five online friendships. Only 3 percent reported having a romantic relationship with a person that they met online, with 9 percent being with peers and 2 percent with an adult. Finally, only 4 percent reported having any sexual contact online (Walsh, Wolak, & Mitchell, 2013).

In examining which youth are more likely to form online relationships with strangers, past research has indicated that it is often troubled adolescents who seek to make these connections. This has included youth who have psychological issues (Valkenburg & Peter, 2007; Ybarra, Alexander, & Mitchell, 2005), have trouble with peers (Smahel, Helsper, Green, Kalmus, Blinka, & Ólafsson, 2012) and parents, have experienced depression and victimization from peers (Wells & Mitchell, 2008; Wolak et al., 2003; Walsh et al., 2013), and also were delinquent (Walsh et al., 2013). It may also be that these youth are lonely or suffer from a lack of social skills and use the Internet as a reach out (Bonetti, Campbell, & Gilmore, 2010; Ybarra et al., 2005). They are trying to reach out and find a sense of belonging that they lack in their offline lives. The online relationships can provide a way for individuals to grow close with others and have social ties (Lee, 2009; Reich, Subrahmanyam, & Espinoza, 2012).

The creation and expanded use of the Internet to more people worldwide has allowed for the formation of relationships online. It varies by individual how and why they seek out individuals in cyberspace to talk to or connect with. However, the constant is that there is the need for a human connection in us, and this new venue is allowing people to reach out and start relationships in new ways that in past decades would not have been imaginable. This is not without its pitfalls, such as infidelity committed via the Internet and inappropriate relationships between youth and adults.

Cybercrime

With all the benefits the Internet provides us in regard to our professional and personal lives, it is difficult to imagine our lives without it. Never again will there be a generation that is not constantly "plugged in" to technology. With this growth of dependence to the Internet, the emergence of a new form of criminality has grown: cybercrime. Broadly, cybercrime is defined as "the destruction, theft or unauthorized or illegal use, modification, or copying of information, programs, services, equipment, or communication networks" (Perry, as cited in Rosoff et al., 2002, p. 417). Essentially, it is any form of crime committed using technology, which includes computers, smart phones, etc. Further, we can categorize cybercrimes into three categories based on the continuum of their development.

The first generation of cybercrime involves the illegal exploitation of mainframe computers and operating systems (Wall, 2010). These types of cybercrimes may be performed for financial gain or to destroy information. These are often "low-end" crimes, where the technology is simply used to prepare for crime commission. For example, an individual may use a YouTube video to learn how to make methamphetamine or build a bomb.

The second generation of cybercrime uses networks, like hacking. Essentially, these are crimes that are classified as "hybrid." In other words, they existed before creation of the Internet, but have been enhanced and adapted to be performed online (Wall, 2007; McQuade, 2006). Before the online evolution, hackers stole long distance telephone service. Now, they may participate in unauthorized access to information online, as well as malicious destruction of the information.

Lastly, the third generation of cybercrime is those crimes that have come into existence solely because of the Internet. Malware attacks (i.e., viruses, worms, Trojan horses) and digital piracy are truly classified as third generation cybercrimes. Further, many would argue that third generation cybercrimes are the only true behaviors that should be labeled a cybercrime (Wall, 2010).

Examining the Relationship between Cybercrime and Intimate Partner Abuse

Despite the categorization of cybercrime, there is a multitude of different criminal behaviors a person can commit online. The purpose of this book is to examine the specific cybercrimes that facilitate intimate partner abuse and will best explain the interaction through the flow of the chapters throughout the text. Chapter 2 will explore the definition of intimate partner abuse (IPA) in the United States, as well as discuss the historical timeline of legislation of IPA. There will be a brief discussion of crimes considered IPA, as well as a comparison of male and female experiences. Chapter 3 will then discuss how the Internet allows an individual to form platonic and romantic relationships online. Discussion will also include how/where/frequency of relationships formed online and dating websites. Further, discussion will include information on the positive and negative repercussions of using the Internet to form relationships. Finally, Chapter 4 will discuss the criminological theories that can be applied to various forms of cybercrimes occurring between (current/former) intimate partners.

The book will then progress onto an examination of specific IPA behaviors performed with the use of technology, as well as a look at the offenders and victims of these crimes. Chapter 5 will discuss the virtual offender who engages in various forms of cybercrime from a psychological and forensic consultant perspective. Discussion will include how technology has negatively impacted individuals overall as well as the relationships individuals form with each other. A section on the applicable types of cybercrime will be included as well as information on definitions, frequencies of occurrence, and victims and offenders. Chapter 6 will include an overview of the research on cyberharassment and cyberstalking, including studies focused on youth and adults. This chapter will also include information on victim risk factors for experiencing these cybercrimes as well as perpetrator characteristics. Moreover, discussion will focus on "high-tech" forms of cyberstalking and cyberharassment (e.g., malware) and "low-tech" forms (e.g., electronic dumpster diving). In addition, Chapter 7 will include an overview of sexual offenses on the Internet involving intimate partners, the frequency and also the current literature and information. This chapter will include a detailed discussion of a variety of sexual offenses, the offenders and the victims.

The remainder of the book will provide an examination of the current state of these crimes in our criminal justice system. Chapter 8 will discuss the initiatives currently used by police to combat and arrest cybercriminals, while Chapter 9 will discuss the history and current state of legislation of these offenses and the effect on negative relationships. Lastly, Chapter 10 will provide a thoughtful discussion of potential future directions of criminal justice processing of these offenders, as well as the treatment of victims and offenders.

References

Baym, N. K. (2010). *Personal connections in the digital age*. Malden, MA: Polity Press.

Ben-Ze'ev, A. (2004). *Love online: Emotions on the Internet*. New York City, NY: Cambridge University Press.

Ben-Ze'ev, A. (2005). 'Deattachment': the unique nature of online relationships. In Y. Amichai-Hamburger (Ed.), *The Social Net; Human Behavior in Cyberspace* (pp. 115–138). New York City, NY: Oxford Press.

Bonetti, L., Campbell, M. A., & Gilmore, L. (2010). The relationship of loneliness and social anxiety with children's and adolescent's online communication. *Cyberpsychology, Behavior, and Social Networking, 13*, 279–285. doi: http://dx.doi.org/10.1089/cyber.2009.0215.

Boyd, D. (2014). *It's complicated: The social lives of networked teens*. New Haven, CT: Yale University Press.

Cacioppo, J. T., Cacioppo, S., Gonzaga, C. G., Ogburn, E. L., & VanderWeele, T. J. (2013). Marital satisfaction and break-ups differ across on-line and off-line meeting venue. *Proceedings of the National Academy of Sciences of the United States of America*, 110 (25) 10135–10140.

Derlega, V., Metts, S. M., Petronio, S., & Margulis, S. T. (1993). *Self-Disclosure*. Newbury Park, CA: Sage.

Hale, J. L., Lundy, J. C., & Mongeau, P. A. (1989). Perceived relational intimacy and relational message content. *Communications Research Report, 6*, 94–99.

Internet World Stats. (2014). *Internet usage statistics*. http://www.internetworldstats.com/stats.htm.

Kleinrock, K. (1964). *Communication nets: Stochastic message flow and delay*. New York: McGraw-Hill.

Lee, S. J. (2009). Online communication and adolescent social ties: Who benefits more from Internet use? *Journal of Computer-Mediated Communication, 14*, 509–531. doi: http://dx.doi.org/10.1111/j.1083-6101.2009.01451.x.

Leiner, B., Cerf, V., Clark, D., Kahn, R., Kleinrock, L., Lynch, D., Postel, J., Roberts, L., & Wolff, S. (2003). A brief history of the Internet. *Internet Society*. Retrieved September 24, 2006 from: http://www.isoc.org/internet/history/brief.shtml.

McKenna, K. Y. A., Green, A. S., & Gleason, M. E. J. (2002). Relationship formation on the Internet: what's the big attraction? *Journal of Social Issues 58* (I) 9–31.

McKenna, K., & Seidman, G. (2005). You, me and we: Interpersonal processes in electronic groups. In Y. Amichai-Hamburger (Ed.), *The Social Net:*

Human Behavior in Cyberspace (pp. 191–218). New York City, NY: Oxford Press.
McQuade, S. C. (2006). *Understanding and managing cybercrime.* Boston, MA: Allyn and Bacon.
Moore, D.W. (2000). Americans Say Internet Makes Their Lives Better.*Gallup News Service.* http://www.gallup.com/poll/3202/americans-say-internet-makes-their-lives-better.aspx.
Pennebaker, J.W. (1989). Confession, inhibition and disease. In L. Berkowitz (Ed.), *Advances in Experimental Social* Psychology (Vol. 22, pp. 211–244). New York: Academic.
Reich, S. M., Subrahmanyam, K., & Espinoza, G. (2012). Friending, IMing, and hanging out face-to-face: adolescents' online and offline social networks. *Developmental Psychology 48*, 356–368. doi: http://dx.doi.org/10.1037/a0026980.
Rosoff, S., Pontell, H., & Tillman, R. (2002). *Profit without honor: White-collar crime and the looting of America.* Upper Saddle River, NJ: Prentice Hall.
Rubin, Z. (1975). Disclosing oneself to a stranger; Reciprocity and its limits. *Journal of Experimental Social Psychology,* 11, 233–260.
Smahel, D., Helsper, E., Green, L., Kalmus, V., Blinka, L., & Ólafsson, K. (2012). *Excessive Internet use among European children.* EU Kids Online, London School of Economics & Political Science, London, UK.
Stenovec, T. (2011, June 29). MySpace history: A timeline of social network's biggest moments. *Huffington Post Tech.* Retrieved from http://www.huffingtonpost.com/2011/06/29/myspace-history-timeline_n_887059.html#s299496title=August_2003_Myspace.
Strickland, J. (2009, October 12). How Classmates.com Works. *HowStuffWorks.com.* Retrieved from: http://computer.howstuffworks.com/internet/socialnetworking/networks/classmates-com.htm.
Valkenburg, P., & Peter, J. (2007). Preadolescents' and adolescents' online communication and their closeness to friends. *Developmental Psychology, 43,* 267–277. doi: http://dx.doi.org/10.1037/0012-1649.43.2.267.
Wall, D. S. (2007). Policing cybercrime: Situating the public police in networks of security in cyberspace. *Police Practice and Research: An International Journal, 8(2),* 183–205.
Wall, D. S. (2010). Micro-Frauds: Virtual robberies, stings and scams in the information age. In T. Holt & B. Schell (Eds.), *Corporate Hacking and Technology-Driven Crime: Social Dynamics and Implications.* Hershey, PA (USA): Information Science Reference, pp. 68–85.
Walsh, W. A., Wolak, J., & Mitchell, K. J. (2013). Close relationships with people met online in a national U.S. sample of adolescents. *Cyberpsychol-*

ogy: Journal of Psychosocial Research on Cyberspace, 7(3), article 4. doi: 10.5817/CP2013-3-4.

Wells, M., & Mitchell, K. J. (2008). How do high-risk youth use the Internet? Characteristics and implications for prevention. *Child Maltreatment, 13,* 227–234. doi: http://dx.doi.org/10.1177/1077559507312962.

Wolak, J., Mitchell, K. J., & Finkelhor, D. (2002). Close online relationships in a national sample of adolescents. *Adolescence, 37*(147), 441–455.

Wolak, J., Mitchell, K. J., & Finkelhor, D. (2003). Escaping or connecting? Characteristics of youth who form close online relationships. *Journal of Adolescence, 26,* 105–119. doi: http://dx.doi.org/10.1016/S0140-1971(02)00114-8.

Ybarra, M. L., Alexander, C., & Mitchell, K. J. (2005). Depressive symptomatology, youth Internet use, and online interactions: A national survey. *Journal of Adolescent Health, 36,* 9–18. doi: http://dx.doi.org/10.1016/j.jadohealth.2003.10.012.

Chapter Two

Exploration of Intimate Partner Abuse

Lindsey Blumenstein and Xavier Guadalupe-Diaz

Introduction

Intimate partner abuse (IPA), also commonly referred to as intimate partner violence (IPV), describes a wide range of behaviors meant to inflict harm and are perpetrated within the context of an intimate relationship. These abusive behaviors include physical, sexual, emotional, psychological, and financial harms that typically occur in a repetitive pattern. The term intimate partner refers to a current or former spouse, dating, or otherwise romantically involved individual. These relationships may include individuals of opposite or same-sex/gender (i.e., heterosexual or gay/lesbian relationships) and involve those who exist outside of the gender binary (i.e., transgender).

IPA is a significant criminal and public health concern within the United States as well as globally, which has lasting negative ramifications on victims (Tjaden & Thoennes, 2000). Prevalence rates of IPA within the U.S. vary significantly due to underreporting and disparity in data collection methods (Gunter, 2007). However, regardless of underreporting, the numbers are alarmingly high. Findings indicate that more than 33 percent of women and approximately 25 percent of men have experienced some form of abuse during their lifetime (Black et al., 2011).

When looking at these violent acts separately, estimates indicate that slightly more than two percent of men, and more than ten percent of women, have been stalked in their lifetimes (Black et al., 2011). Statistics regarding other forms of abuse perpetrated by intimate partners are equally as alarming: approximately 50 percent of men and women have been psychologically abused, approximately 10 percent of women have been raped, and more than 10 percent (of men and women) have experienced severe physical violence at the hands of those closest to them (Black et al., 2011). These statistics become much more disturbing when one considers that a substantial percentage (nearly

40 percent) of all homicides perpetrated in the U.S. are actually domestic homicides (Campbell et al., 2003). Overall, IPA has resulted in 2 million injuries and 1,300 deaths annually for women alone in the U.S. (Centers for Disease Control and Prevention, 2003).

Case Study 2.1

Recently, IPA has dominated news outlets. Many high profile cases are coming to light, and media are focusing on this horrific violence more and more. Jared Remy, who is the son of the Boston Red Sox broadcaster Jerry Remy, recently pled guilty to killing his fiancée Jennifer Martel (Crook, 2014; Moskowitz, 2014). According to several news outlets, this murder occurred only days after he was arrested for assaulting his fiancée, and after she had filed for a restraining order from him (Crook, 2014; Moskowitz, 2014). Unfortunately, even though Remy was arrested for the assault on Martel, he was released the next day after posting just $40 dollars for the bail fee. The very next day, he returned to the home the two shared, along with the couple's daughter, and stabbed Martel multiple times, while the daughter was at home (Crook, 2014). As a result of his crime, Remy was sentenced to life without the possibility of parole (Crook, 2014).

One of the most common risk factors for lethal IPA is previous abuse (Campbell, Glass, Sharps, Laughon, & Bloom, 2007). According to family members, the relationship between Martel and Remy was only a fling until an unplanned pregnancy occurred (Moskowitz, 2014). Friends and family described Martel as self-assured and outgoing; however, once Martel and Remy became more serious, they saw a much more tentative and unsure side of Martel. Family members reported that at times Remy was cruel to Martel and cut her down about her weight and looks (Moskowitz, 2014). Remy was able to create a wedge between Martel and her family by belittling her family members to her. The abusive and controlling behavior led to physical assault following an argument in which Remy grabbed Martel's neck and slammed her head against a bathroom mirror (Crook, 2014; Moskowitz, 2014). Fearing for her life, Martel fled to her neighbors and Remy was promptly arrested. However, the bail set for Remy was so small that he was released shortly after his arrest and he subsequently murdered Martel.

This case brings up many questions on how domestic abuse cases are handled and, in fact, the district attorney's office conducted an internal review that resulted in some countywide procedural changes. Many wonder if this death could have been prevented. According to Martel when she filed for the restraining order, Remy had been previously arrested for assault charges on an ex-girlfriend (Moskowitz, 2014). A greater and more in-depth look into Remy's past shows a trail of victims which started when he was 17 years of age. Police reports and court case files revealed that at least five previous girlfriends were terrorized by Remy; however, the courts repeatedly let him off with as little punishment as a promise to fix this behavior and at most probation (Moskowitz, 2014).

The consequences of IPA are numerous and far reaching. Many survivors of this violence report not only physical injuries but also serious mental health consequences such as anxiety, depression, and low self-esteem (Black et al., 2011). Both men and women who have been a victim of IPA are more likely to report difficulty sleeping, chronic pain issues, frequent headaches, and poorer physical and mental health (Black et al., 2011). Additionally other health consequences have been reported such as substance abuse, gastrointestinal disorders, and sexually transmitted diseases, as well as gynecological or pregnancy complications (Black et al., 2011). Many of these consequences can lead to disability, hospitalization and, at the worst end of the spectrum, death.

Generally, state laws pertaining to IPA vary in criminal scope and definition. Overall, despite the emotional and psychological abuse realms of IPA, legal definitions are focused on bodily harm (Buzawa, Buzawa, & Stark, 2012). These laws do not capture the ongoing patterns of control, manipulation, and domination that are often central dynamics to abusive relationships. For example, Massachusetts law (MGL c. 209A) defines IPA as:

> "abuse," the occurrence of one or more of the following acts between family or household members: (a) attempting to cause or causing physical harm; (b) placing another in fear of imminent serious physical harm; (c) causing another to engage involuntarily in sexual relations by force, threat or duress.

Some IPA crimes or charges include assault and battery, threat of harm, criminal coercion, sexual assault, and rape. Criminal codes also specify crimes such as kidnapping, hostage taking, false imprisonment, stalking, and intimidation as behaviors that can fall under the spectrum of IPA (FBI, 2012). Unfortunately, this leaves out psychological/emotional, spiritual, economic, and technological abuses that can occur in intimate relationships. However, self-report surveys such as the most recent national survey, the National Intimate Partner and Sexual Violence Survey (NISVS), include a much wider range of behaviors that fall along the spectrum of IPA: made to penetrate, sexual coercion, unwanted sexual contact, non-contact unwanted sexual experiences, psychological aggression, expressive aggression, coercive control, control of reproductive or sexual health, as well as physical violence rape, and stalking (Black et al., 2011). While these crimes may not be defined or prosecuted criminally, researchers, advocates, and public health professionals shed light on the fact that there are a multitude of abuses that can occur in intimate relationships.

Only in recent decades has IPA been framed as a contemporary social problem. Prior to the 1970s, violence between intimate partners remained largely a private issue not to be discussed or addressed by the public. Since then, legislative progress, changes in public perceptions as well as changes in policing, victim services, and the criminal justice system response have taken place. Among these advances are the inclusion of same-sex relationships and discussions on male victims of IPA. This chapter will provide a historical review of IPA as well as an overview of current controversies and contemporary issues within the IPA field.

Intimate Partner Abuse: A Historical Overview

For much of Western history, IPA was not considered a social problem and was in fact largely regarded as an accepted means for husbands to discipline wives. One of the earliest examples of this is reflected in "The Laws of Chastisement" that date as far back as 753 BCE. These Roman laws included provisions that granted husbands the right to beat their wives for any reason they deemed necessary as long as the husband utilized a branch, stick, or rod that was no thicker than the girth of his thumb (Lemon, 1996). To this day, the common idiom "Rule of Thumb" is historically rooted in the law that continued beyond the Roman Empire and into English Common Law.

Subsequently, the foundation of the American government was largely influenced by English Common Law and prior legal practices across England and Western Europe. In an early departure from the acceptance of wife beating, Puritan settlers in Massachusetts proclaimed that every married woman should be free from bodily harm at the hands of her husband; however, violence in the home was not an acceptable reason for divorce (Buzawa, Buzawa, & Stark, 2012). In another example, the 1824 Mississippi Supreme Court case *Bradley v. State* limited a husband's right to beat his wife to moderate discipline only to be used in cases of emergency (Martin, 1976). It would be another 47 years before the first two states would completely remove the right of a husband to beat his wife; Alabama first, followed by Massachusetts (Schechter, 1982).

Case Study 2.2

Until the late 1970s, marital rape was considered exempt from rape laws in all states across the U.S. As previously mentioned, the foundational laws of the U.S. were heavily influenced by English Common Law, much of which guided early laws on IPA. In 1857, a court in Massachusetts became the first to hear a case of spousal rape in *Commonwealth v. Fogerty*. The court relied primarily on citing Lord Hale's statement, a jurist in the 1600s, which indicated that married women had given themselves up to their husbands and therefore could not claim rape (Schecter, 1982). This is also largely informed by Judeo-Christian readings of Biblical text, including 1 Corinthians verses 4-5 that state: "The wife hath not power over her own body, but the husband; and likewise also the husband hath not power over his own body, but the wife." Through this perspective, marital partners are exempt from requiring consent prior to engaging in sexual acts.

In a significant case, *People v. Liberta*, a court in New York heard the case of Mario Liberta who had been indicted for raping his wife, Denise Liberta. Denise and Mario had been married for two years before the abuse began. In 1980, Denise requested and obtained an order of protection that forced Mario to vacate their home. Mario was granted visitation rights to their only child. In early 1981, Mario requested a visitation from their son, and Denise agreed as long as he could pick them up and take them to the hotel in which the visit would take place. She requested that a friend of Mario's be present for the duration of the visit. Once they had arrived to the hotel, the friend left, giving Mario the opportunity to attack Denise. Mario threatened to kill her and raped her, demanding that she make their son watch. As a defense, Mario claimed marital exemption to rape and sodomy laws. While the trial court dismissed the charge, the appellate court argued that marriage was not a legitimate defense to rape or sodomy and found him guilty. The court stated " ... a marriage license should not be viewed as a license for a husband to forcibly rape his wife with impunity. A married woman has the same right to control her own body as does an unmarried woman" (People v. Liberta, 64 N.Y.2d 152, 474 N.E.2d 567, 485 N .Y.S.2d 207, 1984).

In the wake of the second wave of feminism, women across the country began sharing once unspeakable truths about their experiences with violent victimization at the hands of the men in their lives. These early beginnings, fueled in part by the counter-cultural atmosphere of the late 1960s and early 1970s, led to the development of a collective feminist response to rape, sexual assault, and "wife beating" or "wife battery." The response that emerged from these intellectual exchanges and theorizations about women's place in society provided the foundation for the development of the sociopolitical or sociocultural explanations of the existence of IPA. These arguments generally framed IPA as we know it today as violence against women which was a "natural consequence of women's powerless position vis-a-vis men in patriarchal societies and the sexist values and attitudes that accompany this inequity" (Martin, 1976, xxi).

After years of advocacy for IPA, specifically against women, legislation came about in the form of the Violence Against Women Act of 1994 (VAWA). The passage of VAWA led to the proliferation of research in the area of IPA (Boba & Lilley, 2009; Moore Parmley, 2004). Congress passed VAWA as part of the Violent Crime Control and Law Enforcement Act of 1994. There were two main goals associated with the passage of this act. The first was to criminalize and increase prosecution and penalties for acts of violence against women, including rape, assault, stalking and other types of violent behavior (Boba & Lilley, 2009; Ford, Bachman Friend, & Meloy, 2002). The second goal was to allocate monies in order to increase the amount of research and evaluation being done within this area to more fully understand the problem (Boba & Lilley, 2009; Ford, Bachman Friend, & Meloy, 2002). According to Ford et al. (2002), policy makers hoped to change public opinion and attitudes towards violence against women and those who would traditionally have seen these crimes as less serious than other types of criminal acts. With the passage of VAWA, Congress sent a message to the public that IPA was not a private matter and that these acts were punishable criminal behaviors that deserved national attention and support. Since the passage of the VAWA legislation, more than $1.6 billion dollars has been allotted to research and develop various prevention and intervention programs in an attempt to reduce IPA (Moore Parmley, 2004). In 2012, the VAWA reauthorization addressed new disparities in services for LGBTQ populations as well as other marginalized groups, i.e., immigrants and Native Americans (Moore Parmley, 2004).

Definitional Issues Surrounding Intimate Partner Abuse

The field of IPA is growing rapidly every day. Indeed, since the inception of the battered women's movement (1970s), scholars have increasingly focused on investigating IPA (DeKeseredy & Schwartz, 2001). However, due to the lack of a standardized definition and varied measurement practices, there is no clear consensus about its magnitude (Saltzman, 2004). It is a challenge to keep up not only empirically, but also theoretically with a social problem that spans the world. Yet these are very important issues in the field of IPA, because the way in which we define and explain acts of abuse have major effects on subsequent methodological techniques, research on prevalence, policy initiatives, and ultimately the lives of many (Renzetti et al., 2010). Unfortunately, the IPA field continues to be plagued by various definitional controversies.

Controversies Concerning the Definition of Intimate Partner Abuse

The nature of the definitional controversy is twofold. One of the biggest debates on the definition of IPA has been whether a narrow versus broad definition of violence in intimate relationships should be used (Kilpatrick, 2004). In describing the debate about whether to define violence as broad or narrow, Kilpatrick (2004) points out that this debate "is old, fierce, and unlikely to be resolved in the near future" (p. 1218). The second part of the definitional controversy, which is a more recent issue, is whether IPA should be labeled using gender-specific or gender-neutral terms (who are the people involved in this debate).

Narrow versus Broad Definitions

One of the challenges with IPA is the tendency, among various populations, to focus on only physical or sexual assaults (Renzetti et al., 2010). There is a long-standing history of discounting other forms of abuse, such as psychological, verbal, and economical, from the equation. There are several arguments for not including these other forms of abuse. Some proponents of a narrow definition argue that by including these other forms of abuse it is too difficult to determine what is actually causing the abuse (Gelles & Cornell, 1985). Others, such as political conservatives, argue that by including forms of abuse other than just physical and sexual abuse, researchers are able to artificially inflate the rates of abuse overall in order to make political points (Dutton, 2006; Fekete, 1994; Gilbert, 1994). Similar attacks have been seen from feminists who argue that when all types of abuse are combined together, it actually trivializes the most serious forms of violence (Fox, 1993). In other words, psychological and emotional abuse is seen as less harmful and therefore not as important.

However, there are some major issues in only using narrow legalistic definitions of violence. Research has shown that unless victims label hurtful behaviors, such as physical assault, rape, or stalking, as being "criminal," they will be much less likely to report them on surveys, even if the violence occurred (Koss, 1996; Schwartz, 2000). In surveys that use such techniques and definitions, there is a much lower incidence rate of violence conveyed, which creates major reporting differences for surveys that do not operationalize victimization in this way (Fisher, 2009). By using operational definitions of IPA in the realm of criminality, we will uncover much less intimate violence. By only uncovering low rates of violence, especially on studies sponsored by the government, it may be less likely to get policy makers to listen and take action. Some government officials may not be willing to provide funding to a problem that does impact large numbers of victims. Thus, narrow definitions of IPA may exacerbate the problem of underreporting (Renzetti et al., 2010).

Other problems remain with using narrow definitions of abuse. Some victims may feel that their problems are being trivialized (DeKeseredy, 2000). Those victims that are experiencing real life abuses may not feel that anyone cares about their issues. Because of these feelings, they may be discouraged from seeking help. If a victim's abuses do not coincide with the conduct that criminal justice officials, government officials, researchers, and even the general public refer to as abuse, then they themselves may not define it as abuse (DeKeseredy, 2000). If a victim does not classify him or herself as a victim, they likely will not seek help and will continue to remain in a violent and destructive relationship.

Perhaps the most significant problem with utilizing narrow definitions is that rarely do abusers utilize only one form of violence (Renzetti et al., 2010). Many times victimization can take multiple forms including physical violence, psychological abuse, sexual abuse that may not include penetration, or economic abuse. Some have even argued that in fact psychological abuse is just as, if not more so, injurious than physical violence (Adams, Sullivan, Bybee, & Greeson, 2008) particularly when examining coercive control in a relationship.

A new body of research has shown growing concern for the problem known as coercive control (Johnson, 1995; Kelly & Johnson, 2008; Stark, 2007). According research, coercive control describes a pattern of abusive behavior, such as intimidation or threats, which is typically paired with physical violence in order to enact further control over the victim (Kelly & Johnson, 2008). In addition to intimidation and threats, coercive control may entail the utilization of isolation, emotional abuse, use of children, and/or economic abuse (Kelly & Johnson, 2008; Pence & Paymar, 1993). Coercive control is particularly dangerous for victims, because (given its non-violent nature) it may not be readily visible to outside parties (Kelly & Johnson, 2008). In fact, taking into account its "hidden" nature, researchers have noted that coercive control is actually more dangerous and more frequent than many other forms of abuse (Kelly & Johnson, 2008). Unfortunately, women who are not familiar with these tactics may consider these abuses forgivable even though abusers are likely making conscious efforts to suppress their partner's freedom (Kernsmith, 2008; Renzetti et al., 2010; Stark, 2007). These reasons are why many researchers assert that definitions of IPA should be broader and include multiple types of abuses, as well as multiple types of intimates. Aside from this controversy concerning broad versus narrow definitions, another equally contentious conversation has arisen regarding whether IPA is largely a male-to-female perpetrated social problem or whether both genders (e.g., male/female) utilize violence equally in relationships.

Gender-Specific versus Gender-Neutral

One of the most substantive controversies in the field of IPA has been the argument over gender symmetry. For nearly four decades, scholars have debated whether men and women commit equal rates of IPA. This debate, described as "longstanding and often rancorous" by Johnson (2008, pg. 3), has divided the field into two opposing sides—feminist theorists and family violence researchers.

Feminist theorists view IPA, or violence against women, as gender asymmetrical in recognition of research that indicates men are overwhelmingly represented among perpetrators (Dobash, Dobash, Wilson, & Daly, 1992; Dutton, 1994; Yllö, 1993). Beyond the gendered pattern, they describe the existence of IPA as a phenomenon that exists directly as a result of a patriarchal power structure that fosters a hostile cultural climate against women, and enables men to perpetrate violence against them as a means of controlling women in our society (Dobash, Dobash, Wilson, & Daly, 1992; Dutton, 1994; Yllö, 1993). Conversely, family violence researchers, sometimes referred to as "family conflict" scholars, argue that men and women perpetrate IPA equally. Further, many of these scholars argue that women are equally as likely to initiate the violence, be equally as physical in their violence, and even claim that women's violence partially causes their own victimization (Bland & Orn, 1986; Demaris, 1992; Morse, 1995; Stets & Straus, 1990; Straus, 1974; Straus, Gelles, & Smith, 1990).

This debate is particularly controversial as feminists have successfully politicized violence against women and have done so influentially through the construction of the "battered woman." The potential for gender symmetry poses a threat not only to the larger feminist paradigm, but also to the programs, policies, and legal structures that have already been influenced by a gender asymmetrical perspective (i.e., the naming of the Violence Against Women Act). Among various challenges to this "either/or" debate, Johnson (1995, 2000, & 2008) argued that the debate over gender symmetry is simply one that is rooted in a difference of sample. Indeed, Johnson (1995, 2000, & 2008) argued that opposing sides obtained results for different definitional forms of IPA, specifically intimate terrorism and situational couple violence.

Feminist approaches to intimate partner abuse. Most of the earlier studies in IPA provided qualitative accounts of "battered women." In arguably one of the most cited pioneering works, Dobash and Dobash (1979) sought to examine the experiences of battered women in a Scottish shelter through a feminist perspective. Commonalities in the women's experiences led to the conclusions that batterers held rigid patriarchal family ideals (Dobash & Dobash, 1979). When these victims were perceived to be out of line by their abusers, they would reassert their patriarchal authority in the relationship through violent means (Dobash & Dobash, 1979).

These findings have roots in works prior by Martin (1976) and Brownmiller (1975) who both discussed a sociohistorical foundation to the problem of violence against women that was echoed in the Dobashes' 1979 work. One key element that both Martin (1976) and Brownmiller (1975) cite is the very construct of marriage itself. Brownmiller (1975) conceptualized marriage as arising not because of the "voluntary desire" for institutional monogamy but rather a product of the constant fear of rape that women faced. She argued that marriage was therefore an exchange of women as property—an exchange that provided the illusion of protection for women against the fear of rape and violence by other men (Brownmiller, 1975). Likewise, as Martin stated, "wives were inescapably slaves to their husbands' lust" (1976, p. 27). Weitzman (1974) added further, " … the very being or legal existence of a woman is suspended during the marriage, or at least incorporated and consolidated into that of the husband, under whose wing, protections, and cover she must perform everything" (p. 1173). Given this perspective, battered women within the context of heterosexual marital relationships were the primary source from which to gather information.

In addition to these key theoretical foundations and early qualitative works, findings from Kersti Yllö and Maury Straus that utilized the first national family violence survey in 1980 further supported the link between patriarchy, or internalized patriarchal norms, and the perpetration of wife beating. This survey utilized the Conflict Tactics Scale (CTS) that measured counts of physical violence used in families (Straus, 1979). In the earliest study, Yllö (1983) examined states for their "egalitarian" qualities between men and women. The results illustrated a curvilinear relationship between how egalitarian a state was and the perpetration of wife beating or a rate of violence (Yllö, 1983). States that were the least egalitarian yielded the highest rate of wife beating while the most egalitarian came second (Yllö, 1983).

While there were a multitude of other studies that showed support for the feminist perspective on IPA, these were key pivotal findings that shaped the early direction of inquiry. Through empirical validation, both qualitatively and quantitatively, feminists were successful in framing the violence as a gendered phenomenon. Not only did men commit the overwhelming amount of violence, but they did so because of the larger patriarchal power structure that constructed women as property in marriage, a legal system that supported or tolerated this view, and the gender socialization that fostered hostile beliefs against women in our society. However, during this same time period, other scholars were gathering research which they would claim showed that men and women were equally violent in intimate relationships.

Family violence approach to intimate partner abuse. During the same time that feminist approaches were gaining momentum in research, theorization, and applied outcomes, several key family violence scholars were collecting and presenting their own findings. Arguably one of the most known works came from Steinmetz in 1977 with her article "The Battered Husband Syndrome." In this work, Steinmetz (1977) examined previous data, cultural views, or what she called "misconceptions," about husbands, and reviewed other studies. Among her controversial claims, Steinmetz (1977) argued that men underreported their victimization, were more often the victims of violence by wives than our culture recognizes, and could not escape out of destructive relationships as easily as the mainstream public thought.

To examine violence within the family, a colleague of Steinmetz, Straus (1979), led the first nationally representative family violence study called the National Family Violence Survey utilizing the CTS tool he developed. In addition to prevalence rates, Straus and others sought to explore severity, reasons for violence, initiation of violence and whether their previous prevalence findings had potential error (1979). In an early investigation into the potential biases in the data, Straus, Gelles, and Steinmetz (1981) "… deliberately interviewed the husbands in a random half of the sample and the wives in the other half to be able to obtain data on the different perspectives of men and women, and to check on possible biases in the data" (p. 682). What they found was that the data were in fact not biased and that rather than attempting to cover up violence, the "rates for each spouse were slightly higher when the computation was based on data provided by the spouse of that sex" (Straus et al., 1980, p. 682). Additionally, Straus, Gelles, and Steinmetz (1980) then explored the victim-aggressor relationship to determine who was directing the violence. By separating violent couples from non-violent couples, they then found that in 49.5% of the violent families both the husband and wife had committed at least one violent act which indicated that the violence was in fact mutual (Straus et al., 1980).

Additionally, Straus and colleagues found that, in both his 1980 and 1985 studies, no significant differences existed between men and women on who first initiated violence (Straus, Gelles, & Smith, 1990). Straus, Gelles, and Smith (1990) further added that "the main conclusion to be drawn from these findings is that women not only engage in physical violence as often as men, but they also initiate violence about as often as men" (p. 155). This led them to conclude that because of these repeated findings, violence committed by women is not motivated by self-defense (Straus et al., 1990). Women's reactions to the spousal abuse also illustrated that they were more likely than men to respond to violence with more violence (Straus et al., 1990). However, while these findings further demonstrated equal rates between men and women, significant differences were found in that women were more likely to need hospitalization and time off from work when compared to men (Straus et al., 1990). Additionally, depression and stress were more likely to be reported by women as a consequence of men's violence against them than when men were assaulted by women (Straus et al., 1990). The gender symmetry in violent perpetration evident in Straus's national surveys continued to be replicated in other studies, even in different samples (Carrado, George, Loxam, Jones, & Templar, 1996; Demaris, 1992; Gryl, Stith, & Bird, 1991; Sorenson & Telles, 1991).

To date, there have been hundreds of studies that have found gender symmetry in the perpetration of physical violence against intimate partners (Cercone, Beach, & Arias, 2005; Dutton & Nicholls, 2005; Felson, Ackerman, & Yeon, 2003; Straus, 1999). For family violence scholars, the interest lies in obtaining representative prevalence of physical violence and potential causes or stressors for conflict, they continue to rely on general population samples. To compile and examine findings across several hundred of these studies, Archer (2000) conducted a meta-analysis to explore gender difference in aggression within the context of heterosexual intimate relationships. Archer's (2000) meta-analysis covered 82 articles from 1976 to 1997 with the keywords: "marital or dating" and "aggression or violence" but excluding "sexual," "rape," and "pornography." Filtering specifically for those studies that examined gender, aggression, conflict, and consequence of violence, Archer's (2000) findings revealed that women were significantly more likely than men to use physical aggression in intimate relationships. However, the findings did indicate that women were more severely injured when men used physical violence against them (Archer, 2000).

As Holtzworth-Munroe (2005) stated as a result of many of these findings, "some in the field have suggested that women might be introducing violence into their relationships, allowing their male partners to believe that violence is an acceptable relationship behavior" (p. 252). Support for the gender symmetry evident in marital and cohabiting relationship expanded to dating relationships in the 1980s (Arias & Beach, 1987; Henton et al., 1983; Sigelman,

Berry, & Wiles, 1984). In a more recent study, Cercone, Beach, and Arias (2005) utilized the revised second CTS, called CTS2, to examine the issue of gender symmetry in a sample of dating undergraduate students. Additionally, they examined the participants' perceptions of their own physically aggressive behavior in terms of whether it was expressive (i.e., reactionary or in the moment) or relatively instrumental (i.e., necessary to reach solution or end) and fear of their partner (Cercone et al., 2005). These results illustrated once again that not only was gender symmetry evident in dating relationships as well, but, in this sample, women were also significantly more likely to utilize severe physical violence than men (Cercone et al., 2005).

As previously mentioned, in contemporary attempts to explore the debate regarding gender symmetry and IPA, Johnson (1995, 2000) examined both quantitative and qualitative datasets to examine work from both feminist and family violence researchers and presented an argument that these opposing arguments may in fact be presenting findings from two distinct types of IPA. To illustrate these forms of IPA, Johnson (1995, 2000) developed a theoretical typology which included what he referred to as: "patriarchal terrorism" and "common couple violence." Johnson (1995) stated, "patriarchal terrorism, a product of patriarchal traditions of men's right to control 'their' women, is a form of terroristic control of wives by their husbands that involves the systematic use of not only violence, but economic subordination, threats, isolation, and other control tactics" (p. 284). This type of IPA is what Johnson (1995) argued is found in feminist research. Because feminist scholars focused primarily on battered women's shelter samples, they analyzed an extreme aspect of IPA that was mainly men's violence against women and involved more than physical violence. This type of IPA incorporated those aspects of manipulation, control, and power that were often linked to emotional and psychological abuses as well (Johnson, 1995). While this type of IPA was mainly men's violence against women, Johnson (1995) emphasized that the use of the terms "wife beating," "battered woman," or "wife battery" are still quite limiting. He proposed that these terms placed the focus on victims and not perpetrators—as he believed they should—and also excluded the body of research on cohabiting and dating couples as well as same-sex IPA (Johnson, 1995).

Johnson's (1995) second type of IPA (i.e., common couple violence) " ... is less a product of patriarchy, and more a product of the less-gendered causal processes discussed at length by Straus and his colleagues working in the family violence tradition" (Straus & Smith, 1990, p. 285). Johnson (1995) makes the distinction here between feminist and family violence researchers by introducing the idea that the scholars had long been studying two very different manifestations of IPA. He argued that these occurrences of violence typically arose out of the escalation of conflict in relationships and are most often "minor" in their severity.

A key pitfall, Johnson (1995) argued, in the controversial debate on gender symmetry is that opposing sides claimed to know the absolute true and only true "nature" of IPA. Instead, Johnson (1995) argued that because these two perspectives utilized two distinct types of samples; they were in fact analyzing two different types of IPA. Through this perspective, it would be erroneous, for example, for family violence scholars to claim that husband battering was on par in severity, consequence, and outcome as wife battering because in their general population data, there existed no "patriarchal terrorism" or extremely gendered example of violence. Indeed, as Johnson stated (1995), " ... the two information sources deal with nearly no overlapping phenomena" (p. 286). Further, a simple tally or count of acts of physical violence would not get to the issue of power and control in the dynamics of abusive relationships; in other words, by simply "counting" acts of violence, important contextual details of *why* the violence was occurring were missed. Similarly, it would be erroneous for feminist scholars to claim that only women were the "real" victims of IPA when in fact an aspect of IPA does include those physical acts of aggression which have repeatedly been found to be gender-symmetrical (Johnson, 1995).

Later, Johnson (2000) added two additional types of violence found in relationships: violent resistance and mutual violent control. Violent resistance was a term Johnson (2000) used in place of "self-defense," which he argued had more legal connotations. Violent resistance was conceptualized as primarily women's resistance against abuse from men (Johnson, 2000). Finally, Johnson (2000) expanded his notion of intimate terrorism to include the possibility that both men and women could be involved in control and violence, which he referred to as a relationship marked by "mutual violent control."

By solidifying his argument that general population surveys primarily captured situational couple violence, which was largely gender-symmetrical, and that shelter surveys captured mainly intimate terrorism, Johnson (2000) addressed the long-standing debate regarding gender symmetry in IPA. He argued that the aspect of power and control in relationships is what ultimately distinguished intimate terrorism from situational couple violence (Johnson, 2000). Because of his specific attention to control in the dyad or relationship context, this presented a slight departure from the more structurally connected feminist perspective. However, because he also called attention to the importance of context and respondent samples, he also shed an important light on family violence scholars' findings. Although the debate regarding gender symmetry is likely to continue unabated for some time, there have been considerable attempts made to establish a uniform definition of IPA.

Attempts to Create a Uniform Definition

As previous sections underscore, a fundamental problem in the IPA field is accurately measuring the size and scope of the problem (Saltzman, 2004). This challenge persists because scholars vary in how IPA is defined and measured, which then subsequently affects prevalence rates (Saltzman, 2004). To help address the lack of consistency, the U.S. Centers for Disease Control and Prevention (CDC) undertook the mission of creating a uniform definition (Saltzman, 2004).

In order to help create consistency in identifying the prevalence and incidence of IPA, the CDC published a uniform definition and guidelines for IPA surveillance in 1999 (Saltzman, Fanslow, McMahon, & Shelley, 1999). The CDC (1999) recommends that when it is not possible to use their definitions, that the individuals specify how the definition they used differs from the CDC's definition in order to help facilitate interpretation of findings across studies. According to the CDC, an intimate partner is defined as current or former spouses, boyfriends/girlfriends, dating partners, and same- or opposite-sex partners (Saltzman et al., 1999). The CDC defines violence to include physical and sexual violence, the threat of physical or sexual violence, and emotional or psychological abuse that occurs in the context of physical or sexual violence or threats of such violence (Saltzman et al., 1999). The CDC then gives a definition for each form of violence. According to the CDC, stalking is not a form of IPA. In addition to providing a uniform definition of IPA, the CDC also provided a set of 50 recommended guidelines for the surveillance of IPA. In 2002, the CDC continued its path to consistency by providing a uniform definition and surveillance guidelines for sexual violence (Basile & Saltzman, 2002). This publication followed a similar consultative process to the one used for IPA.

The CDC was the first to attempt to provide a uniform definition of IPA. In order to monitor the incidence of IPA and examine trends over time a consistent definition is necessary. By creating consistency in the definition, it helps to compare the problem across jurisdictions and determine the magnitude of the problem. If consistent definitions are used, then researchers are better able to identify risk and protective factors. Ultimately, a consistent definition helps inform intervention and prevention efforts.

Definitions, Moving Forward

Progress has been made toward a consistent definition of IPA; however, we do not yet have uniformity across the discipline. There is still no gold standard in definitional or methodological strategies in the field of IPA, and this will continue to cause controversy in the field. As the field continues to grow and more research is evaluated, it becomes increasingly more important for a consistent and standardized definition of violence to be used. This lack of a firm definition causes controversies in all parts of a research design. The definitions one uses have a direct impact on the methodological strategies that are chosen for a study. The methodological design has bearing on the prevalence rates, risk and protective factors, and the overall magnitude of the problem that is uncovered in a study. The findings that are uncovered inform policy and prevention efforts. The variation in rates of prevalence and disputes over the interpretation of the problem create a serious problem in our prevention and intervention efforts. In order to make an impact on the problem we must be trying to accurately measure and assess the violence. The discussion of prevention of IPA must not be overshadowed by disagreements on definitions and methodologies. We must come together to identify a gold standard for the definition and methodologies used, and the CDC's definition seems as a good a place as any to start.

Summary of Controversies

These arguments make up the nature of the controversies of the definitional and gender symmetry issues in the IPA field. There are problems with using both narrow and broad definitions as well as with using gender-specific and gender-neutral definitions. The definitions used to describe violence affect all parts of the research on IPA, but specifically have an impact on methodological decisions, which in turn have a direct impact on prevalence rates. Similarly, drawing conclusions regarding whether men and women utilize violence in intimate relationships equally using data derived from tools that may fail to draw out important contextual differences also have far-reaching implications for the family violence field and, thus, should be approached cautiously.

Contemporary Issues in Intimate Partner Abuse

As the approaches to IPA have expanded and evolved, several key issues emerged in the field. The proceeding section highlights some fundamental debates, expansions, and subareas addressed by scholarly theorization and research that deal directly with definitional and gender issues. As noted, early researchers struggled with the issue of gender symmetry, or the notion that men and women committed equal acts and amounts of violence against each other in intimate relationships. And, while scholars today continue to assess issues of gender symmetry and attempt to explain male and female victimization in various ways, recognition of IPA at the "margins" has also begun. Indeed, for much of its history, the IPA movement has been dominated by a focus on heterosexual relationships while seemingly overlooking violence within relationships outside of the gender binary. However, beginning in the 1980s, scholars have since expanded research and theorization around IPA that occurs within the context of same-sex relationships.

IPA in Same-Sex Relationships

While nationally representative samples are obtainable for estimating heterosexual IPA rates, the same is not necessarily true for same-sex relationships. For same-sex IPA, obtaining prevalence rates presents many challenges. First, our current heterosexist and homophobic culture marginalizes and isolates the gay and lesbian community (Merrill, 1996). Much of the early research did not bother to seek lesbian, gay, bisexual, transgender or queer (LGBTQ) participants, and violence within same-sex relationships went unexamined. Further, as a result of our hostile cultural climate, many gays and lesbians may not be "out" enough to ever be within any possible sampling frame. While nationally representative samples can assume that most, or sometimes all, of their participants will be heterosexual, the same is not true when attempting to reach the LGBTQ community (Owen & Burke, 2004). Despite the limitations, a multitude of scholars have proposed that same-sex intimate IPA rates are similar to heterosexual rates (Bograd, 1999; McClennen, 2003, 2005; Renzetti et al., 2010). Among gay men, studies have shown a wide range from prevalence rates from 14 percent to up to 50 percent (Oringher & Samuelson, 2011; Tjaden, Thoennes, & Allison, 1999; Stanley, Bartholomew, Taylor, Oram, & Landolt, 2006).

Utilizing the National Violence Against Women survey, Tjaden and Thoennes (2000) examined lifetime prevalence of rape and physical assault by intimate partners for a sample of women. When compared to women with male intimate partners, they found that women with female intimate partners had significantly lower rates of rape and physical assault (Tjaden & Thoennes, 2000). Women with female partners had a rate of 11.4 percent while women with male intimate partners had nearly double the rate at 20.3 percent (Tjaden & Thoennes, 2000). These findings were different than the previous study, which showed higher victimization for women in same-sex relationships (Tjaden, Thoennes, & Allison, 1999). Despite the limitations of the data for exploring same-sex IPA, Messinger (2011) most recently utilized the data to perform what he referred to as the "first multivariate analyses of the NVAW data to compare same-sex vs. opposite-sex partners" (p. 2229). As previously mentioned, these data included only 144 *assumed* gays and lesbians—65 men with same-sex intimate partners and 79 women with same-sex intimate partners (Messinger, 2011). While he stated that there "is reason for caution" with his methods, he goes on to conclude that his findings illustrate that "IPV is significantly more prevalent among GLB individuals than heterosexuals. Indeed, GLB IPV is startlingly *twice* as prevalent" (Messinger, 2011, p. 2239).

While the literature reflects a wide range of prevalence rates, it is apparent that this is due to methodological, measurement, and sampling differences (West, 2002). As West (2002) stated, the same-sex IPA literature "has been plagued by methodological problems" (p. 122). However, it is generally accepted that rates for both same-sex and heterosexual IPA fall between approximately 25% to 35%" (McClennen, 2005). As more comparison studies utilize the same methods, measurements, and sampling frame and find consistent rates, the estimate will continue to be refined.

Unique Aspects of Same-Sex IPA

Erbaugh (2007) argued that the victim-perpetrator gendered binary in dominant IPA theorizing is another central factor in the silencing of LGBTQ victims. As a result of this dominant framework and limited explanation of violence, the cultural construct of "victim" is gendered—always female (Erbaugh, 2007). This cultural construct of victim extends beyond the victim's gender when applied to IPA. This gendered heterosexist assumption behind perpetrator-victim dynamics assumes that the victim is passive and submissive; it assumes effeminacy. Within the context of same-sex relationships, this pervasive construct of victim assumes that the victim in the relationship is the "woman" or the passive and submissive member. Conversely, it assumes that the perpetrator is the "man" or the aggressive and dominating member. While this may be commonly assumed, this is not empirically supported (Marrujo & Kreger, 1996). As Erbaugh (2007) explains, "the gender identities of the participants in a given relationship may counter normative gender stereotypes, and first impressions based on gender-normative assumptions will not reliably reveal which partner has the upper hand in an abusive dynamic" (p. 454). This cultural construct has consequences in police reaction that may approach lesbian battering as a "cat fight" or gay battering as a fight between roommates.

Homophobia and heterosexism also present unique barriers to help-seeking for survivors of same-sex IPA (Erbaugh, 2007). First, homophobia may play a role in whether or not victims of same-sex IPA even come forward. Because LGBTQ relationships are already marginalized and characterized as inferior, the literature illustrates evidence for a reluctance of both the community and individuals to report victimization (Bornstein, Senturia, Shiu-Thornton, 2006; Erbaugh, 2007; Girshick, 2002; Merril & Wolfe, 2000; McLaughlin & Rozee, 2001; Renzetti, 1992, 1998; Ristock, 2002). Disclosing same-sex IPA victimization sheds negative light onto an already oppressed population and, thus, scholars such as McLaughlin and Rozee (2001) explain that this "maintains the silence about same-sex IPA and reflects an acute awareness of societal homophobia" (p. 44).

In a slightly more recent study, Bornstein and colleagues (2006) found across their sample of LGBTQ that some participants attributed the community's lack of attention to same-sex IPA to the conscious suppression of the discussion. They also stated that their reluctance to even discuss the problem of same-sex IPA was linked directly to the "negative attention to relationships that are already unsupported by a homophobic and transphobic culture" (Bornstein et al., 2006, p. 169). It is evident in the literature that homophobia directly affects same-sex IPA victims' ability to seek help (Merrill & Wolfe, 2000). As a result, interventions should continue to work on discussing the issue of same-sex IPA and also challenging homophobic attitudes through public outreach and community education.

Studies have also found that LGBTQ victims of IPA consistently had negative experiences with the police or negative perceptions of the police that influenced reporting (Guadalupe-Diaz & Yglesias, 2013; McClennen, 2005; McClennen, Summers, & Vaughan, 2002). These factors all play a role in the fear of "revictimization" by police as documented by other studies (Balsam, 2001; Herek, Cogan, & Gillis, 2002). In more recent national findings, the National Coalition of Anti-Violence Projects (2011) found that, in 2010, almost a fourth of their sample experienced a "misarrest" by the police in which either the victim or both the victim and the perpetrator were arrested, and 29.7 percent called the police and received no arrest. Further, among these incidents, 7 percent reported police misconduct in which they reported homophobic abuse on behalf of the police (NCAVP, 2011). Unfortunately, even when police interventions are successful, LGBTQ face unique challenges in the courtroom as well (Leventhal & Lundy, 1999).

Additionally, IPA shelters have typically been a haven of resources for battered women seeking to leave violent relationships. For battered lesbians, and especially battered gay men, shelters have not historically been helpful resources (Renzetti, 1992). The research is heavily skewed, only focusing on lesbian women's use or perceptions of battered women's shelters. Several studies show that lesbians do not feel welcome in IPA shelters because they perceive them to be only for heterosexual women (McLaughlin & Rozee, 2001; Renzetti, 1992; Ristock, 2002; West, 2002).

Very much absent from the literature are experiences by transgender victims of IPA. Bornstein and colleagues (2006) have stated that "'trans' refers to a wide range of people whose gender identity or expression varies from the cultural norm for their birth sex" (p. 160). Few estimates have tried to propose that 25–43 percent of transgender people have reported being the victim of violence at the hands of an intimate partner; however, these estimates are not meant to be generalized and did not focus solely on IPA (Lombardi et al., 2001; Xavier, 2000). Therefore, as in the case of LGBTQ victims of IPA, transgender victims also face unique barriers to help-seeking avenues and the criminal justice system compared to those who are cisgender.[1]

Summary

Overall, IPA is a relatively new and expanding field relative to other topics in sociological and criminological research. Throughout our social and legislative histories, IPA has evolved from a largely private, individualized issue to a larger and much broader social problem. Through the mobilized efforts of women's groups and successful politicization of wife battering, expansions have now moved forward to include victims of both genders as well as protections for same-sex couples.

As a conceptual issue, progress has been made toward a consistent definition of IPA; however, uniformity has yet to emerge across the discipline. Although the CDC's efforts are valiant, there is still no evidence to suggest that researchers are using, or will use, this definition. As a result, there is still no gold standard in definitional or methodological strategies in the field of IPA, and this will likely cause the controversies discussed in this chapter to continue. Moreover, as the field of IPA continues to grow and more research is evaluated, increased attention needs to be paid to long overlooked marginalized populations also experiencing violence within relationships (e.g., same-sex couples). Without resolving these controversies regarding definitions, measurements, and what violence "looks like" in various types of relationships (e.g., cisgender, LGBTQ, trans), the family violence field will be unable to truly understand the prevalence and magnitude of this problem.

---

1. Cisgender describes an individual whose gender identity matches that of their biologically determined sex.

References

Adams, A. E., Sullivan, C. M., Bybee, D., & Greeson, M. R. (2008). Development of the scale of economic abuse. *Violence Against Women, 15*, 563–588.

Archer, J. (2000). Sex differences in aggression between heterosexual partners: a meta-analytic review. *Psychological bulletin, 126*(5), 651.

Arias, I., & Beach, S. R. (1987). Validity of self-reports of marital violence. *Journal of family violence, 2*(2), 139–149.

Balsam, K. F. (2001). Nowhere to hide: Lesbian battering, homophobia, and minority stress. *Women & Therapy, 23*(3), 25–37.

Basile, K. C., & Saltzman, L. E. (2002). *Sexual violence surveillance: Uniform definitions and recommended data elements* (version 1.0). Atlanta, GA: CDC, national Center for Injury Prevention and Control.

Black, M. C., Basile, K. C., Briedling, M. J., Smith, S. G., Walters, M. L., Merrick, M. T., Chen, J., and Stevens, R. (2011). *The National Intimate Partner and Sexual Violence Survey (NISVS): 2010 Summary Report*. Atlanta, GA., National Center for Injury Prevention and Control, Centers for Disease Control and Prevention.

Bland, R. C., & Orn, H. (1986). Family violence and psychiatric disorder. *The Canadian Journal of Psychiatry/La Revue canadienne de psychiatrie*.

Boba, R., & Lilley, D. (2009). Violence Against Women Act (VAWA) funding: A nationwide assessment of effects on rape and assault. *Violence Against Women, 15*(2), 168–185.

Bograd, M. (1999). Strengthening domestic violence theories: Intersections of race, class, sexual orientation, and gender. *Journal of Marital and Family Therapy, 25*(3), 275–289.

Bornstein, D. R., Fawcett, J., Sullivan, M., Senturia, K. D., & Shiu-Thornton, S. (2006). Understanding the experiences of lesbian, bisexual and trans survivors of domestic violence: A qualitative study. *Journal of Homosexuality, 51*(1), 159–181.

Brownmiller, S. (1975). *Against Our Will: Men, Women and Rape*. Pearson Education: New Zealand.

Buzawa, E. S., Buzawa, C. G., & Stark, E. D. (2012). *Responding to domestic violence: The integration of criminal justice and human services*. Sage Publications.

Campbell, J., Webster, D., Koziol-McLain, J., Block, C., et al. (2003). Risk Factors for Femicide in Abusive Relationships: Results from a Multisite Case Control Study. *American Journal of Public Health, 93*(7), 1089–1097.

Campbell, J. C., Glass, N., Sharps, P. W., Laughon, K., & Bloom, T. (2007). Intimate Partner Homicide: Review and Implications of Research and Policy. *Trauma, Violence, & Abuse, 8*(3), 246–269.

Carrado, M., George, M. J., Loxam, E., Jones, L., & Templar, D. (1996). Aggression in British heterosexual relationships: A descriptive analysis. *Aggressive Behavior, 22*(6), 401–415.

Cercone, J. J., Beach, S. R., & Arias, I. (2005). Gender symmetry in dating intimate partner violence: does similar behavior imply similar constructs? *Violence and victims, 20*(2), 207–218.

Crook, L., III. (2014, May 27). Jared Remy, son of Red Sox announcer, pleads guilty to killing fiancée. *CNN*, http://www.cnn.com/2014/05/27/justice/red-sox-announcer-son-guilty-murder/.

DeKeseredy, W. S. (2000). Current controversies on defining nonlethal violence against women in intimate heterosexual relationships. *Violence Against Women, 6*(7), 728–746.

DeKeseredy, W. S., & Dragiewicz, M. (2007). Understanding the complexities of feminist perspectives on woman abuse: A commentary on Donald G. Dutton's *Rethinking domestic violence. Violence Against Women, 13*, 874–884.

_____. (2009). *Shifting public policy direction: Gender focused versus bidirectional intimate partner violence.* Report prepared for the Ontarios Womens Directorate. Toronto: Ontario Women's Directorate.

DeKeseredy, W. S., & Schwartz, M. D. (2001). Definitional Issues. In C. M. Renzetti, J. L. Edleson, & R. L. Bergen (Eds.), *Sourcebook on Violence Against Women* (pp. 23–34). Thousand Oaks, CA: Sage.

_____. (2009). Patterns of Violence in the Family. In M. Baker (Ed.), *Families: Changing Trends in Canada* (pp. 179–205). Whitby, ON: McGraw-Hill Ryerson.

DeKeseredy, W. S., Saunders, D. G., Schwartz, M. D., & Alvi, S. (1997). The meaning and motives for women's use of violence in Canadian college dating relationships: Results from a national survey. *Sociological Spectrum, 17*, 199–222.

DeMaris, A. (1992). Male versus female initiation of aggression: The case of courtship violence. *Intimate violence: Interdisciplinary perspectives*, 111–120.

Dobash, R. E., & Dobash, R. (1979). *Violence against wives: A case against the patriarchy* (pp. 179–206). New York: Free Press.

Dobash, R. P., Dobash, R. E., Wilson, M., & Daly, M. (1992). The myth of sexual symmetry in marital violence. *Social problems*, 71–91.

Duffy, A., & Momirov, J. (1997). *Family Violence: A Canadian Introduction.* Toronto: Lorimer.

Dutton, D. G. (1994). Patriarchy and wife assault: The ecological fallacy. *Violence and victims, 9*(2), 167–182.

Dutton, D. G. (2006). *Rethinking Domestic Violence*. Vancouver: University of British Columbia Press.
Dutton, D. G., & Nicholls, T. L. (2005). The gender paradigm in domestic violence research and theory: Part 1—The conflict of theory and data. *Aggression and violent behavior*, 10(6), 680–714.
Erbaugh, E. (2007). Queering approaches to intimate partner violence. *Gender Violence: An Interdisciplinary Perspective*. Ch 32, pp. 451–459. New York University Press.
Federal Bureau of Investigation. (2012). *National Incident-Based Reporting System, 2012*. United States Department of Justice, Inter-University Consortium for Political and Social Research 30770.
Fekete, J. (1994). *Moral Panic: Biopolitics Rising*. Montreal: Robert Davies.
Felson, R. B., Ackerman, J., & Yeon, S. J. (2003). The infrequency of family violence. *Journal of Marriage and Family*, 65(3), 622–634.
Fisher, B. (2009). The Effects of Survey Question Wording on Rape Estimates: Evidence from a Quasi-Experimental Design. *Violence Against Women*, 15, 133–147.
Ford, D. A., Bachman, R., Friend, M., & Meloy, M. (2002). Controlling violence against women: A research perspective on the 1994 VAWA's criminal justice impacts. *Washington, DC: National Criminal Justice Reference Service*.
Fox, B. J. (1993). On Violent Men and Female Victims: A Comment on DeKeseredy and Kelley. *Canadian Journal of Sociology*, 18, 320–324.
Gelles, R. J., & Cornell, C. P. (1985). *Intimate Violence in Families*. Beverly Hills, CA: Sage.
Gilbert, N. (1994). Miscounting Social Ills. *Society*, 31, 18–36.
Girard, A. (2009). Backlash or equality? The influence of men's and women's rights discourses on domestic violence legislation in Ontario. *Violence Against Women*, 15, 5–23.
Girshick, L. B. (2002). No Sugar, No Spice Reflections on Research on Woman-to-Woman Sexual Violence. *Violence Against Women*, 8(12), 1500–1520.
Gryl, F. E., Stith, S. M., & Bird, G. W. (1991). Close dating relationships among college students: Differences by use of violence and by gender. *Journal of Social and Personal Relationships*, 8(2), 243–264.
Guadalupe-Diaz, X. L., & Yglesias, J. (2013). "Who's Protected?" Exploring Perceptions of Domestic Violence Law by Lesbians, Gays, and Bisexuals. *Journal of Gay & Lesbian Social Services*, 25(4), 465–485.
Gunter, J. (2007). Intimate Partner Violence. *Obstetrics and Gynecology Clinics of North America*, 34(3), 367–388.
Henton, J., Cate, R., Koval, J., Lloyd, S., & Christopher, S. (1983). Romance and violence in dating relationships. *Journal of Family Issues*, 4(3), 467–482.

Herek, G. M., Cogan, J. C., & Gillis, J. R. (2002). Victim experiences in hate crimes based on sexual orientation. *Journal of Social Issues, 58*(2), 319–339.

Holtzworth-Munroe, A. (2005). Male versus female intimate partner violence: Putting controversial findings into context. *Journal of Marriage and Family, 67*(5), 1120–1125.

Jiwani, J. (2000). *The 1999 general social survey on spousal violence: An analysis*. Retrieved from http://www.casac.ca/survey99.htm.

Johnson, M. P. (1995). Patriarchal terrorism and common couple violence: Two forms of violence against women. *Journal of Marriage and the Family*, 283–294.

_____. (2008). *A typology of domestic violence: intimate terrorism, violent resistance, and situational couple violence*. Boston, MA: Northeastern University Press.

Johnson, M. P., & Ferraro, K. J. (2000). Research on domestic violence in the 1990s: Making distinctions. *Journal of Marriage and Family, 62*(4), 948–963.

Kelly, J. B., & Johnson, M. P. (2008). Differentiation among types of intimate partner violence: Research update and implications for interventions. *Family Court Review, 46*, 476–499.

Kernsmith, P. (2008). Coercive Control. In C.M. Renzetti & J.L. Edleson (Eds.), *Encyclopedia of interpersonal violence* (pp. 133-134). Thousand Oaks, CA: Sage.

Kilpatrick, D. (2004). What is violence against women? Defining and measuring the problem. *Journal of Interpersonal Violence, 19*(11), 1209–1234.

Koss, M. P. (1996). The Measurement of Rape Victimization in Crime Surveys. *Criminal Justice and Behaviors, 23*, 55–69.

Lemon, N. K. (1996). *Domestic violence law: A comprehensive overview of cases and sources*. Austin & Winfield Publishers.

Lundy, S., & Leventhal, B. (Eds.). (1999). *Same-sex domestic violence: Strategies for change*. Sage Publications.

Lombardi, E. (2001). Enhancing transgender health care. *American Journal of Public Health, 91*(6), 869–872.

Marrujo, B., & Kreger, M. (1996). Definition of roles in abusive lesbian relationships. *Journal of Gay & Lesbian Social Services, 4*(1), 23–34.

Martin, D. (1976). *Battered wives*. Volcano Press.

McClennen, J. C. (2003). Researching gay and lesbian domestic violence: The journey of a non-LGBT researcher. *Journal of Gay & Lesbian Social Services, 15*(1-2), 31–45.

McClennen, J. C. (2005). Domestic violence between same-gender partners recent findings and future research. *Journal of interpersonal violence, 20*(2), 149–154.

McClennen, J. C., Summers, A. B., & Vaughan, C. (2002). Gay men's domestic violence: Dynamics, help-seeking behaviors, and correlates. *Journal of Gay & Lesbian Social Services, 14*(1), 23–49.

McLaughlin, E. M., & Rozee, P. D. (2001). Knowledge about heterosexual versus lesbian battering among lesbians. *Women & Therapy, 23*(3), 39–58.

Merrill, G. S. (1996). Ruling the exceptions: Same-sex battering and domestic violence theory. *Journal of Gay & Lesbian Social Services, 4*(1), 9–22.

Merrill, G. S., & Wolfe, V. A. (2000). Battered gay men: An exploration of abuse, help seeking, and why they stay. *Journal of homosexuality, 39*(2), 1–30.

Messinger, A. M. (2011). Invisible victims: Same-sex IPV in the national violence against women survey. *Journal of interpersonal violence, 26*(11), 2228–2243.

Moffit, T. E., Capsi, A., Rutter, M., & Silva, P. A. (2001). *Sex differences in antisocial behaviors.* Cambridge: Cambridge University Press.

Moore Parmley, A. M. (2004). Violence against women research post VAWA: Where have we been, where are we going? *Violence Against Women, 10*(12), 1417–1430.

Morse, B. J. (1995). Beyond the Conflict Tactics Scale: Assessing gender differences in partner violence. *Violence and victims, 10*(4), 251–272.

Moskowitz, E. (2014, March 23). For Jared Remy, leniency was the rule until one lethal night. *The Boston Globe,* http://www.bostonglobe.com/metro/2014/03/22/remy/xFRaOQqrnZ1S1pfLa2eKgK/story.html.

National Center for Injury Prevention and Control. (2003). *Costs of intimate partner violence against women in the United States.* Atlanta, GA: Centers for Disease Control and Prevention.

NCAVP (2011). "Lesbian, Gay, Bisexual, Transgender, Queer and HIV-Affected Intimate Partner Violence 2010: A Report from the National Coalition of Anti-Violence Projects." Technical Report.

Oringher, J., & Samuelson, K. W. (2011). Intimate partner violence and the role of masculinity in male same-sex relationships. *Traumatology, 17*(2), 68.

Owen, S. S., & Burke, T. W. 2004. "An exploration of prevalence of domestic violence in same sex relationships". *Psychological Reports, 951,* 129–132.

Pence, E., & Dasgupta, S. D. (2006). *Re-examining battering: Are all acts of violence against intimate partners the same?* Duluth: Praxis International. Retrieved from http://www.praxisinternational.org/pages/library/files/pdf/ReexaminingBattering.pdf.

Pence, E., & Paymar, M. (1993). *Education groups for men who batter: The Duluth model.* New York, NY: Springer.

People v. Liberta (1984). 64 N.Y.2d 152, 474 N.E.2d 567, 485 N.Y.S.2d 207. URL: http://faculty.law.miami.edu/zfenton/documents/Peoplev.Liberta.pdf.

Renzetti, C. M. (1992). *Violent betrayal: Partner abuse in lesbian relationships*. Sage Publications, Inc.

Renzetti, C. M. (1998). Violence and abuse in lesbian relationships. *Issues in intimate violence*. p. 117–127. Sage: Thousand Oaks, CA.

Renzetti, C., Edleson, J., & Bergen, R. (Eds). (2010). *Sourcebook on Violence Against Women*. Thousand Oaks, CA: Sage.

Ristock, J. L. (2002). *No more secrets: Violence in lesbian relationships*. Psychology Press.

Saltzman, L. E, Fanslow, J. L., McMahon, P. M., & Shelley, G. A. (1999). *Intimate partner violence surveillance: Uniform definitions and recommended data elements* (version 1.0). Atlanta, GA: CDC, National Center for Injury Prevention and Control.

Saltzman, L. E. (2004). Definitional and methodological issues related to Transnational Research on Intimate Partner Violence. *Violence Against Women*, 10(7), 812–830.

Schechter, S. (1982). *Women and male violence: The visions and struggles of the battered women's movement*. Boston: South End Press.

Schwartz, M. D. (2000). Methodological issues in the use of survey data for measuring and characterizing violence against women. *Violence Against Women*, 6(8), 815–838.

Sigelman, C. K., Berry, C. J., & Wiles, K. A. (1984). Violence in College Students' Dating Relationships. *Journal of Applied Social Psychology*, 14(6), 530–548.

Sorenson, S. B., & Telles, C. A. (1991). Self-reports of spousal violence in a Mexican-American and non-Hispanic white population. *Violence and victims*, 6(1), 3–15.

Stanley, J. L., Bartholomew, K., Taylor, T., Oram, D., & Landolt, M. (2006). Intimate violence in male same-sex relationships. *Journal of Family Violence*, 21(1), 31–41.

Stark, E. (2007). *Coercive control: How men entrap women in personal life*. New York: Oxford University Press.

Steinmetz, S. K. (1977). The battered husband syndrome. *Victimology*, 2(3-4), 499–509.

Stets, J. E., & Straus, M. A. (1990). Gender differences in reporting marital violence and its medical and psychological consequences. *Physical violence in American families: Risk factors and adaptations to violence in*, 8(145), 151–165.

Straus, M., & Gelles, R. G. (1986). Societal change and change in family violence from 1975 to 1985 as revealed by two national surveys. *Journal of Marriage and Family*, 48, 465–479.

Straus, M. A. (1974). Leveling, civility, and violence in the family. *Journal of Marriage and the Family*, 13–29.

Straus, M. A. (1979). Measuring intrafamily conflict and violence: The conflict tactics (CT) scales. *Journal of Marriage and the Family*, 75–88.

Straus, M. A., & Smith, C. (1990). Family patterns and primary prevention of family violence. In M. A. Straus & R. J. Gelles (Eds.), *Physical violence in American families* (pp. 507–526). New Brunswick, NJ: Transaction Publishers.

Straus, M. A., Gelles, R. J., & Smith, C. (1990). *Physical violence in American families: Risk factors and adaptations to violence in 8,145 families* (pp. 29–47). New Brunswick, NJ: Transaction Publishers.

Straus, M. M. A., Gelles, R. J., & Steinmetz, S. K. (Eds.). (1982). *Behind closed doors: Violence in the American family*. Transaction Publishers.

Straus, M., Gelles, R. G., & Steinmetz, S. (1981). *Behind Closed Doors: Violence in the American Family*. New York: Anchor Press.

Straus, M. A. (1990). The Conflict Tactics Scale and its critics: An evaluation and new data on validity and reliability. In M. A. Strauss & R. A. Gelles (Eds.). *Physical violence in American families: risk factors and adaptations to violence in 8,145 families* (pp. 49–73). New Brunswick, NJ: Transaction Publishing.

Straus, M. A. (1999). The controversy over domestic violence by women: A methodological, theoretical, and sociology of science analysis. In X. Arriage & S. Oskamp (Eds.), *Violence in intimate relationships* (pp. 17–44). Thousand Oaks, CA: Sage.

Tjaden, P., Thoennes, N., & Allison, C. J. (1999). Comparing violence over the life span in samples of same-sex and opposite-sex cohabitants. *Violence and victims*, 14(4), 413–425.

Tjaden, P., & Thoennes, N. (2000). *Full report on the prevalence, incidence, and consequences of violence against women: Findings from the National Violence Against Women Survey* (NCJ183781). Washington DC: National Institute of Justice, Office of Justice Programs, U.S. Department of Justice and the Centers for Disease Control and Prevention.

Weitzman, L. J. (1974). Legal Regulation of Marriage: Tradition and Change: A Proposal for Individual Contracts and Contracts in Lieu of Marriage. *California Law Review*, 1169–1288.

West, C. M. (2002). Lesbian intimate partner violence: Prevalence and dynamics. *Journal of Lesbian Studies*, 6(1), 121–127.

Xavier, J. M. (2000). The Washington, DC, Transgender Needs Assessment Survey final report for Phase Two: Tabulation of the survey questionnaires; presentation of findings and analysis of the survey results; and recommendations.

Yllö, K. (1983). Sexual equality and violence against wives in American states. *Journal of Comparative Family Studies*, 67–86.

Yllö, K. (1993). Through a feminist lens. *Current controversies in family violence*, 47–62.

Chapter Three

Relationship Formation and Maintenance via the Internet

Steven J. Seiler and Brad Ictech

Introduction

In the early-1990s, the Internet took off in mainstream America, and people found new means of remotely interacting with others. Fast-forward nearly a quarter of a century, the Internet is a mainstay in social life, and online interaction has become normalized into the everyday life through email, social networking sites (SNS), micro-blogs, and even dating websites. Moreover, with Internet-capable mobile devices such as smartphones and tablet computers, online social life is increasingly managed on the go. The sea change in the technological structure of everyday social life has dramatically transformed the ways in which relationships arise and are managed. In particular, the Internet, as well as the mobile nature of the social technology, has altered the structure and dynamics of courtship and, ultimately, the life course of romantic relationships. In this chapter, we provide a sociological perspective, generally, and social psychological perspective, specifically, of relationship formation and maintenance with and through the Internet.

Romance in the 21st Century

By the mid-1980s, personal computers were becoming a popular household item, video game consoles, with the introduction of the Nintendo, were experiencing a resurgence, and the first mobile phones were introduced to the general public (Hanson, 2007). Yet such devices were largely limited to the wealthy, as the least expensive personal computers cost around $500 (roughly $1,300 in 2014), a Nintendo cost around $250 (roughly $550 in 2014), and the first mobile phone cost around $4,000 (roughly $9,000 in 2014). Social networks were managed through face-to-face interaction, landline telephones, and letters—

either handwritten or typed on a typewriter—sent through what is now referred to as "snail mail." The grocery store, places of worship, and newspaper classified ads were common places to look for a romantic partner. In large part, everyday social life was limited to people's local milieu, and strategies for finding a romantic partner were limited to people's local social networks or a handful of physically located and proximally convenient locations. Moreover, romantic relationships, once established, were primarily negotiated within face-to-face interactions or through landline telephone calls. People's methods for communication other than face-to-face interaction were limited and situation-like—not involving mutual monitoring (Goffman, 1979). For a period in history, the letter seemed to be a dying communication medium while other communication technologies such as the telephone and pager gained popularity. However, there was a revival of the letter in the mid-1990s as the Internet was commercialized and the average person gained access to e-mail services. By the time Joe Fox's (Tom Hanks) e-mail romance with Kathleen Kelly (Meg Ryan) in the 1998 movie *You've Got Mail* captured the hearts of romantics, the Internet was already transforming the social nature of romance in America.

The Internet is now an essential aspect of everyday social life. Approximately 70 percent of homes in America have broadband Internet service (Zickuhr & Smith, 2013); 87 percent of adults in America use the Internet; and 90 percent of them own cell phones (Fox & Raine, 2014). Moreover, 53 percent of all American adults play video games either on a console or a computer, 81 percent of adults between the ages of 18 and 29 and nearly 97 percent of teenagers play video games (Lenhart, Jones, & Macgill, 2008). Not only are people's daily lives connected to the Internet, but also their social networks now expand far beyond their immediate social setting, as nearly 75 percent of online adults use at least one SNS (Duggan & Smith, 2014). For example, on SNS such as LinkedIn and Facebook, people are able to connect with each other and share information regardless of spatial proximity. Some take advantage of this benefit to find romantic interests as nearly 40 percent of Americans who are single and seeking a partner use online dating services (Smith & Duggan, 2013). However, romantic encounters on the World Wide Web are not limited to any particular website or virtual world. They can occur anywhere online where two people can communicate with each other.

Romantic Relationship Formation and Maintenance in an Internet Era

Sociologically, a relationship is not a "thing"; rather, it is a complex social process. To understand the impact of the Internet on romantic relationships, it is first necessary to examine the basic structure and dynamics of a romantic relationship. A personal relationship is a frequent, reoccurring social interaction with another person, through which each interlocutor develops a relatively high degree of emotional closeness and/or familiarity with the other (Blumstein & Kollock, 1988). A romantic relationship, then, is a personal relationship that includes a relatively mutual and expressed sexual attraction between the two interlocutors.

Romantic relationships in the 21st century can be further defined by the centrality of social technology in the relationship. Baker (2008) defines an online relationship as two people with romantic interest in each other that first meet online. This definition, of course, does not capture relationships that initiate offline and subsequently are taken online through the use of cell phones and SNS in the relationship. Wright (2004, p. 239–40) delineated "exclusively Internet-based relationships," i.e., relationships formed and maintained online without any face-to-face interactions, from "primarily Internet-based relationships," i.e., relationships that rely on social technology to supplement face-to-face interactions. Although some romantic relationships are sustained exclusively online for a substantial amount of time, very few relationships remain solely online. Furthermore, underlying such definitions is a rather dichotomous logic of either online or offline. Even "primarily Internet-based" is problematic in relationships in which multiplexing, i.e., using two or more media for interacting with a significant other, is normalized (Baym, 2010). Turkle (2008) suggests that mobile technologies, in particular, create an environment in which people are perpetually in both a digital and physical space at the same time. Therefore, it is reasonable to conclude that most romantic relationships have an online component. With this in mind, it is possible to categorize relationships based upon the directionality of online and offline interactions within the life course of a relationship. That is, exclusively online romantic relationships, albeit uncommon, are relationships initiated and maintained wholly within online social environments. Online-to-offline romantic relationships are initiated within an online forum or online fora with the goal of taking the relationship offline. Finally, offline-to-online romantic relationships constitute the overwhelming majority of romantic relationships initiated in the 21st century, as most relationships that are initiated offline incorporate various forms of social technology for managing the relationships (Höflich & Linke, 2012; Ling, 2000).

Beyond developing a basic conceptual definition of a romantic relationship are the complex dynamics of relationship formation and maintenance. On a fundamental level, a relationship of any sort involves two interdependent participants engaged in social interaction in which "the behavior of each affects the outcomes of the other"; moreover, a relationship becomes such when it "is comprised of a series of related interactions, each affected by past episodes and in turn affecting future interactions" (Blumstein & Kollock, 1988, p. 468). Thus, personal relationships arise through frequent, effectual interaction between two people over the course of time. No personal relationship suddenly appears. All relationships have a life-course, and they are always in a state of flux.

At the heart of a relationship is sense of selfhood. The self consists of the sum total of all of one's identities (James, 1890). Sociologically, the self is a process located at the intersection of the mind and social life; it is a reflexive process through which the individual experiences external stimuli, interprets it, and reacts to it (Sandstrom, Lively, Martin, & Fine, 2014). The ways in which people see themselves (i.e., self-conceptions) are filtered through interpretations of how people think others view them (i.e., self-appraisal) in light of their social performances aimed at giving off a certain impression of self to others (i.e., self-presentation) within situated interaction. The necessity of self-presentation is related to the connection between an identity and the self.

Throughout daily life, people maintain a vast array of social statuses (i.e., positions relative to others within groups), and within each status they engage in a prescribed set of performances (i.e., roles) (Stryker, 1980). However, within each status, people develop a unique sense of self as a holder of the particular status, i.e., a personal identity. Yet other people also develop a unique perception of people within each particular status, i.e., a social identity, which might or might not be consistent with people's personal identities (Owens, 2006). That is, the self is populated by the numerous situational and relational identities one maintains at all times. People constantly evaluate the connection between their ideal self-presentations, i.e., the performances they feel are necessary for others to see them the way they want to be seen, and their actual self-presentations, i.e., the real social performances (Stryker, 1980). A *self*, then, is one's theory of oneself, i.e., self-concept, based upon the sum total of all of one's self-presentation assessments (i.e., self-appraisal) (McCall & Simmons, 1966; Stryker, 1980). The extent to which people's actual self-presentations align with their ideal self-presentations will determine the extent to which their self-concepts are modified. If the ideal self-presentation and actual self-presentation do not align, self-concept is modified accordingly, which would, consequently, affect one's self-esteem (Cooley, 1967; McCall & Simmons, 1966). Should they feel their actual self-presentations exceed their ideal self-presentations, their theories of themselves are likely to be positively reevaluated, thus, producing higher self-esteem. Alternatively, should their actual self-presentations not fulfill the expectations in their ideal self-presentations, they are likely to negatively reevaluate their self-concepts and, thus, have lower self-esteem.

From the point when two people engage in effectual interaction with each other, they begin a complex dialectical process of, on the one hand, *developing* unique identities associated for the other within the relationship and, on the other hand, *managing* the construction each other's own identity for the other (O'Sullivan, 2000). In other words, within every romantic relationship, a *relational identity* for each interlocutor is constructed and maintained. Formally stated, a relational identity is an identity constructed by and for the other within the context solely of a personal relationship—an identity that is couched solely within the specific relationship, not within any given situated interaction.

Therefore, regardless if a relationship is developed online or offline, the process of relationship formation is always equally a self-process (McCall & Simmons, 1966; O'Sullivan, 2000). In commonsensical terms, people often express their relationships in terms of emotional closeness. All personal relationships have an inherently social element, which is subjectively related to the extent to which the two interlocutors "know" each other. However, to "know" someone involves a complex self-other dynamic. Ethnomethodologically, people commonsensically identify the level of "knowing" someone along a continuum ranging from the most rudimentary firsthand knowledge to the most intimate sense of understanding of the other. Temporality of social interaction is a necessary pre-requisite for "knowing" someone, yet it is not a zero-sum game; that is, the level of closeness or "knowing" does not necessary increase as the frequency of interaction increases. A personal relationship cannot arise without frequent social interaction, but it is not simply the frequency of social interaction that defines the closeness of a relationship. It is the extent to which people establish relatively stable relational identities for their significant others. To "know" another is to confidently predict the other person's behaviors, likes, dislikes, as well as the various other idiosyncrasies; furthermore, knowing another person also involves a confident understanding of a rather stable and consistent personal history of the other.

No relationship arises outside of the relational identity formation, and relational identity maintenance is an ongoing process throughout the course of the relationship. This, of course, suggests that identities, like relationships, are processual. In fact, they must be so! No identity can be guaranteed. McCall and Simmons (1966, p. 168) claims,

> Identity must be won and rewon continually. Audiences are fickle, and we must continually induce them anew to support our roles and legitimate our claims to particular identities ... a spouse cannot rest upon the laurels of honeymoon romance and intimacy to hold her mate ... The struggle to legitimate one's identities is never-ending ...

Identities, then, are performances, and such performances require constant attention to ensure that others see the person the way she or he sees himself or herself. Yet such identity performance, or, more generally, *self-presentation*, occurs regardless if a person is attentively and strategically engaging in it. That is, whenever people are in the presence of others, they are, by default, engaged in self-presentation (Goffman, 1959). Even people's inaction contributes to other people's perception of them (McCall & Simmons, 1966).

Regardless of circumstance, a personal relationship arises not only through frequent and reoccurring interaction, but also through the continuous and reciprocal exchange of a variety of verbal and non-verbal information supportive of each person's self-concept. Therefore, the two interlocutors' reflect appraisals, i.e., the extent to which they see the other person as complementary to their senses of self, become the foundation of the relationship. As the two interlocutors interact, they develop an image of the other as well as evaluate that image in light of their senses of self. As long as the image of the other coincides with each person's ever-changing sense of self, the relationship will continue. However, information introduced about the other that is not compatible with one's sense of self puts the relationship at risk of dissolution.

Romantic relationship formation, then, involves the tacit establishment of relational identities — a process that involves both performance and evaluation on each person's part (McCall & Simmons, 1966). People often refer to the initial courting stages as "getting to know the other." By "getting to know the other," people mean that they establish a baseline reference for the other person's social, emotional, and behavioral dispositions. Such a baseline reference develops through the frequent, reoccurring, and effectual interactions in which they not only engage in overt conversations about themselves, but also acclimate to each other's behavior patterns (Blumstein & Kollock, 1988). The formation stage of the relationship is often considered the most formidable stage because each person is working to establish an identity for the other and, based upon the identity formed of the other, determining if it is conducive to one's sense of self. In other words, the relationship can be sustained to the extent that each person finds consistent *identity support* from the other (McCall & Simmons, 1966).

As a romantic relationship develops, each person actively seeks information about the other to establish — and constantly reassess — if the other is complimentary of one's own sense of self (Gibbs, Ellison, & Heino, 2006; Gibbs, Ellison, & Lai, 2011; Utz & Beukeboom, 2011; Whitty, 2007). One of the many functions of relationships is that they provide consistent sources of identity support. They provide a stable source of confirmation on a person's sense of self (McCall & Simmons, 1966).

The formidability of the initial stage of a romantic relationship is confounded by the performance element of relationship development. At the same time they are seeking to establish an identity for the other, they are also actively engaging in a form of self-presentation, which relationship scholars refer to as *relationship maintenance* (Canary & Stafford, 1994; Wright, 2004). All relationships require maintenance; otherwise, they would simply dissolve (Canary & Stafford, 1994; McCall & Simmons, 1994). Relationship maintenance involves both active strategies as well as mundane or otherwise routine behaviors that sustain the relationship (Canary & Stafford, 1994; Dainton & Stafford, 1993; Duck, 1988; Wright, 2004). It refers to the frequent, routine, and meaningful interactions within the normal course of the personal relationship that contribute to the stability and continuance of the relationship (Blumstein & Kollock, 1988); it consists of those "actions and activities used to sustain desired relational definitions ... that indicate the character of the relationship" (Canary & Stafford, 1994, p. 5). Among the challenges of relationship maintenance is the management of two common logistical problems in personal relationships. McCall and Simmons (1966, p. 187) claim that people must, first, "juggle the claims" associated with their relationships and, second, "manage events pertinent to any given relationship in such a way as to preserve and cultivate it." That is, people must manage the naturally arising demands associated with their relationships in order to nurture and preserve them (e.g., frequent communication, affirmation of the relationship, confidence in the significant other's character), as well as manage their relationships in a manner in which the expectations associated with each of them are met. If these problems are not properly managed then the relationship could begin to deteriorate or simply end.

Stafford and Canary (1991) identified five significant maintenance behaviors: positivity (e.g., complimenting, cheerfulness, courtesy and politeness), openness (e.g., honesty, willingness to talk about the relationship), assurances (e.g., expressions of love, confirmations of the future of the relationship), social networks (e.g., be surrounded by close friends, family, and people supportive of the relationship), and sharing tasks (e.g., balancing chores and responsibilities). Underlying such behaviors is self-presentation (Derlega, Winstead, Wong, & Greenspan, 1987). Relationship maintenance strategies involve conveying a particular image to the other of oneself. Of equal importance to relationship maintenance, then, is information control—or strategic self-disclosure (Toma, Hancock, & Ellison, 2008; Whitty, 2008a). That is, in the development and management of particular relational identities, each person has a vested interest in controlling the amount and type of information about oneself that is made available to others. Most people are familiar with the first-date conversational taboos: do not talk about politics, religion or past relationships. Underlying such common advice is the strategic self-disclosure. The goal, of course, is to give a positive first impression, which would be the foundation of any future relational identities within the given relationship.

Relationship maintenance, then, involves engaging in consistent self-presentation to the other (Canary & Stafford, 1994; O'Sullivan, 2000). As relational identities develop, the feeling of "knowing the other" arises and deepens. Knowing the other effectively means that a person understands the other in a rather stable and predictable manner, as the relational identity is based upon a set of expectations of the other. The trajectory of the relationship is, in many ways, contingent upon the extent to which the expectations consistent with the relational identities are maintained (McCall & Simmons, 1966).

Finally, not only do relationships provide a consistent source of identity support, but also they become part of a person's sense of self (Aron & Aron, 1986, 1996; Carpenter & Spottswood, 2013; McCall & Simmons, 1966). When people state that they feel close to another person, they mean that they identify strongly with others, they feel as if they "know" others, and that other people, to a certain extent, are an extension of themselves. The relational identity with a romantic partner often becomes a central identity in a person's sense of self. The more central an identity is to an individual, the more the person will seek to protect and sustain it. People often talk about emotional investment in relationships. The essence of such emotional investment is found in their identity investment, i.e., their perception of themselves as partners of the other. Identity investment is based upon the subjective return from the other; that is, the extent to which the other person provides subjectively positive identity support.

Romantic Relationships, Online and Connected

Connected social technology is a game-changer for romantic relationship formation and maintenance, as now two people can be together without physically being together (Gergen, 2002; Turkle, 2011). To substantiate this point, it is important to review the structure of copresence as well as general interface parameters for social interactions mediated through social technology. In all social environments, people tacitly establish a sense of copresence, which is the mutual awareness of present others (Goffman, 1963; Zhao, 2003). In face-to-face social interactions, people are corporeally, or physically, copresent. However, electronically mediated interactions produce various forms of telecopresence (Zhao, 2003, 2005). Telecopresence is the technology-supported reciprocal interaction with others who are not physically present (Zhao, 2003). For example, in a conversation via instant messages, people establish a sense of telecopresence with others based, first, on their others' online statuses and, second, solely on text-based exchanges. Additionally, Gergen (2002) argues that as mobile technologies are incorporated into people's relationships they develop absent present others; that is, people establish a sense of perpetual telecopresence. Consequently, if people establish a sense of absent presences, they assume that their significant others are available all of the time and anywhere (Gergen, 2002; Turkle, 2008). All forms of telecopresence are predicated on a very high degree of genuineness, honesty, and trust.

The unique structure of telecopresence is conditioned upon the interface parameters of each particular medium for a given interaction (Zhao, 2003) as well as the multiplexed interface parameters through which a unique, relationship-specific sense of perpetual telecopresence arises. Zhao (2003, p. 450) conceptualizes interface parameters as technologically structured "ways in which co-located individuals come into contact with each other." He outlines such interface parameters that structure copresence as the following: (1) embodiment, (2) immediacy, (3) scale, and (4) mobility (Zhao, 2003). The level of embodiment refers to the extent to which the physical, human body is incorporated into the interaction (Zhao, 2003). Face-to-face social interaction is considered corporeal copresence, as it is premised upon totally embodied interaction. Social interaction through the majority of social technology is considered disembodied because participants in such interactions are physically dislocated and the interaction is, thus, void of the corporeal bodies of the participants. The exception to this rule is, of course, any forms of social interaction involving avatars, as avatars are considered, to a certain extent, to be embodied. Avatars are digital recreations of the corporeal body. Second, the level of immediacy references the rapidity of reciprocations within a social interaction (Zhao, 2003). Whereas face-to-face interaction is considered highly synchronous, the level of immediacy within various telecopresent online environments can vary from asynchronous (e.g., email) to highly synchronous (e.g., massively multiplayer online role-playing games). Third, the scale of the social environment pertains to "the number of people enabled by a given interface to interact with one another" (Zhao, 2003, p. 451). Whereas face-to-face interactions allow for only a small number of people to effectually interact, in various telecopresent environments, the scale of participants vary dramatically from one-to-one interactions (e.g., instant messaging, text messaging, private chats) to one-to-many interactions (e.g., wall comments on Facebook, Tweets). Finally, the level of mobility refers to the "capacity of copresent individuals to carry the interactions around" (Zhao, 2003, p. 451). Although face-to-face interactions are situated within physical spaces, Zhao (2003) distinguishes between stationary, portable, and wearable mobility conditions within telecopresence.

Conventional desktop computing constitutes stationary telecopresence (Zhao, 2003). Laptop computers and devices requiring a Wi-Fi connection constitute mobile telecopresence, as they allow users to establish telecopresence at various situated locations (Zhao, 2003). Cell phones, smartphones, and digitally connected tablets constitute wearable telecopresence, whereby the users can maintain fluid telecopresence while navigating and moving through various social environments (Zhao, 2003). The trajectories of romantic relationships are unconditionally impacted by the structures of telecopresence produced through the unique interface parameters of the social environments within which the relationships are initiated and maintained. In practice, since the overwhelming majority of romantic relationships involve multiplexing, every relationship involves a unique configuration of interface parameters (Baym, 2010). Although it would be impossible to outline all of the possible configurations of interface parameters shaping a variety of structures of telecopresence, the point here is that connected romantic relationships are developed and managed within a highly complex social environment. At this point, it is necessary to take a closer look at the unique structures and dynamics of the relationship-self processes involved in the development and maintenance of exclusively online romantic relationships, online-to-offline romantic relationships, and offline-to-online relationships.

Exclusively online relationships. Resembling interactions amongst people offline, online interactions can also lead to platonic and romantic relationships. In the virtual world of Azeroth, Arixi Fizzlebolt and Weulfgar McDoal discovered their mutual attraction for each other during their campaign leading up to the successful defeat of Prince Malchezaar in the video game World of Warcraft (Rosenbloom, 2011). Following the defeat of the evil Prince, Arixi and Weulfgar found a quiet virtual space in the game to talk (Rosenbloom, 2011). After hours of this in-game conversation, they both felt a new romance developing (Rosenbloom, 2011). For months following their defeat of the prince, the couple dated within the expansive virtual world, ultimately fell in love and lived happily ever after (Rosenbloom, 2011). This narrative echoes stories we hear about people falling in love in the "real" or offline world, courtship and all. Although the online courtship of Arixi and Weulfgar eventually led to a face-to-face meeting, it is not uncommon for online relationships to stay online, indefinitely.

An exclusively online relationship is a relationship maintained by two individuals, who have never met face-to-face, entirely online through various Internet mediums such as e-mail, social media, and online video games. Exclusively online relationships offer many benefits that offline relationships do not, such as sexual encounters without the fear of disease or pregnancy, anonymity, and privacy. These relationships adhere to most of the same rules and norms that are associated with offline relationships. However, the few differences between exclusively online relationships and face-to-face relationships can influence how these relationships develop online. First, online relationships tend to begin with the discovery of similarities and self-disclosure and not physical attraction (Cooper & Sportolari, 1997). Exceptions to this are relationships maintained through popular social media websites and apps (e.g., Myspace, Tumblr, Facebook, Instagram) where the presentation of self takes place primarily on a profile page with pictures of the individual and through statuses or posts. Popular television shows such as Catfish have addressed the many problems associated with online dating and the authenticity of presentation of self. Second, spatial proximity is a less important determinant for online relationships (Cooper & Sportolari, 1997). The distance between individuals can vary from only a few miles to across the world. Although, exclusively online relationships lack the element of physical copresence they are equally as "real" as offline relationships. Third, the Internet provides individuals with a sense of anonymity that allows them to feel more comfortable with sharing personal information online compared to face-to-face interactions (Wysocki, 1998). Anonymity allows the individual to be in more control over their presentation of self and thus gives them the freedom to express themselves as they desire. These three factors make the exclusively online relationship a very complex and dynamic phenomenon. The virtual worlds of World of Warcraft and Second Life, two types of massively multiplayer online role-playing games, are prime examples of social environments that are conducive to exclusively online relationships.

Online gaming functions as an important element of many people's leisure lifestyles or free time (Bryce & Rutter, 2003). Massively multiplayer online role-playing games (MMORPGs) are detailed virtual worlds inhabited by player-controlled characters, non-player characters (NPCs), and mobiles (mobs) that contain vast amounts of visual and auditory elements that are inspired by science fiction, fantasy, and life on earth. Individuals who participate in MMORPGs are referred to as players, and as players they control the actions and behaviors of their characters also known as avatars. Before MMORPGs there were text-based games online called MUDs (Multi User Dungeons). MUDs allowed players to experiment with new roles and identities from behind the safety of the screen (Turkle, 1995). Similarly, MMORPGs are a relatively new medium for computer-mediated communication (CMC) that affords new ways to explore social identities and interactions (Yee, 2006a).

The virtual worlds present in MMORPGs are social environments that provide opportunities for players to form friendships and close relationships. MMORPGs are designed to encourage social interaction with others and group collaboration (Krotoski, 2004). Indeed, platonic and romantic relationships form frequently in MMORPGs (Yee, 2006b). Cole and Griffiths (2007) found in their survey study that approximately three quarters of all individuals who play MMORPGs become good friends with other players, and that the amount of hours played per week is positively associated with the number of friends an individual has within a game. In addition, they found that one third of gamers are attracted to another player at least once in their gaming career and that female players are significantly more likely to be attracted to another player (Cole & Griffiths, 2007). Indeed, players can be attracted to each other in MMORPGs and form relationships although they may never result in a face-to-face encounter. These relationships can always potentially escalate in importance. In the early 2000s, players began to have in-game marriages (Wu, Fore, Wang, & Ho, 2007). In-game marriages are very similar to offline marriages in that they symbolize the love and unity between two players. For example, MMORPGs such as *Final Fantasy XI* allow players to obtain a formal coat, wedding dress, and wedding bands inscribed with their partner's name for their wedding ceremony. However, in-game marriages like the one abovementioned often lack any strategic benefit for the players (e.g., tax credits, larger loans), and in-game marriages can last for years exclusively online never to result in a face-to-face interaction.

Without the ability to be physically next to each other players must perform relationship maintenance techniques regularly to keep their relationships at a satisfactory level. Players can perform relationship maintenance via many activities. The most common ways are private messaging, guild voice client, exploring, questing, player versus player (PvP) arenas, and raiding. Raiding is a very popular activity in MMORPGs. Raiding is an activity in which players form a group or an alliance to eradicate monsters while traveling through a cave, tower, or castle-like structure ultimately arriving at the most powerful monster whom they must all work together to destroy. During in-game activities, players interact with each other through either text or audio and can potentially become closer because of their interaction.

Interactions online are fundamentally not so different from interactions offline. Evidence suggests that individuals communicate online with each other as they would offline (Jordan, 2014; Ward & Tracey, 2004). Most interactions in MMORPGs proceed about the same as they do offline. Individuals interacting with each other for the first time in an MMORPG may have little to no information about the other at first, but they are by no means starting from a blank slate. That is, they are not interacting in a vacuum and bring to the table all the knowledge and lessons they have gained through previous life experiences, online and offline. They build upon that initial interaction with subsequent interactions online. During MMORPG interactions, in which individuals give a presentation of self, they often have ample time to prepare their performance (Yee, 2006b). They are allowed this time, because individuals are typically not expected to respond in real-time except for instances in which players are communicating via voice over Internet protocol (VoIP) clients. Individuals form an impression of the other by interpreting the information that the other has prepared and communicated to them. Since they do not have to worry about non-verbal gestures and their appearance, they can concentrate on the content and structure of the message in hopes of influencing its interpretation (Yee, 2006b). Having greater control over presentation of self is not unique to MMORPGs and in fact is the case in almost all forms of computer-mediated communication (Walther, 1996).

MMORPGs allow players to have hyperpersonal interactions—interactions that have greater levels of intimacy, intensity, and saliency than face-to-face interactions because of the individual's ability to strategically construct their presentation of self (Walther, 1996). Studies have shown that there are many factors influencing the quality of online relationships. Closeness in online friendships is contingent on many factors such as social similarity, content, frequency and variation of activities, and length of the friendship (Mesch & Talmud, 2006). Those who disclose more personal information to their online friends report greater closeness to online friends than face-to-face friends (McKenna, Green, & Gleason, 2002).

MMORPG social interactions are not immune to the forms of oppression that exist offline. Computer gaming has long been dominated by males, and, thus, it is no surprise that sexism, misogyny, and sexual harassment are a part of MMORPG social interactions. Female characters are often overwhelmed with attention, sexual advances, and offers of assistance from players who assume they cannot do anything for themselves (Bruckman, 1999; Turkle, 1995). Furthermore, hyperpersonal interactions within online games can sometimes be problematic, especially for youths. Youths can be intensely trusting of their online relationships to the point that they hastily share personal information (Mishna, McLuckie, & Saini, 2009). Anonymity combined with trust in online interactions can place youths at risk for victimization (Ybarra & Mitchell, 2004), which often goes unreported to parents or adults (Finkelhor, Mitchell, & Wolak, 2000; O'Connell, Price, & Barrow, 2004). Although youths can get into unfavorable situations by being too trusting of online partners, they are not the only ones victimized by those they feel close to online.

Case Study 3.1

Catfish, the MTV television show, is a key example of how the combination of hyperpersonal interactions and online relationships can result in someone getting hurt emotionally and financially. In Season 2 Episode 11 of Catfish, Aaliyah, the 'catfishee,' was hoping that she would be able to express, face-to-face, her true feelings to her first love Alicia, the 'catfish' (Schulman & Joseph, 2013). Aaliyah tells the co-hosts of the show that the two initially met on Facebook and eventually moved their conversation over to text messaging. While both women lived in Oakland, California, they were unable to meet because Alicia had yet to reveal her homosexuality to her family and friends (Schulman & Joseph, 2013). Alicia, unfortunately, had an ulterior motive for their relationship. Over approximately one year, she received a total of $600 and a new iPhone from Aaliyah, who was currently experiencing financial hardship (Schulman & Joseph, 2013). When the two online lovers finally met face-to-face, it was an unpleasant ordeal: Alicia cruelly laughed in Aaliyah's face, stating that she never had romantic feelings for Aaliyah, she used her, and that she is not homosexual. Afterword, Alicia admitted to Nev Schulman, one the co-hosts and producers, that she was conning multiple people online in the same manner (Schulman & Joseph, 2013). In this situation, hyperpersonal interactions through Facebook and text messaging allowed one individual to carefully construct their self-presentation in order to manipulate and con the other out of money, despite the victim's financial hardship. This case is evidence of the influence hyperpersonal interactions have on an individual's behaviors. If Alicia was not a con artist and had genuine romantic feelings toward Aaliyah, then their relationship might have continued offline, thus becoming an online-to-offline relationship.

Online-to-Offline Relationships

Online-to-offline relationships consist of people who met in an online forum, but chose to continue the relationship offline. Many people who are seeking romantic partners turn to popular social media as well as online dating services (Baker, 2008; Gunter, 2013). The objective is to meet someone online, and, if everything goes well, continue the relationship offline. People seek such relationships through various media. Baker (2008) broadly distinguishes between two online fora in which relationships arise: (1) virtual communities, which are online groups of people interacting for various purposes other than romance or dating purposes (e.g., SNSs, MMORPGs, chatrooms, online news groups, blogs), and (2) online dating sites, which are online websites devoted strictly to development of relationships, geared toward romantic interests (e.g., Match.com, eHarmony, ChristianMingle.com). However, online dating sites vary significantly according to the means through which people search for potential partners. Fiore and Donath (2004, p. 1397) identified three such types of online dating sites: (1) "search/sort/match systems," characterized by a profile, search engine through which others meeting specific criteria can be identified, and private messaging capabilities (e.g., Match.com, Lavalife.com), (2) "personality-matching systems," through which people are matched based upon the results of users' personality tests (e.g., eHarmony.com), and (3) "social network systems," within which people are encouraged to have their friends and family log into the site to suggest potential matches (e.g., Friendster.com).

Online dating sites were once considered taboo or not the norm for seeking relationships, but are now a commonly used service (Gibbs et al., 2011). The motivations for seeking relationships online range from individual personality factors to social factors (Muise, Christofides, & Desmarais, 2009; Utz & Beukeboom, 2011). Early research on online dating focused largely on individual personality factors, suggesting that people who used online dating services struggle with basic social skills and often experienced social anxiety (Erwin, Turk, Heimberg, Fresco, & Hantula, 2004; Kraut, Keisler, Boneva, Cummings, Helgeson, & Crawford, 2002; Kraut, Patterson, Lundmark, Keisler, Mukhopadhyay, & Scherlis, 1998; McKenna et al., 2002; Morahan-Martin & Schumacher, 2003; Scharlott & Christ, 1995). However, a substantial amount of more recent research provides evidence that people who use online dating sites are quite social offline (Bargh & McKenna, 2004; Gunter, 2013; Shaw & Gant, 2002; Valkenburg, Peter, & Schouten, 2006). Although online dating sites have proven relatively useful for people who feel uncomfortable in face-to-face interactions, social factors largely motivate people to use online dating services (Baker, 2005; Barraket & Henry-Waring, 2008). Barraket and Henry-Waring (2008) outline five such social factors:

1. An avenue for developing a new social network after relocating for work.
2. A means of coping with the isolation felt as a result of single-parenting.
3. A solution to the limited possibilities for traditional courtship due to one's work commitment and obligations.
4. A means of finding new romance after a breakup of a long-term relationship.

Although many people who use online dating sites seek some degree of intimacy (Baker, 2008), other people use it primarily as a means for alleviating loneliness (Lawson & Leck, 2006). In fact, people often use online dating sites as a means for connecting with others following various life crises, such as coping with the death of a close family member, friend, or significant other or attempting to move on following a divorce (Lawson & Leck, 2006).

People also use online dating sites as a strategy for coping with the challenges of meeting a romantic partner offline (Baker, 2002, 2008). Specifically, online dating sites provide greater control over various aspects of self-presentation (Gibbs et al., 2011; Lawson & Leck, 2006). They allow people to meet others outside of their local environment and social network (Baker, 2008). Moreover, given the disembodiment of online dating sites and disconnection from their local social environments, people often feel a greater freedom in their self-presentations as well as liberation from stereotypical roles (Gibbs et al., 2011; Lawson & Leck, 2006; Rabby, 2007).

Although online dating sites are popular and useful fora for meeting others, relationship initiation in online dating sites come with a substantial amount of uncertainty and a variety of unique challenges. Much of the current research focuses on the centrality—and, thus, the challenge—of self-presentation and self-disclosure in online relationship formation (Baker, 2008; Ellison et al., 2006; Gibbs et al., 2011; Toma et al., 2008). Unlike offline self-presentation, self-presentation online is disembodied and dislocated, which means that people have more freedom to present their *ideal* selves, i.e., the "representation of how you or another would like to see yourself" (Whitty, 2007, p. 2). In online dating sites, people often embellish characteristics of themselves; however, they rarely consider it deceitful, as they feel it is a means of "selling themselves" to others (Ellison et al., 2006; Gibbs et al., 2006; Gibbs et al., 2011). That is, such subjectively slight embellishments are effectively marketing strategies for selling their product—in this case, it is themselves (Guadagno, Okdie, & Kruse, 2012; Toma & Hancock, 2010). Although people often embellish themselves online, most people are quite cognizant of the potential for offline meeting, should the relationship develop (Ellison et al., 2006). Therefore, they often seek to balance their self-presentation between their ideal selves, their actual selves, and their "ought to" selves (Ellison et al., 2006; Higgins, 1987; Toma & Hancock, 2010). Whereas the actual selves are the characteristics people are in actual possession of, and the "ought to" selves reflect the characteristics people feel they should possess (Ellison et al., 2006; Higgins, 1987).

Case Study 3.2

In a 2013 *Ted.com* lecture, Amy Webb, a statistically minded 30-year-old award-winning journalist and CEO of a digital strategies group, described her experience with online dating. After a good, yet ultimately failed, relationship, she found herself in a conundrum about how to not only meet her Prince Charming, but also meet him in time to fall in love, marry, and ultimately have a child by the time she's 35. To complicate matters, she had a very clear idea about what she was—and was not—looking for in a partner: among other things, he must be between the ages of 30 and 36, be culturally Jewish, enjoy "non-cruise ship" travelling, and be a non-sport-loving man. However, she crunched the numbers and determined that, statistically speaking, only around 35 men in Philadelphia, where she lived at the time, fit her criteria. Therefore, following the advice of friends and family, she turned to online dating websites.

Ms. Webb quickly not only discovered the critical importance of online self-presentation, but also the complexity of online self-presentation. She completed her profile, and she filled out the characteristics in the ideal partner. However, after a number of bad dates, she began reflecting upon, and ultimately systematically studying, profiles of other women on the dating websites in order to figure out how to meet her Prince Charming online. She collected data, developed spreadsheets, ran some analyses, and she ultimately concluded that the algorithms used in online dating sites are not flawed; rather, she claimed,

> The real problem here is that, while the algorithms work just fine, you and I don't, when confronted with blank windows where we're supposed to input our information online. Very few of us have the ability to be totally and brutally honest with ourselves. The other problem is that these websites are asking us questions like, are you a dog person or a cat person? Do you like horror films or romance films? I'm not looking for a pen pal. I'm looking for a husband. Right? So there's a certain amount of superficiality in that data (Webb, 2013).

In this sense, she recognized that people tend to present certain ideal images of themselves online, which, complicated by the superficial nature of the profile questionnaire, meant that, although people might be able to convey positive images of themselves, they face the second challenge of attracting a partner who compliments their images of self. She ultimately created a number of fake male profiles, in order to collect "data on the women who were going to be attracted to the type of man that I really, really wanted to marry" (Webb, 2013). She stated,

> So I was looking at qualitative data, so what was the humor, the tone, the voice, the communication style that these women shared in common? And also quantitative data, so what was the average length of their profile, how much time was spent between messages? (Webb, 2013)

From her research, she determined that "content matters a lot" (Webb, 2013); the ideal profile consisted of around 97 words, with optimistic, non-specific content that conveys to others approachability; furthermore, the more photos, the better. Finally, she found that the timing at which people contact others on the site is important:

> Just because you have access to somebody's mobile phone number or their instant message account and it's 2 o'clock in the morning and you happen to be awake, doesn't mean that that's a good time to communicate with those people. The popular women on these online sites spend an average of 23 hours in between each communication. And that's what we would normally do in the usual process of courtship (Webb, 2013).

Based on her research, she developed what she called the "super profile" focusing on the aforementioned strategies. Ultimately, she successfully met, married, and had a child with her Prince Charming. She concluded,

> Well, as it turns out, there is an algorithm for love. It's just not the ones that we're being presented with online. In fact, it's something that you write yourself. So whether you're looking for a husband or a wife or you're trying to find your passion or you're trying to start a business, all you have to really do is figure out your own framework and play by your own rules, and feel free to be as picky as you want (Webb, 2013).

Although she concluded that people must figure out their own approaches and play by their own rules, she was actually acknowledging that you must understand that strategic self-presentation is important and that rules absolutely matter when meeting others online. That is, although algorithms might connect people with others, it does not replace the critical importance of self-presentation in online dating sites. In addition to the algorithms, she effectively emphasizes the importance of strategic self-disclosure and self-presentation. One interpretation of her experience is that, rather than presenting an ideal self or an actual self—a self that simply reflect as precisely as possible who a person really is or who a person would like to be—the "super profile" focuses on the ought self, which focuses on conveying general, positive, and optimistic information about oneself through a brief narrative and an array of photos. Such an ought self is not a rejection of the actual self; rather, it conforms to the norms of the online social environment.

Unlike offline relationships, an online relationship in an online dating site relies solely on self-presentation (Whitty, 2008b). Offline, people can have circumstantial run-ins that could serendipitously result in a romantic relationship. Although self-presentation even in the most random of meetings is crucial for a relationship to arise, happenchance meetings in online dating sites do not happen. Consequently, the foundation of any form of potential interaction within such sites is solely people's self-presentations. Therefore, consideration must be made to strategically present oneself in a manner that would attract or otherwise produce matches with some degree of similarity (Toma et al., 2008; Whitty & Carr, 2006). Since people's self-presentations must fit within the constraints of the particular site's technological format, people often use creative, colorful language as well as selected photos to "give off" a particular impression to the other (Ellison et al., 2006; Goffman, 1959). In this sense, people must focus on accentuating themselves in the information they provide, but they also must cautiously self-disclose (Gibbs et al., 2006; Sprecher, 2009). That is, they want to provide enough information to attract potential partners, but they do not want to provide so much information, which could potentially discourage potential partners from contacting them (Baker, 2005; Toma & Hancock, 2010). The verdict is still out about the importance of physical appearance in online dating sites. Whereas some researchers argue that physical appearance is not as important in online dating fora as it is in offline meetings (Baker, 2008; McKenna & Bargh, 2000), a substantial amount of research suggests that physical appearance is, in fact, just as important as in offline meetings (Gunter, 2013; Toma & Hancock, 2010). The major difference is that physical appearance is only displayed in a small number of select pictures the user chooses to disclose. Therefore, although physical appearance is important in online dating fora, it is largely a "gating" feature (McKenna & Bargh, 2000). If the physical appearance is generally attractive to the other, the relationship could move forward with emphasis on other aspects of the person's self-presentation (Toma & Hancock, 2010).

Although strategic self-presentation is challenging enough, users also must be cautious about the others they meet in online dating fora. Numerous mass media reports account for online daters, primarily women, who have become victims of rape and sexual assault by people they met in online dating sites (Adams, 2014; Matyszczyk, 2011; McMillian, 2014; Meyer, 2012). Therefore, accepting a person's profile for proverbially face value comes with much greater risk than meeting a person offline. Most online daters are very concerned about the authenticity of the potential partner (Ellison et al., 2006; O'Sullivan, 2000; Toma et al., 2008), as well as their safety should they meet their potential partner face-to-face. Therefore, "warranting" is a common practice in online relationship formation. Warranting is "the capacity to draw a reliable connection between a presented persona online and a corporeally anchored person in the physical world" (Walther, Van Der Heide, Hamel, Shulman, 2009, p. 232). Unlike offline meetings, information seeking—that is, seeking information to help develop an accurate impression of the other person—occurs outside of the other's purview (Gibbs et al., 2011; Ramirez, Walther, Burgoon, & Sunnafrank, 2002); consequently, the accuracy on one's impression of the other is an elusive idea and undoubtedly subjective determination—as the many reports of rape and sexual assault perpetrated by people met online confirm (Cornwell & Lundgren, 2001).

Although online daters are concerned about safety, they are also concerned about compatibility of the other. Researchers often refer to the importance of identifying similarities in determining compatibility (Anderson & Emmers-Sommer, 2006). Similarities, however, are not limited to basic interests. Rather, the similarities begin with basic structural characteristics of the other person—race, age, height, income or occupation, marital status. Beyond such basic characteristics, people seek similarities in regards to interests, hobbies, as well as personality dispositions (Barnes, 2003). However, ultimately, compatibility involves a basic assessment of the other in terms of one's self-conception (Anderson & Emmers-Sommer, 2006). Aside from online dating sites, online-to-offline relationships can also develop through the utilization of virtual communities.

Virtual communities constitute a very wide range of online fora—from chatrooms to Second Life—and relationship formation within such communities can occur in a wide variety of ways. Rather than surveying all of the possible non-dating site fora in which relationships could arise, a few general characteristics of relationship formation in virtual communities will be reviewed. Needless to say, relationship formation in virtual communities is far less structured and predictable than in online dating sites. People rarely enter general virtual communities with the primary goal of meeting a romantic partner (Baker, 2008); rather, people enter various virtual communities with a wide range of objectives. Consequently, courtship often occurs serendipitously as people happen to meet, for example, through a friend of a friend's Facebook page or while playing World of Warcraft. Baker (2008) identifies four ways in which relationships arise differently in virtual communities than in online dating sites.

First, whereas people in online dating sites meet through a filtering process based upon what characteristics the person feels are desirable, people in virtual communities interact with everyone else who is online at that time. Instead of reviewing simply profiles of others one-at-a-time, in virtual communities, everyone interacts—potentially in real time—with all others who are logged in at that time (Baker, 2008). Second, the selection of a potential partner can occur quite rapidly in an online dating site; however, people in virtual communities only get to know each other through repeated social interactions within the given fora (Baker, 2008). Third, in online dating sites, people are matched with others automatically through matching software applications. In virtual communities, Baker (2008, p. 172) argues, "matching is completely under the control of the individual participant." Finally, online daters have to follow a proscribed protocol when communicating to potential dates, as online dating sites restrict access to personal contact information until each person communicates through the site and subsequently consents to revealing contact information to the other. Conversely, in virtual communities, people use "backchanneling," i.e., communication outside of the specific medium in which the two met, to communicate with each other and, thus, express interest in each other (Baker, 2008, p. 172).

In virtual communities, once relationships are initiated, people face similar, yet qualitatively different, challenges to self-presentation, self-disclosure, as well as information-seeking that online daters experience. First, self-presentation in virtual communities is far more restrictive (Gibbs et al., 2011). For example, in Second Life, where people interact through highly individualized avatars, interaction is synchronous, and users can speak to each other directly, self-presentation is highly dynamic with a wide range of rich cues (Williams, Kennedy, & Moore, 2011; Zhao, 2003). People are able to develop an avatar that expresses just about anything about themselves—or absolutely nothing about themselves. For example, one of the authors of this chapter taught a class partially through Second Life in which his avatar resembled Shrek in a nice business suit with a blunt in one hand and a large growler in the other hand. Nonetheless, unlike online dating sites, self-presentation is multi-faceted. However, in such a forum, users have substantial control over the information provided to others, and anonymity is the norm (Williams et al., 2011).

In more mainstream virtual communities such as SNS, participants engage in self-presentation in a less-synchronous fashion. For example, in Facebook and Twitter, people commonly interact with others through text-based communication, emojis, and digital photos. SNS allow the individual to carefully construct a self-image through less-synchronous means for others to view at their leisure. If relationships arise within such media, they often switch to other, more personal media to get to know one another such as text messaging (Turkle, 2008, 2011). Text messaging allows individuals in a relationship to have more direct and immediate means to get to know each other before a face-to-face meeting. This sequence can often flow in the opposite direction from the initial face-to-face interaction to a combination of an online and offline relationship.

Offline-to-Online Relationships

Throughout the course of most people's everyday experiences, they often seamlessly move between their offline and online lives—from face-to-face interactions to interacting, for example, via email, Facebook, text messages, Twitter, Snapchat, Instagram, or Skype (Humphreys, 2005; Turkle, 2011). Since the Internet has become so deeply normalized in everyday life, it is virtually impossible for relationships of any sort to be exclusively offline (Turkle, 2011). Since Internet-based technologies are integrated into most areas of our work, social, and personal lives, people tend to integrate technology into their relationships very early in the offline relationship formation process—if not instantaneously (Turkle, 2011). In this sense, people not only become tethered to their devices but also to the relationships they manage through their devices (Turkle, 2008).

McCall and Simmons (1966) claim that as close relationships develop they move toward totality; that is, in the process of developing relational identities, people begin sharing more about who they are in different environments and begin incorporating the other into these other relationships. In a similar way, social technologies exacerbate this move toward totality. In most romantic relationships, people engage in multiplexing, whereby they interact with their significant others through various online media (Baym, 2010). Multiplexing produces a relational environment in which both interlocutors are assumed to be perpetually available to each other at all times (Baym, 2010; Turkle, 2008). Within each romantic relationship arises a unique set of relational norms associated with the relational identity of each interlocutor. They become accustomed to the their partner's idiosyncratic uses, which ultimately become the norms of reciprocity within the relationship (Horstmanshof & Powers, 2005).

Internet-based mobile devices cut across traditional relational boundaries that were once upheld by physical boundaries and proximate situated interactions. Prior to the popularity of such devices, social interactions were not only situated largely in physical spaces, but also those physical spaces established relatively stable relational boundaries within which information to others about oneself could be more easily controlled. However, with mobile devices that provide instantaneous (or at least potentially instantaneous) digital connection to others, people can be called upon to simultaneously negotiate multiple "front stages" (Goffman, 1959; Palen, Salzman, & Youngs, 2000; Turkle, 2008). Romantic relationships that are taken online become premised on a sense of continual copresence—the sense that they and their significant others are perpetually copresent through their social technologies (Gergen, 2002; Turkle, 2011). That is, not only can they be available to their partners, but also they should be available to their partners; moreover, not only can their partners be available to them, but also they should be available to them. Such an astringent move toward totality arising from a sense of continual copresence presents complex challenges for managing information control, self-presentation, and self-disclosure within romantic relationships (Ling & Campbell, 2012). In this sense, social technologies are inherently Janus-faced—both immensely useful for and potentially detrimental to the development and maintenance of romantic relationships.

On the one hand, taking romantic relationships online provides a vast array of opportunities for self-presentation, relationship maintenance, and constructing relational identities, which could greatly contribute to developing and sustaining the relationship. Research suggests that people use text messages as forms of gift-giving (Taylor & Harper, 2002). Sending brief statements (e.g., "Just thinking about you"; "I love you"; "Hope you have a good day") or even a simple emoji serve as small gifts to the recipients to let them know, at the very least, that the senders are thinking about them (Taylor & Harper, 2002; Ramirez & Broneck, 2009).

Facebook, too, allows for a disembodied self-presentation for the other. Once people "friend" their partners, the status update to "in a relationship" confirms to their partners, as well as all of their other Facebook friends, that they identify with their now romantic significant other. Furthermore, posting comments directly to their partners, posting comments to others with the intent of their partner seeing the comments, or even posting pictures of the two of them together serve as self-presentation and relationship maintenance strategies (Ellison et al., 2006; Gibbs et al., 2011; Toma et al., 2008).

Even instant messaging programs (e.g., Skype, Facebook Chat) contribute to a sense of closeness by seeing that their partners are at least online (i.e., available to them) or posting an away message for the other that reaffirms the relationship (e.g., "Wrapping up work; can't wait to see my honey") (Baron, Squires, Tench, & Thompson, 2005; Baym, 2010). Moreover, even email provides a means for engaging in relationship maintenance (Johnson, Haigh, Becker, Craig, & Wigley, 2008; Stafford, Kline, & Dimmick, 1999).

McCall and Simmons (1966, p. 189) once claimed that the move toward totality within romantic relationships "is hard to comply with at great distance, for it is impossible to include all one's life in letters and rare visits." Moreover, they argue, "Frequent face-to-face interaction seems to be a necessary condition for a strong and viable relationship" (McCall & Simmons, 1966, p. 189). Although this might have been true 50 years ago, social technologies allow for remote relationship development and maintenance.

On the other hand, while social technologies provide new and very useful means for engaging in self-presentation and relationship maintenance, they also—and always—have potential for hindering the development of the relationship and undermining relationship maintenance strategies. First, maintaining the expectations associated with continual copresence is monumentally challenging, particularly in the early stages of a romantic relationship (Horstmanshof & Powers, 2005). That is, in the development of relational identities, information control, relationship maintenance, and self-presentation strategies are critical. One such expectation that becomes embedded within the relational identities is that of constant availability—that the other should be able to get in touch with their partner anytime and anywhere. Although such expectations are unreasonable in practice, they become normative to the relational identity. Therefore, people must develop boundary work strategies (Turkle, 2011). Such strategies might consist of providing information about where one will be for roughly how long prior to the event itself, which serves as a disclaimer in the event a text message is not immediately reciprocates or a cell phone call goes unanswered. However, other such boundary work involves strategic accounting for not answering a call, text message, or instant message at times when they are normally available—or when their partners expect them to be available or when they do not have an away message posted. Violation of these norms of reciprocity could strain the relationship, as they are inconsistent with their relational identities.

Second, when romantic relationships are taken online, a new, vast array of information about the other becomes available—regardless if such information is overtly sought or unwanted. Initiating a romantic relationship offline is intimidating and formidable enough; however, once the relationship is taken online, particularly on SNS, a substantial amount of information about the other becomes available, which could be interpreted as discrediting to or inconsistent with the relational identities being developed. Furthermore, on SNS such as Facebook, the presence of information about a partner's friends, comments the partner made to others, and comment exchanges are readily available, which has been found to produce jealousy (Muise et al., 2009). Therefore, people's control over their own self-disclosure—a characteristic critical to relationship formation and maintenance—decreases. This decreasing control over self-disclosure is a consequence of the unpredictable interpretations of the information available on such SNS. Having an ex-girlfriend or boyfriend as a Facebook friend could potentially be interpreted by the new romantic interest as perfectly harmless or as potentially threatening to the relationship. Self-disclosure, then, becomes a complex process of managing the information available to the other through incoming calls, text messages, Facebook posts, Twitter tweets, et cetera. The more social technologies people use, the more complex information control becomes (Gergen, 2002; Muise et al., 2009; Turkle, 2011).

Additionally, as more online sources for information are made available, people often use the Internet for developing a relational identity for the other. Facebook, in particular, has become a ripe environment for warranting (Baym, 2010). A number of studies establish a link between Facebook use and jealousy (Muise et al., 2009; Marshall, Benjanyan, Di Castro, & Lee, 2013). Jealousy is a result of finding new information about a significant other that is void of definitive meaning. That is, as people seek information about their significant other, they come upon information that raises question about the other person's commitment, honesty, or integrity, such as a comment from an ex-partner on their significant other's Facebook page. Since such information-seeking tasks are completed when people's partners are not around, the new information is open to interpretation. The other person has no involvement in helping their significant other interpret the questionable posts; therefore, the possibility of jealousy cannot be ruled out. The randomness of interpretations of such information is largely associated with the viewers' understanding of their significant others' relational identity as well as the person's self-efficacy, personal history, and the relational history.

Since online interactions are disembodied, people are unable to adjust their self-presentations to increase the likelihood of their partners interpreting information in a manner most consistent with, and conducive to, the relational identities constructed within the romantic relationships. As online technologies are integrated into relationships, people relinquish a certain degree of control over self-presentation and self-disclosure, as the expectations for remote reciprocation increase and the potential for indiscriminate appearance of unintended information that could challenge the relational identities increase (Hjorth, 2012; Höflich, & Linke, 2012).

Conclusion

With the rapid advancement in social technology, the means through which people establish and manage their relationships is dramatically changing (Baym, Zhang, Kunkel, Lin, & Ledbetter, 2007; Baym, Zhang, & Lin, 2004). The courtship process as well as the general process of relationship development in the 21st century is far more complex, as couples commonly navigate their relationships within and through various social technologies. Navigating social life in a technologically connected society allows for numerous historically new ways of meeting others and managing romantic interests; however, despite the numerous benefits, social technologies present a vast array of challenges to relationship formation and maintenance.

The process through which all romantic relationships develop is a complex process involving both developing relational identities with the other as well as managing the relationship based upon the expectations of the relational identities. All relationships involve a complex self-other process, in which each person in the relationship must engage in self-presentation, self-disclosure, and relationship maintenance. When the relationship arises solely online, arises online then is taken offline, or arises offline and is taken online, the complexity of the aforementioned processes are compounded. Although the Internet has provided a wealth of new opportunities for initiating and/or managing relationships, it presents a volatile environment that could potentially threaten the relationship itself.

With the rapid advent of new and innovative social technologies, the structure and dynamics of romantic relationships will continue to change—and could do so quite rapidly. Romantic relationships are likely to become increasingly hybridized, as social technologies are only increasing in popularity; moreover, among a generation of children who have no firsthand experience of a social world without the Internet, hybrid online-offline relationships are normalized. Since social technology is still relatively new in our social experience, researchers are only beginning to understand the consequences of the Internet on romantic relationships.

References

Adams, A. (2014, June 24). Man Found Guilty in Christian Mingle Rape Case. *NBC San Diego*. Retrieved from: http://www.nbcsandiego.com/news/local/Verdict-Reached-in-Christian-Mingle-Rape-Case-Sean-Banks-264292301.html.

Anderson, T., & Emmers-Sommer, T. (2006). Predictors of relationship satisfaction in online romantic relationships. *Communication Studies, 57*(2), 153–172.

Aron, A., & Aron, E. (1986). *Love as the expansion of self: Understanding attraction and satisfaction.* New York, NY: Hemisphere.

Aron, A., & Aron E. (1996). Love and the expansion of the self: The state of the model. *Personal Relationships, 3,* 45–58.

Baker, A. (2002). What makes an online relationship successful? Clues from couples who met in cyberspace. *CyberPsychology & Behavior, 5*(4), 363–375.

Baker, A. (2005). *Double Click: Romance and Commitment Among Online Couples*. Cresskill, NJ: Hampton Press.

Baker, A. (2008). Down the rabbit hole: The role of place in the initiation and development of online relationships. In A. Barak (Ed.), *Psychological Aspects of Cyberspace: Theory, Research, Applications* (pp. 163–184). New York, NY: Cambridge University Press.

Bargh, J. A., & McKenna, K. Y. (2004). The Internet and social life. *Annual Review of Psychology, 55*, 573–590.

Barnes, S. (2003). *Computer-Mediated Communication: Human-to-Human Communication Across the Internet*. Boston, MA: Allyn & Bacon.

Barraket, J., & Henry-Waring, M. S. (2008). Getting it on (line) Sociological perspectives on e-dating. *Journal of Sociology, 44*(2), 149–165.

Baron, N. S., Squires, L., Tench, S., & Thompson, M. (2005). Tethered or mobile? Use of away messages in instant messaging by American college students. In Mobile Communications (pp. 293–311). Springer London.

Baym, N. (2010).*Personal Connections in the Digital Age*. Malden, MA: Polity Press.

Baym, N., Zhang, Y., Kunkel, A., Lin, M., & Ledbetter, A. (2007). Relational quality and media use in interpersonal relationships. *New Media & Society, 9*, 735–752.

Baym, N., Zhang, Y., & Lin, M.C. (2004). Social interactions across media: Interpersonal communication on the Internet, telephone, and face-to-face. *New Media and Society,6*, 299–318.

Blumstein, P., & Kollock, P. (1988). Personal relationships. *Annual Review of Sociology, 14*, 467–490.

Bruckman, A. S. (1999). Gender swapping on the Internet. In V. J. Vitanza (Ed.), *Cyberreader* (2nd ed., pp. 418–425). Boston, MA: Allyn & Bacon.

Bryce, J., & Rutter, J. (2003). The gendering of computer gaming: Experiences and space. In S. Fleming & I. Jones (Eds.), *Leisure culture: Investigations in sport, media and technology* (pp. 3–22). Eastbourne, UK: Leisure Studies Association.

Canary, D. J., & Stafford, L. (1994). Maintaining relationships through strategic and routine interaction. In D. Canary & L. Stafford, *Communication and Relational Maintenance* (pp. 3–19). San Diego, CA: Academic Press.

Carpenter, C. J., & Spottswood, E. L. (2013). Exploring romantic relationships on social networking sites using the self-expansion model. *Computers in Human Behavior, 29*(4), 1531–1537.

Cole, H., & Griffiths, M. D. (2007). Social interactions in massively multiplayer online role-playing gamers. *CyberPsychology & Behavior, 10*(4), 575–583.

Cooley, C. H. (1967). *Human nature and the social order, 2nd ed.* New York, NY: Schocken Books.

Cooper, A., & Sportolari, L. (1997). Romance in cyberspace: Understanding online attraction. *Journal of Sex Education and Therapy, 22,* 7–14.

Cornwell, B., & Lundgren, D. C. (2001). Love on the Internet: Involvement and misrepresentation in romantic relationships in cyberspace vs. realspace. *Computers in Human Behavior, 17*(2), 197–211.

Dainton, M., & Stafford, L. (1993). Routine maintenance behaviors: A comparison of relationship type, partner similarity and sex differences. *Journal of Social and Personal Relationships, 10,* 255–271.

Derlega, V., Winstead, B., Wong, P., & Greenspan, M. (1987). Self-disclosure and relationship development: An attributional analysis. In M. E. Roloff & G. R. Miller (Eds.), *Interpersonal Processes: New Directions in Communication Research* (pp. 172–187). Newbury Park, CA: Sage.

Duck, S. (1988). Maintaining relationships. In S. Duck (Ed.), *Relating to Others* (pp. 84–101). Chicago, IL: Dorsey Press.

Duggan, M., & Smith, A. (2014). *Media update 2013.* Pew Research Center's Internet Life Project. Retrieved from http://www.pewinternet.org/2013/12/30/social-media-update-2013/.

Ellison, N., Heino, R., & Gibbs, J. (2006). Managing impressions online: Self-presentation processes in the online dating environment. *Journal of Computer-Mediated Communication, 11*(2), 415–441.

Erwin, B. A., Turk, C. L., Heimberg, R. G., Fresco, D. M., & Hantula, D. A. (2004). The Internet: home to a severe population of individuals with social anxiety disorder?. *Journal of Anxiety Disorders, 18*(5), 629–646.

Finkelhor, D., Mitchell, K., & Wolak, J. (2000). *Online victimization: A report on the nation's youth.* Retrieved from http://www.unh.edu/ccrc/pdf/jvq/CV38.pdf.

Fiore, A. T., & Donath, J. S. (2004, April). Online personals: An overview. In *CHI'04 Extended Abstracts on Human Factors in Computing Systems* (pp. 1395–1398). ACM.

Fox, S., & Raine, L. (2014). The web at 25. Pew Research Center's Internet & American Life Project. Retrieved from http://www.pewinternet.org/2014/02/25/the-web-at-25-in-the-u-s.

Gergen, K. (2000). *The saturated self: Dilemmas of identity in contemporary life.* New York, NY: Basic Books.

Gergen, K. (2002). The challenges of absent presence. In J. E. Katz & M. Aakhus. *Perpetual Contact: Mobile Communication, Private Talk, Public Performance.* (pp. 227–242). New York, NY: Cambridge University Press.

Gibbs, J., Ellison, N., & Lai, C. H. (2011). First comes love, then comes Google: An investigation of uncertainty reduction strategies and self-disclosure in online dating. *Communication Research, 38*, 70–100.

Gibbs, J. L., Ellison, N. B., & Heino, R. D. (2006). Self-presentation in online personals the role of anticipated future interaction, self-disclosure, and perceived success in Internet dating. *Communication Research, 33*(2), 152–177.

Goffman, E. (1959). *The Presentation of Self in Everyday Life*. Garden City, NY: Anchor.

Goffman, E. (1963). *Behavior in public places: Notes on the social organization of gatherings*. New York, NY: Free Press.

Goffman, E. (1979). *Gender Advertisements*. New York, NY: Harper and Row.

Guadagno, R., Okdie B., & Kruse, S. (2012). Dating deception: Gender, online dating, and exaggerated self-presentation. *Computers in Human Behavior, 28*, 642–647.

Gunter, B. (2013). The study of online relationships and dating. In W. Dutton, *The Oxford Handbook of Internet Studies*. (pp. 173–94). Oxford, England: Oxford University Press.

Hanson, J. (2007). *24/7: How cell phones and the Internet change the way we live, work, and play*. Westport, CN: Praeger.

Higgins, E. T. (1987). Self-discrepancy: A theory relating self and affect. *Psychological Review, 94*(3), 319–340.

Horstmanshof, L., & Power, M. R. (2005). Mobile phone, SMS, and relationships. *Australian Journal of Communication, 32*, 33–52.

Hjorth, L. (2012). Mobile specters of intimacy: A case study of women and mobile intimacy. In R. Ling and S. Campbell, *Mobile Communication: Bringing Us Together and Tearing Us Apart*. (pp. 37–60). New Brunswick, NJ: Transactions Publisher.

Höflich, J., & Linke, C. (2012). Mobile communication in intimate relationships: Relationship development and the multiple dialectics of couples' media usage and communication. In R. Ling and S. Campbell, *Mobile Communication: Bringing Us Together and Tearing Us Apart*. (pp. 107–126). New Brunswick, NJ: Transactions Publisher.

Humphreys, L. (2005). Cellphones in public: social interactions in a wireless era. *New Media &Society, 7*(6), 810–833.

James, W. (1890). *The Principles of Psychology, Vol I*. New York, NY: Henry Holt and Co.

Johnson, A., Haigh, M., Becker, J., Craig, E., & Wigley, S. (2008). College students' use of relational management strategies in email in long-distance and geographically close relationships. *Journal of Computer-Mediated Communication, 13,* 381–404.

Jordan, N. (2014). World of Warcraft: A family therapist's journey into scapegoated culture. *Qualitative Report, 19*(31), 1–19.

Kraut, R., Kiesler, S., Boneva, B., Cummings, J., Helgeson, V., & Crawford, A. (2002). Internet paradox revisited. *Journal of Social Issues, 58,* 49–74.

Kraut, R., Patterson, M., Lundmark, V., Kiesler, S., Mukhopadhyay, T., & Scherlis, W. (1998). The Internet paradox: A social technology that reduces social involvement and psychological well-being. *American Psychologist, 53,* 1017–1032.

Krotoski, A. (2004). *Chicks and joysticks: An exploration of women and gaming.* London, UK: Entertainment and Leisure Software Publishers Association.

Lawson, H. M., & Leck, K. (2006). Dynamics of Internet dating. *Social Science Computer Review, 24*(2), 189–208.

Lenhart, A., Jones, S., & Macgill, A. (2008). Adults and video games. Research Center's Internet & American Life Project. Retrieved from: http://www.pewinternet.org/Reports/2008/PIP_Adult_gaming_memo.pdf.

Ling, R. (2000). Direct and mediated interaction in the maintenance of social relationships. In Sloane, A. & van Rijn, F. (Eds.), *Home Informatics and Telematics: Information, Technology and Society.* (pp. 61–86). Boston, MA: Kluwer.

Ling, R., & Campbell, S. (2012). *Mobile Communication: Bringing Us Together and Tearing Us Apart.* New Brunswick, NJ: Transactions Publisher.

Marshall, T., Benjanyan, K., Di Castro, G., & Lee, R. (2013). Attachment styles as predictors of Facebook-related jealousy and surveillance in romantic relationships. *Personal Relationships, 20*(1), 1–22.

Matyszczyk, C. (2011, April 15). Match.com sued after alleged sexual assault. CNet. Retrieved from: http://www.cnet.com/news/match-com-sued-after-alleged-sexual-assault/.

McCall, G. J., & Simmons, J. L. (1966). *Identities and Interactions.* New York, NY: The Free Press.

McKenna, K., & Bargh, J. (2000). Plan 9 from cyberspace: The implications of the Internet for personality and social psychology. *Personality and Social Psychology Review, 4*(1), 57–75.

McKenna, K., Green, A. S., and Gleason, M. E. G. 2002. Relationship formation on the Internet: What is the big attraction. *Journal of Social Issues, 58*(1), 9–31.

McMillian, R. (2014, July 30). Online date arrested for sexual assault. ABC7 Los Angeles. http://abc7.com/news/online-date-arrested-for-sexual-assault/229101/.

Mesch, G., & Talmud, I. (2006). The quality of online and offline relationships: The role of multiplexity and duration of social relationships. *Information Society, 22*(3), 137–148.

Meyer, E. (2012, November 22). Sexual predators turn to web to snare victims. Chicago Tribune. Retrieved from: http://articles.chicagotribune.com/2012-11-22/news/ct-met-online-dating-20121122_1_spark-networks-truecom-online-relationship-site.

Mishna, F., McLuckie, A., & Saini, M. (2009). Real-world dangers in an online reality: A qualitative study examining online relationships and cyber abuse. *Social Work Research, 33*(2), 107–118.

Muise, A., Christofides, E., & Desmarais, S. (2009). More information than you ever wanted: Does Facebook bring out the green-eyed monster of jealousy?. *CyberPsychology & Behavior, 12*(4), 441–444.

Morahan-Martin, J., & Schumacher, P. (2003). Loneliness and social uses of the Internet. *Computers in Human Behavior, 19*(6), 659–671.

O'Connell, R., Price, J, & Barrow, C. (2004). *Cyber stalking, abusive cyber sex and online grooming: A programme of education for teenagers.* Lancashire, England: Cyberspace Research Unit, University of Central Lancashire.

O'Sullivan, P. (2000). What you don't know won't hurt me: Impression management functions of communication channels in relationships. *Human Communication Research, 26*(3), 403–431.

Owens, T. (2006). Self and identity. In Delamater, J. (Ed.), *Handbook of Social Psychology, Vol. 3.* (pp. 205–232). New York, NY: Springer.

Palen, L., Salzman, M., & Youngs, E. (2000, December). Going wireless: behavior & practice of new mobile phone users. In Proceedings of the 2000 Association of Computer Machinery conference on computer supported cooperative work (pp. 201–210). Association of Computer Machinery, Philadelphia, PA.

Rabby, M. (2007). Relational maintenance and the influence of commitment in online and offline relationships. *Communication Studies, 58*(3), 315–37

Ramirez, A., & Broneck, K. (2009). IM me': Instant messaging as relational maintenance and everyday communication.*Journal of Social and Personal Relationships, 26*(2–3), 291–314.

Ramirez, A., Walther, J., Burgoon, J., & Sunnafrank, M. (2002). Information-seeking strategies, uncertainty, and computer-mediated communication: Toward a conceptual model. *Human Communication Research, 28*, 213–228.

Rosenbloom, S. (2011, April 22). It's Love at First Kill. In The New York Times. Retrieved From http://www.nytimes.com/2011/04/24/fashion/24avatar.html?pagewanted=all&_r=1&.

Sandstrom, K.L., Lively, K. J., Martin, D. D., &Fine, G. A. (2014). *Symbols, Selves, and Social Reality: A Symbolic Interactionist Approach to Social Psychology and Sociology*, 4th ed. New York, NY: Oxford University Press.

Scharlott, B. W., & Christ, W. G. (1995). Overcoming relationship-initiation barriers: The impact of a computer-dating system on sex role, shyness, and appearance inhibitions. *Computers in Human Behavior, 11*(2), 191–204.

Schulman, N., & Joseph, M. (Producer). (2013). Catfish: The TV Show [Online video]. MTV. Retrieved from http://www.mtv.com/shows/catfish/catfish-the-tv-show-season-2-ep-11-aaliyah-amp-alicia/1713855/playlist/#id=1713855.

Shaw, B., & Grant, L. (2002). In defense of the Internet: The relationship between Internet communication and depression, loneliness, self-esteem, and perceived social support. *Cyberpsychology & Behavior, 5*, 157–171.

Smith, A., & Duggan, M. (2013). Online dating & relationships. Pew Research Center's Internet & American Life Project. Retrieved from: http://pewinternet.org/Reports/2013/Online-Dating.aspx.

Sprecher, S. (2009). Relationship initiation and formation on the Internet. *Marriage & Family Review, 45*(8), 761–782.

Stafford, L., Kline, S. L., & Dimmick, J. (1999). Home e-mail: Relational maintenance and gratification opportunities. *Journal of Broadcasting & Electronic Media, 43*(4), 659–669.

Stafford, L., & Canary, D. (1991). Maintenance strategies and romantic relationship type, gender and relational characteristics.*Journal of Social and Personal Relationships, 8*, 217–242.

Stryker, S. (1980). *Symbolic interactionism: A social structural version*. Menlo Park, CA: Benjamin/Cummings Publishing Company.

Taylor, A. S., & Harper, R. (2002, April). Age-old practices in the 'new world': A study of gift-giving between teenage mobile phone users. In Proceedings of the SIGCHI conference on Human factors in computing systems (pp. 439–446). Association of Computer Machinery, New Orleans, LA.

Toma, C., & Hancock, J. (2010). Looks and lies: The role of physical attractiveness in online dating self-presentation and deception. *Communication Research, 37*, 335–351.

Toma, C., Hancock, J., & Ellison, N. (2008). Separating fact from fiction: An examination of deceptive self-presentation in online dating profiles. *Personality and Social Psychology Bulletin, 34*(8), 1023–1036.

Turkle, S. (1995). *Life on the Screen: Identity in the Age of the Internet*. London: Weidenfeld & Nicolson.

Turkle, S. (2008). Always-on/always-on-you: The tethered self. In J. Katz (Ed.), *The Handbook of Mobile Communications Studies* (pp. 121–138). Cambridge, MA: MIT Press.

Turkle, S. (2011). *Alone together: Why we expect more from technology and less from each other.* New York, NY: Basic Books.

Utz, S., & Beukeboom, C. J. (2011). The role of social network sites in romantic relationships: Effects on jealousy and relationship happiness. *Journal of Computer-Mediated Communication, 16*(4), 511–527.

Valkenburg, P.M., Peter, J., & Hampton, A. P. (2006). Friend networking sites and their relationship to adolescents' well-being and social self-esteem. *Cyberpsychology & Behavior, 9,* 584–590.

Walther, J. B. (1996). Computer-mediated communication: Impersonal, interpersonal, and hyperpersonal interaction. *Communication Research, 23*(1), 3–43.

Walther, J., Van Der Heide, B., Hamel, L., & Shulman, H. (2009). Self-generated versus other-generated statements and impressions in computer-mediated communication: A test of warranting theory using Facebook. *Communication Research, 34,* 28–49.

Ward, C. C., & Tracey, T. J. G. (2004). Relation of shyness with aspects of online relationship involvement. *Journal of Social and Personal Relationships, 21*(5), 611–623.

Webb, A. (2013, April). How I hacked online dating. *Ted.* Retrieved from: http://www.ted.com/talks/amy_webb_how_i_hacked_online_dating.

Webb, A. (2013). *Data, A Love Story: How I Cracked the Online Dating Code to Meet My Match.* New York, NY: Penguin Group.

Whitty, M. (2007). Revealing the 'real' me, searching for the 'actual' you: Presentations of self on an Internet dating site. *Computers in Human Behavior, 24*(4), 1707–1723.

Whitty, M. (2008a). Liberating or debilitating? An examination of romantic relationships, sexual relationships and friendships on the Net. *Computers in Human Behavior, 24,* 1837–1850.

Whitty, M. (2008b). Revealing the 'real' me, searching for the 'actual' you: Presentations of self on an internet dating site. *Computers in Human Behavior, 24*(4), 1707–1723.

Whitty, M., & Carr, A. (2006). *Cyberspace Romance: The Psychology of Online Relationships.* Hampshire, England: Palgrave-Macmillan.

Williams, D., Kennedy, T., & Moore, R. (2011). Behind the avatar: The patterns, practices, and functions of role playing in MMOs. *Games & Culture, 6*(2), 171–200.

Wright, K. (2004). On-line relational maintenance strategies and perceptions of partners within exclusively internet-based and primarily internet-based relationships. *Communication Studies,55*, 239–53.

Wu, W., Fore, S., Wang, X., & Ho, P. S. Y. (2007). Beyond Virtual Carnival and Masquerade: In-Game Marriage on the Chinese Internet.*Games and Culture, 2*(1), 59–89.

Wysocki, D. K. (1998). Let your fingers do the talking: Sex on an adult chat-line. *Sexualities, 1*(4), 425–452.

Ybarra, M. L., & Mitchell, K. J. (2004). Online aggressor/targets, aggressors, and targets: A comparison of associated youth characteristics. *Journal of Child Psychology and Psychiatry, 45*(7), 1308–1316.

Yee, N. (2006a). The demographics, motivations, and derived experiences of users of massively multi-user online graphical environments. *Presence, 15*(3), 309–329.

Yee, N. (2006b). The Psychology of MMORPGs: Emotional Investment, Motivations, Relationship Formation, and Problematic Usage. In R. Schroeder & A. Axelsson (Eds.), Avatars at Work and Play: Collaboration and Interaction in Shared Virtual Environments (pp. 187–207). London: Springer-Verlag.

Zhao, S. (2003). Toward a taxonomy of copresence. *Presence: Teleoperators and Virtual Environments, 12*(5), 445–55.

Zhao, S. (2005). The digital self: Through the looking-glass of telecopresent others. *Symbolic Interaction, 28*(3), 387–405.

Zickuhr, K., & Smith, A. (2013). Home broadband 2013. Pew Research Center's Internet & American Life Project. Retrieved from: http://pewinternet.org/Reports/2013/Broadband.aspx.

Chapter Four

Theoretical Explanations of Personal Forms of Online Victimization

Bradford W. Reyns, Billy Henson, and Thomas J. Holt

Introduction

    Researchers have only just begun to investigate the potential reasons behind personal forms of online victimization. Many of the resulting studies have approached this task by identifying factors that are associated with individuals' increased or decreased odds of being victimized while online (see Holt & Bossler, 2014 for review). Generally, which factors have been investigated has been based upon existing theories from victimology and criminology, and the known correlates of *offline* victimization. In other words, theoretical explorations of online victimization have drawn heavily from prevailing theories in the offline victimization literature (Holt & Bossler, 2014).
    Along these lines, empirical research into online victimization has focused almost exclusively on two related but separate theoretical frameworks—the opportunity perspective (Cohen & Felson, 1979; Felson & Clarke, 1998) and the general theory of crime (Gottfredson & Hirschi, 1990). Overall, there is support for the position that these perspectives provide useful explanations for online forms of personal victimization. However, the evidence indicates that explaining online victimization is complex, and support for the theories is far from universal (Holt & Bossler, 2014; Yar, 2005). This suggests that more research and theoretical development are required to better understand the precursors to online victimization.
    Additional theoretical refinement is especially needed in light of gender and the victim-offender relationship. Within the existing body of research, gender has emerged as a robust correlate of online victimization with females reporting higher rates of personal crimes such as cyberbullying (Tokunaga, 2010) and

stalking and harassment (Reyns, Henson, & Fisher, 2012). While these patterns are in keeping with trends in offline victimization, the theoretical explanations accounting for these gendered effects online have remained underdeveloped. Precisely how gender affects victimization risk, even after considering other known correlates of victimization, has for the most part remained an open theoretical question (e.g., Holt & Bossler, 2009; Reyns et al., 2012). A similarly unaddressed question relates to the relationship between the victim and the offender, and the dynamics that contribute to online victimization by an intimate partner. Few studies of online victimization have included the victim-offender relationship in statistical analyses, and none has articulated why risk for victimization may theoretically vary according to different relationships.

This chapter elaborates on these issues by discussing the theoretical role that gender and the victim-offender relationship might play in determining victimization risk. The focus of this discussion is limited to the two more prolific theoretical frameworks in the online victimization literature—the opportunity and self-control perspectives. Further, we address this line of inquiry in the context of personal forms of online victimization in which gender and the victim-offender relationship are more likely to exert some influence. First, the prevailing theories of online victimization are reviewed to provide a foundation for discussing how gender and the victim-offender relationship fit within these perspectives. Second, we discuss how these characteristics should influence victimization risk for personal online crimes within the theoretical frameworks. Third and finally, we provide an example using original data to illustrate some of these theoretical arguments. The chapter closes with a discussion of future directions for research in this area of inquiry.

Theories of Online Victimization

The Opportunity Perspective

The opportunity perspective is one of the most vibrant theoretical frameworks in criminology today. Its central precept is that opportunity is the root cause of all crime and that without criminal opportunities criminal events are significantly less likely to occur. This hypothesis has been strongly supported in the empirical literature for a wide variety of criminal behaviors (for a general overview, see Felson & Clarke, 1998). As a theory of criminal victimization, the opportunity perspective is best illustrated by lifestyle-routine activities theory. Lifestyle-routine activities theory is an integrated theory of victimization that combines two contemporaneous theories under the same conceptual umbrella—lifestyle-exposure theory and routine activity theory (Cohen & Felson, 1979; Hindelang, Gottfredson, & Garofalo, 1978).

Recognizing criminal opportunities as the foundation of criminal events, lifestyle-routine activities theory explains that all criminal opportunities are composed of three essential building blocks that must be present at the same place and at the same time: (1) motivated offenders, (2) suitable targets, and (3) weak or absent guardianship. Motivated offenders are persons who are likely to act upon criminal opportunities. Considered in the context of criminal victimization, exposure (i.e., accessibility or visibility) and proximity (i.e., physical closeness) to motivated offenders are necessary conditions for a target to experience victimization. Suitable targets are persons or other potential targets of motivated offenders, with more suitable targets being theoretically more likely to be victimized. However, it should be noted that the characteristics that make a target suitable or attractive will depend upon the type of crime. Finally, guardianship refers to other persons who discourage crime, either overtly because it is their responsibility to do so (e.g., police officers) or indirectly by merely being present (e.g., bystanders). Therefore, it is hypothesized that when guardians are absent victimization is more likely. A large body of victimization research has investigated how these theoretical elements of opportunity work together to identify factors and circumstances that increase the likelihood of victimization (e.g., Fisher, Cullen, & Turner, 2002; Miethe, Stafford, & Long, 1987; Reyns, Henson, & Fisher, 2011).

Although lifestyle-routine activities theory has demonstrated its value as a theory of *offline* victimization, fewer research studies have utilized it as a theory of *online* victimization (see Holt & Bossler, 2014). Further, doing so has required rethinking some of its central concepts that were originally developed when it was assumed crimes would mostly transpire between victims and offenders within the same physical location and at the same time (e.g., Yar, 2005). Nevertheless, the theory has been adapted to suit online environments (Reyns et al., 2011), and several research studies have found that opportunities play an important role in facilitating online victimization. While all of these studies cannot be reviewed, three representative examples are used to illustrate the current state of the opportunity-based online victimization literature.

First, Holt and Bossler (2009) conducted one of the earliest studies to examine the relationship between individuals' routine activities and their online victimization risk. This study found that visiting chatrooms, engaging in hacking behaviors, and having friends involved in online deviance each significantly increased the odds that a person would experience online harassment victimization. Notably, this study also reported that females were at heightened risks for victimization, even after considering the effects of these other risk factors— a finding that will be discussed further in subsequent sections.

In another study of online victimization, Reyns and colleagues (2011) likewise reported that certain online activities were related to online victimization risk. For example, adding strangers as friends to online social networks was found to be associated with an increased likelihood of unwanted contact, harassment, sexual advances, and cyberstalking. Interestingly, the study also found a significant relationship between gender and online victimization, in which females were more likely than males to experience these types of online victimization.

In the third and final study, Navarro and Jasinski (2012) investigated predictors of cyberbullying within an opportunity framework, reporting that behaviors such as Internet usage, online purchasing activities, and visiting video sharing sites were positively related to victimization. Like the previously discussed studies, females were found to be at significantly greater risk than males, regardless of their online behaviors.

The General Theory of Crime

The general theory of crime was originally developed as an explanation for criminal behavior, and within the field of criminology it has received a great deal of scholarly attention and been the subject of much debate (e.g., Akers, 2008; Pratt & Cullen, 2000). The theory explains that criminal behavior is the result of a propensity to offend. This propensity is represented by an individual's level of self-control, which consists of six dimensions. These six dimensions include: impulsivity, preference for simple tasks, preference for physical activities, risk-seeking, self-centeredness, and having a quick temper (Gottfredson & Hirschi, 1990; Grasmick, Tittle, Bursik, & Arneklev, 1993). According to the theory, criminal events occur when individuals with low self-control are provided with criminal opportunities. In other words, simply possessing low self-control is not sufficient to cause criminality unless such individuals also have criminal opportunity. This highlights the inherent compatibility of the opportunity and self-control theoretical perspectives, and may explain not only why the two theories are often tested together, but also their popularity. Overall, low self-control has been consistently supported as a predictor of criminal behavior within in the empirical research that has tested the theory (Pratt & Cullen, 2000).

Although the general theory of crime provides a fairly straightforward explanation for criminal behaviors, its utility as a theory of victimization may not be so clear-cut. In addition to conceptualizing low self-control as a propensity to act upon criminal opportunities, it has also been argued that individuals possessing low self-control are especially vulnerable to criminal victimization

(Schreck, 1999). For example, individuals who are impulsive may not fully consider the consequences of their behavior before acting, which could ultimately place them in situations that compromise their safety. Similarly, those who seek thrills and take risks may also be unconsciously increasing their victimization risk by placing themselves into vulnerable situations. Parallel arguments have been made for each of the six dimensions of self-control (see, Schreck, 1999). Thus, low self-control ultimately creates opportunities for victimization, thereby placing individuals or their property at risk.

Like the opportunity perspective, a large body of research has reported that low self-control is positively related to *offline* victimization (Pratt, Turanovic, Fox, & Wright, 2014). However, far fewer studies have used the theory to explain *online* victimization, and with somewhat tenuous results—a few such studies are reviewed to demonstrate the current status of this body of research. For example, Bossler and Holt (2010) reported that individuals with low self-control were significantly more likely than others to experience several types of online victimization (e.g., harassment); however, this ceased to be the case when additional variables were considered, including participation in cyber-deviance and peer offending. Research by Reyns, Burek, Henson, and Fisher (2013) conversely found that low self-control was related to single and recurring online personal victimization. The study results indicated that persons with low self-control were put at added risks for experiencing one type (e.g., harassment), two types (e.g., harassment and threats), and three or more types of online victimization (e.g., harassment, threats, and sexual advances). In a related study, Van Wilsem (2013) also reported that low self-control was related to single and recurring victimization, with individuals being more likely to experience hacking, harassment, and both hacking and harassment than persons with higher self-control. Finally, Reyns, Henson, and Fisher (2014) simultaneously examined the effects of opportunity and low self-control upon a related online experience—sexting. The results suggested that both low self-control and elements of opportunity were related to different sexting behaviors (e.g., sending, receiving).

Although the studies assessing the effects of low self-control upon personal forms of online victimization are valuable, they are also small in number. Many other empirical studies, however, have reported that low self-control is a consistent correlate of online criminal behavior and deviance (e.g., Holt & Bossler, 2014), suggesting that more research is needed to explore these effects within an online context for personal victimization. Further, the available evidence reinforces the importance of gender and the victim-offender relationship in explaining online victimization risks. With the exception of Van Wilsem's (2013) study of hacking and harassment, each of the previously discussed studies found gender to exert a significant effect upon the online experiences of cybervictimization and sexting (Bossler & Holt, 2010; Reyns et al., 2013; Reyns et al., 2014). This is noteworthy because it appears that gender has a strong influence on online victimization above and beyond the effects of low self-control. Further, the sexting study by Reyns and colleagues (2014) reported that sexting experiences varied with relationship status, with those in a dating relationship being more likely to receive sext messages. Unfortunately, this is the lone study to consider the impact of relationship status or the victim-offender relationship in conjunction with low self-control. The next sections of the chapter explain how these two characteristics—gender and the victim-offender relationship—fit into the larger theoretical perspectives of opportunity and the general theory of crime.

The Theoretical Importance of Gender and the Victim-Offender Relationship

Researchers in the field of victimology have hypothesized that gender influences victimization risk in several different ways (e.g., Daly & Maher, 1998; Jensen & Brownfield, 1986; Schwartz & Pittz, 1995). Of those working specifically within the opportunity and self-control theoretical frameworks, these hypotheses propose that the relationship between gender and victimization is *mediated* by these theoretical variables, or alternatively, that gender *moderates* the relationship between the theoretical variables and victimization. While mediation and moderation arguments related to gender have generally not been specifically put forth within the cybercrime victimization research literature, studies have begun to implicitly explore these hypotheses. Similar processes could theoretically be operating across different victim-offender relationships, although as yet, research has not tested such hypotheses. In the following sections of this chapter, the concepts of mediation and moderation are reviewed, discussed in light of opportunity and low self-control, and the extant cybercrime victimization studies that provide insights into the mediation and moderation hypotheses are highlighted.

Mediation Processes and Victimization

Lifestyle-exposure theory posits that personal characteristics affect individuals' lifestyles and that lifestyles impact one's likelihood of victimization by exposing would-be victims to victimization risk (Hindelang et al., 1978). Put differently, the theory proposes that characteristics, such as gender, to some de-

Figure 4.1: A Mediation Model of Gender, Victimization, and Opportunity

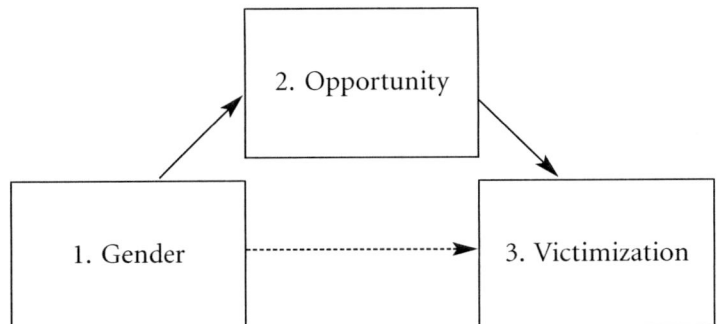

gree dictate lifestyles and routine activities. These behaviors, in turn, create opportunities for victimization. In effect, the theory is suggesting that the relationship between gender and criminal victimization is mediated by lifestyles and routine activities. Gender only matters to the extent that it affects opportunity, and that ultimately it is opportunity that accounts for victimization. It is therefore assumed that certain lifestyles provide more victimization opportunities than others and that these riskier lifestyles are a by-product of personal characteristics. If gender partially determines lifestyles and routines, then theoretically males and females should have differential victimization risk because of their lifestyle differences. This mediation process is visually depicted in Figure 1, which demonstrates how an observed relationship between gender and victimization might actually depend upon opportunity.

Many studies of offline victimization have found support for the mediating role of opportunity in the gender-victimization relationship (e.g., Bunch, Clay-Warner, & Lei, 2012; Henson, Wilcox, Reyns, & Cullen, 2010; Jensen & Brownfield, 1986; Lauritsen, Sampson, & Laub, 1991). Yet, the relationship between the victim and the offender has received much less research attention. Case Study 1 below, describes an incident in which both opportunity and gender influenced online victimization. Theoretically, an individual's relationship status should have effects similar to those of gender in determining lifestyles and routine activities. For example, persons who are single might spend more time in bars or clubs compared to married individuals, who spend more time at home or with their partner. Although research has not examined whether relationship status influences lifestyles, routine activities, and opportunities for victimization, the lifestyle-routine activities perspective suggests that the mediation hypothesis could apply in the same way that it does with gender. As an example, those who are in a relationship with a motivated offender are most likely at increased risks of being victimized due to their greater exposure and proximity to their partner. In this scenario, relationship status with a motivated offender would take the place of gender in Box 1 of Figure 1.

Case Study 4.1

Cyberstalking is typically defined as repeated, unwanted contact, harassment, sexual advances, or threats of violence online. It may involve the use of computer-mediated programs, such as social networking websites or chat programs, or text messaging with cell phones or tablets. In 2014, the Sheriff of Rock Island County, Illinois, pleaded guilty to attempted misconduct, stemming from charges of cyberstalking and harassment. The sheriff sent text messages to a woman he met at the gym, in an attempt to solicit a date. After the woman spurned his advances, the sheriff continued to send the woman intimidating and harassing text messages, even going as far as to threaten her, causing her to fear for her safety.

These same principles also can be applied to the general theory of crime, wherein an apparent relationship between gender and victimization exists, but that this relationship is mediated by self-control. This hypothesis has been tested and supported as it applies to criminal behavior, but not with respect to criminal victimization. For example, Burton, Cullen, Evans, Alarid, and Dunaway (1998) reported that males were more likely to commit crimes than females. However, once indicators of low self-control were added to their statistical models, the effects of gender were eliminated. This implies that the relationship between gender and criminality is mediated by self-control. Applied to Figure 1, in this example low self-control would replace opportunity in Box 2 of the theoretical model. Theoretically, then, the relationship between gender and victimization may also be mediated by self-control, but more research is needed to fully answer this research question. Interestingly, research has also found that males have lower self-control on average than do females, suggesting that gender partially explains one's level of self-control, regardless of the effects of self-control on behavior (Gibson, Ward, Wright, Beaver, & Delisi, 2010). It should also be pointed out that there is no theoretical reason for expecting one's relationship status to affect their level of self-control; however, self-control could impact relationship status. In this example, the mediator variable would be relationship status rather than self-control (in Figure 1, low self-control would be in Box 1 and relationship status in Box 2).

Moderation Processes and Victimization

Like the mediation hypothesis, the moderation hypothesis on victimization also focuses on the theoretical importance of gender in determining victimization

Figure 4.2: A Moderation Model of Gender, Victimization, and Opportunity

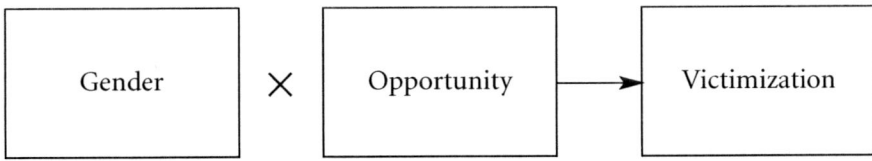

risk. According to the moderation hypothesis, correlates of victimization such as gender interact with theoretically important variables to result in criminal victimization. For example, within the opportunity perspective, the mediation hypothesis suggests that characteristics such as gender or relationship status alter lifestyles and routine activities, thereby dictating one's likelihood of victimization through victimization opportunities. In contrast, the moderation hypothesis argues opportunity interacts with gender or relationship status to produce gender- or relationship-specific victimization risks. In other words, the effects that lifestyles or routine activities have upon victimization risk are unique to males and females and different victim-offender relationships. The moderation hypothesis is depicted in Figure 2, wherein opportunities for victimization are moderated by gender.

Several studies have investigated whether opportunities for victimization are moderated by gender (e.g., Mustaine & Tewksbury, 1998; Tillyer, Wilcox, & Gialopsos, 2010; Popp & Peguero, 2011; Wilcox, Tillyer, & Fisher, 2009). As an example, Tillyer and colleagues (2010) reported that among Kentucky adolescents, delinquent lifestyles had a stronger effect on female victimization risk than they did upon male risk. However, as with the mediation hypothesis, research has not assessed whether relationship status interacts with opportunity in influencing victimization risk—the assumption here being that relationship status changes risk factors for specific types of relationship-based victimization, including intimate partner violence. To carry this premise forward, certain lifestyles and routine activities would increase the risks for intimate partner violence differently across relationship types, such as single (but dating casually), single (but in a serious relationship), married, married (but separated), and so on.

Research investigating how low self-control affects criminal, delinquent, and deviant behaviors has likewise reported that gender interacts with self-control in influencing these outcomes. For instance, a study by LaGrange and Silverman (1999) found that impulsivity, which is a measure of low self-control, was a positive predictor of juvenile delinquency, but only for males. Another dimension of self-control, temper, was positively related to violent behavior for females but not males. These examples illustrate a potential moderation process in explaining relationships between gender, offending, and analogous behaviors, but they do not necessarily demonstrate that such processes affect victimization risks. Further, it is unclear how negative social relationships impact victimization risks. In an informative study, Wilcox, Sullivan, Jones, and Van Gelder (2014) examined how the effects of personality characteristics similar to those reflecting self-control (i.e., agreeableness and conscientiousness) mediated and/or moderated relationships between opportunity, offending, and victimization. Their results suggested that mediation and moderation effects were at work, but importantly that the interaction of personality and opportunity did not impact victimization risk. Overall, however, more research is needed to more fully explore how precisely self-control interacts with gender and/or relationship characteristics to explain personal forms of victimization.

Mediation and Moderation in the Cybercrime Victimization Research

Several studies in the cybercrime victimization literature have emphasized the importance of gender in understanding the dynamics of personal victimization risks (e.g., Henson, Reyns, & Fisher, 2013; Holt & Bossler, 2009; Marcum, Ricketts, & Higgins, 2010; Navarro & Jasinski, 2013; Reyns et al., 2011). However, this body of research is limited in its value for understanding the risks of online victimization by an intimate partner in at least three ways. First, none of these studies have specifically examined intimate partner violence in an online context, instead investigating online personal victimization, such as harassment and cyberbullying generally. Second, most have not included relationship status as an independent variable in the analyses, making it difficult to confirm the hypothesis that relationship status or characteristics influence victimization risk. Third, the majority of these studies have tested for moderation effects, rather than mediation effects. With these caveats in mind, informative studies from the cybercrime victimization research literature are discussed with an eye toward how they can illuminate the roles of gender and relationship characteristics in explaining personal victimization.

The previously reviewed research by Holt and Bossler (2009) into online harassment victimization was among the first cybercrime victimization studies to evaluate how gender conditions victimization risk. Specifically, this study tested for possible moderating relationships between gender and online lifestyle-routine activity behaviors by examining how such behaviors differentially impacted victimization risks for males and females. The results suggested that gender interacts with particular online behaviors to determine risks for online harassment victimization. For example, engaging in computer deviance was correlated with increased odds of victimization for females, but not males. However, the study also found common correlates of victimization for both sexes. For instance, using online chatrooms was associated with online harassment victimization for both males and females. Marcum, Ricketts, and Higgins (2010) also reported that participation in online chatrooms increased victimization risks (i.e., exposure to sexually explicit materials) for males and females. Likewise, certain online activities were positive and significant predictors of victimization for only one gender. As an example, communicating through email increased the likelihood that females would receive sexually explicit materials, but emailing did not have such effects for males.

More recently, Navarro and Jasinski (2013) examined the interaction of gender and opportunity as it applies to cyberbullying victimization. The results of this study indicated that such moderating relationships are useful in differentiating victims from non-victims, but at the same time finding that there are common correlates of victimization regardless of gender. For instance, once again, participation in chatrooms positively affected cyberbullying victimization for males and females; however, online blogging was only associated with male victimization. In contrast, using instant messaging services and perpetrating cyberbullying intensified cyberbullying victimization risks, but only amongst females.

Similarly, Reyns and colleagues (2011) reported that certain opportunity-inducing behaviors, such as the frequency of online social network usage and the use of instant messaging services were associated with an increased likelihood of cyberstalking victimization for females, whereas the number of social networks used was identified as a risk factor for males. Common correlates of victimization, such as adding strangers as friends to online social networks were also found. Henson and colleagues (2013) also investigated the possibility of moderating relationships between gender, opportunity, and online personal victimization, with results indicating that the number of social network updates, flirting behaviors on social networks, and time spent on social networks impacted online victimization, but only amongst females.

Together, these studies offer support for the moderation hypothesis. That is, the contention that gender interacts with opportunity to produce risk factors for victimization that are unique to males or females. Far fewer studies, however, have explored the mediation hypothesis—the argument that gender regulates opportunity, which in turn, influences victimization likelihood—and none of these studies has concentrated on victimization by an intimate partner in an online context. For example, research by Pratt, Holtfreter, and Reisig (2010) indicated that males spent more time online than females, and that time online was affiliated with Internet fraud targeting. This provides some validation of the mediation hypothesis, but unfortunately, the study examined property-based online victimization, so whether this relationship would also be useful in understanding personal victimization is unclear. Case Study 2 below details a case of revenge porn, a form of online victimization that is often specific to females.

Case Study 4.2

"Revenge porn" is a term associated with posting sexually explicit images of an individual online, without his or her consent, often with the intention of embarrassing or humiliating the individual. It typically occurs when relationships end badly.

In 2014, after her relationship with her boyfriend ended, a British woman found sexually explicit images of herself online, posted by her ex-boyfriend. The photos had been taken during their relationship, some by her ex and some by herself which she sent to him. When she confronted her ex-boyfriend, he responded that he posted the photos out of anger, but that he would stop. However, she found that if she failed to speak to him for a period of time, more photos appeared online. She struggled for over six months to have the photos removed.

Research has also not addressed how low self-control impacts online personal victimization, from either mediation or moderation perspectives. Still, the study by Reyns and colleagues (2014) into sexting behavior is somewhat revealing with respect to mediation. Results from this research suggested that the effect of gender on sexting participation is not mediated by either lifestyles and routine activities or low self-control. In other words, gender influenced sexting behaviors above and beyond the effects of these theoretical variables. Further, it appears that opportunity partially mediated the effects of low self-control on different forms of sexting. On the whole, more research is needed to assess the efficacy of both the mediation and moderation hypotheses as they apply to online forms of victimization. To that end, we present results that test both of these hypotheses for online personal victimizations involving unwanted sexual advances.

An Example Using Original Data

Data for the following examples were collected in 2009 as part of a project investigating the online victimization of college students. Undergraduate students attending a large public university in the Midwest were administered an online survey asking them about a number of online experiences and behaviors, including their online routine activities and their online victimization. From these data, several variables were created to reflect the theoretical concepts discussed earlier in this chapter (for more detailed methodological information, see Reyns et al., 2011). In the statistical models presented below, measures of demographic characteristics, opportunity variables, and low self-control were used to test for both mediating and moderating relationships between gender and online victimization. The specific type of online victimization under investigation is unwanted sexual advances. The advantage of exploring this particular type of victimization is twofold. First, gender is most likely an important risk factor for victimization. Second, unwanted sexual advances could potentially be perpetrated by an intimate partner, allowing us to gauge the effects of relationship status on victimization.

Results

The three models included in Table 4.1 provide results related to the mediating effects of opportunity on the relationship between gender and unwanted online sexual advances. In Model 1, as expected, gender is a statistically significant predictor of unwanted sexual advances, with females being over two and a half times more likely to be victimized than males. Interestingly, relationship status did not influence victimization risk. Model 2 includes the four demographic characteristics, along with six opportunity variables. Recall that the mediation hypothesis suggests that gender should have less influence on victimization once opportunity is taken into consideration. Although two online routine activities—number of social network updates and number of friends on social networks—significantly influenced victimization risk, gender also remained a significant influence upon victimization. This suggests that the relationship between gender and victimization is not mediated by online opportunities as hypothesized. The inclusion of opportunity variables also caused age to become significant, suggesting that older individuals were more likely to be victimized.

Finally, Model 3 adds low self-control to the analyses, and the results indicate that individuals with low self-control are more likely to be victimized online. The previously identified relationships regarding technology use and age also remained significant. Finally, gender remains statistically significant at the same level. As a result, opportunity and self-control appear to affect the risk of victimization, though gender is a substantive predictor as well.

Table 4.2 includes these same theoretical variables, but instead examines the possibility of interaction or moderation effects on online victimization. Model 1 in Table 4.2 examines the effects of these variables upon unwanted online sexual advances against males. The results indicate that only low self-control is a significant correlate of victimization against males. Conversely, Model 2, which includes only females, suggests that opportunity (i.e., num-

Table 4.1: Mediation Models: Gender, Opportunity, Low Self-Control, and Unwanted Online Sexual Advances

Variables	Coefficient	SE	Exp(B)	Coefficient	SE	Exp(B)	Coefficient	SE	Exp(B)
Gender (female)	0.98***	0.23	2.68	1.04***	0.24	2.85	1.15***	0.25	3.16
Non-Single	0.20	0.20	1.22	0.18	0.21	1.20	0.13	0.21	1.14
Race (non-White)	0.05	0.28	1.06	-0.12	0.32	0.88	-0.15	0.32	0.85
Age	0.11	0.07	1.12	0.18*	0.07	1.19	0.15*	0.07	1.17
Opportunity Variables									
Live Alone				-0.17	0.40	0.83	-0.17	0.40	0.83
Time Online				0.01	0.04	1.01	0.01	0.04	1.01
Accurate Info				0.08	0.26	1.09	-0.01	0.27	0.98
Number SN Updates				0.07**	0.02	1.07	0.06**	0.02	1.07
Number SN Friends				0.33*	0.13	1.39	0.31*	0.13	1.36
Time on SN				0.01	0.06	1.01	0.002	0.06	1.00
Low Self-Control							0.71*	0.29	2.04
Constant	-5.04***	1.42	0.006	-8.56***	1.82	0.00	-9.45***	1.87	0.00
-2 Log-likelihood	731.42			645.57			639.61		
Model χ²	27.72***			47.39***			53.35***		
Nagelkerke R²	0.05			0.09			0.10		
N	940			853			853		

*$p \leq .05$; ** $p \leq .01$; *** $p \leq .001$

Table 4.2: Moderation Models: Gender, Opportunity, Low Self-Control, and Unwanted Online Sexual Advances

	Model 1: Males			Model 2: Females		
Variables	Coefficient	SE	Exp(B)	Coefficient	SE	Exp(B)
Non-Single	0.17	0.45	1.19	0.13	0.25	1.14
Race (non-White)	-0.94	0.94	0.39	-0.08	0.36	0.91
Age	0.31	0.17	1.36	0.10	0.08	1.11
Opportunity Variables						
Live Alone	-0.22	0.80	0.79	-0.19	0.46	0.82
Time Online	-0.04	0.10	0.95	0.03	0.05	1.03
Accurate Info	0.23	0.53	1.26	-0.06	0.32	0.93
Number SN Updates	-0.01	0.05	0.99	0.09**	0.02	1.09
Number SN Friends	0.43	0.28	1.54	0.26	0.15	1.30
Time on SN	0.11	0.14	1.11	-0.03	0.07	0.96
Low Self-Control	1.58*	0.63	4.87	0.49	0.33	1.63
Constant	-15.14***	4.24	0.00	-6.64***	2.09	0.00
-2 Log-likelihood	155.16			476.00		
Model χ2	17.30***			21.44*		
Nagelkerke R2	0.12			0.06		
N	333			520		

* $p \leq .05$; ** $p \leq .01$; *** $p \leq .001$

ber of social network updates) explains unwanted online sexual advances. Together, these two models support the hypothesis that gender moderates the relationship between opportunity and online victimization as well as the relationship between self-control and victimization.

Conclusion

Taken as a whole, the criminological literature regarding online interpersonal victimization is growing and provides some insights into the potential determinants of victimization. Scholarship utilizing existing theories designed to account for offline victimization have demonstrated some value in explaining trends in various forms of cybercrime victimization. There is, however, a significant relationship between gender and the risk of victimization that may not be easily accounted for through the use of traditional theories involving both opportunity and self-control.

Since the relationship between gender and victimization remains across multiple studies of online personal victimization, there is a need to more carefully investigate the role of gender as a mediating or moderating influence on the risk of victimization. As noted in the analysis presented, females are more likely to be victimized, though we also found that opportunity variables do not completely mediate this relationship. Furthermore the inclusion of low self-control did not affect the relationship between gender and victimization. As a result, the relationship between gender and victimization may not be completely accounted for through the use of existing theories which calls to question how we may better understand this relationship.

In order to better understand this relationship, it is imperative that researchers attempt to refine the existing theoretical frameworks of victimization to more appropriately suit online environments and behavior sets. This can only be achieved through better measurement and identification of the distinct differences in the nature of virtual communications that may serve as an underlying factor that enables an increased risk of victimization in an otherwise faceless virtual environment (see also Holt & Bossler, 2009). For instance, there is some evidence that online communications are gendered, such that various forms of computer-mediated communication are oriented toward more aggressive and masculine patterns of text (Herring, 1999). Those whose communications can be readily distinguished from this expected pattern may stand out, and thereby increase their likelihood of becoming a target for victimization (Holt & Bossler, 2009).

Similarly, there is a need to better measure the extent to which victims of interpersonal online victimization are targeted by former or current intimate others while online. Few studies have attempted to capture the presence or density of intimate connections in online social networks, or the extent to which they affect risk. Though relationship status was non-significant in the model presented above, that is only one way to operationalize the role of intimate peers online. Further assessments are needed to capture the total number of active and prior intimate associations that are present in an individual's online social networks, the interactions between these individuals, and other variables to explore how relationships affect exposure to offenders online.

Further research also is needed to better assess how risky behaviors are perceived and understood in online environments. Low self-control was originally focused on behaviors which were associated with physical risks for harm, such as drug and alcohol use, promiscuity, and aggressive tendencies (Gottfredson & Hirschi, 1990). It is unclear to what extent low self-control affects willingness to engage in different, but still arguably "risky" behaviors, in online spaces, and how those risks are interpreted based on age and technology access. Youth populations who have grown up in a world with the Internet may see no inherent danger in developing large social networks populated in part by individuals they have never met, or constantly sharing information about their day to day activities (Lenhart & Madden, 2007; Lenhart, Purcell, Smith, & Zickuhr, 2010). If such activities occur regardless of an individual's level of self-control, then it will be necessary to revise our understanding of what it means to engage in risky behaviors online. Furthermore, this would require a reconsideration of the ways that self-control and opportunity interact in online spaces to affect the risk of victimization.

Finally, there is a need to better assess the intersection of victimization in online and offline contexts. Research has identified a distinct relationship between the risk of cyberbullying and real world bullying victimization experiences (see Tokunaga, 2010). Few studies to date have, however, considered any association between real world dating or intimate partner violence and experiences with online harassment or stalking. Since females face an increased risk of victimization for these real world offenses (see Fisher et al., 2002), it may be that this also conditions their risk for online victimization. Further research is needed to understand this dynamic and, in turn, improve our understanding of these crimes in a modern context.

References

Akers, R. L. (2008). Self-control and social learning theory. In E. Goode (Ed.), *Out of control: Assessing the general theory of crime* (pp. 77–89). Stanford, CA: Stanford University Press.

Bossler, A. M., & Holt, T. J. (2010). The effect of self-control on victimization in the cyberworld. *Journal of Criminal Justice, 38(3)*, 227–236.

Bunch, J., Clay-Warner, J., & Lei, M. (2012). Demographic characteristics and victimization risk: Testing the mediating effects of routine activities. *Crime and Delinquency*, DOI: 10.1177/0011128712466932.

Burton, V. S., Cullen, F. T., Evans, T. D., Alarid, L. F., & Dunaway, R. G. (1998). Gender, self-control, and crime. *Journal of Research in Crime and Delinquency, 35(2)*, 123–147.

Cohen, L. E., & Felson, M. (1979). Social change and crime rate trends: A routine activity approach. *American Sociological Review, 44(4)*, 588–608.

Daly, K., & Maher, L. (1998). *Criminology at the crossroads: Feminist readings in crime and justice.* Oxford, UK: Oxford University Press.

Dobash, R. P., Dobash, R. E., Wilson, M., & Daly, M. (1992). The myth of sexual symmetry in marital violence. *Social Problems, 39(1)*, 71–91.

Felson, M., & Clarke, R. V. (1998). *Opportunity makes the thief: Practical theory for crime prevention.* London: Home Office.

Fisher, B. S., Cullen, F. T., & Turner, M. G. (2002). Being pursued: Stalking victimization in a national study of college women. *Criminology and Public Policy 1(2)*, 257–308.

Gibson, C. L., Ward, J. T., Wright, J. P., Beaver, K. M., & Delisi, M. (2010). Where does gender fit in the measurement of self-control? *Criminal Justice and Behavior, 37(8)*, 883–903.

Gottfredson, M. R., & Hirschi, T. (1990). *A general theory of crime.* Stanford, CA: Stanford University Press.

Grasmick, H. G., Tittle, C. R., Bursik, R. J., & Arneklev, B. J. (1993). Testing the core empirical implications of Gottfredson and Hirschi's general theory of crime. *Journal of Research in Crime and Delinquency, 30(1)*, 5–29.

Henson, B., Wilcox, P., Reyns, B. W., & Cullen, F. T. (2010). Gender, adolescent lifestyles and violent victimization: Implications for routine activity theory. *Victims and Offenders, 5(4)*, 303–328.

Henson, B., Reyns, B. W., & Fisher, B. S. (2013). Does gender matter in the virtual world? Examining the effect of gender on the link between online social network activity, security and interpersonal victimization. *Security Journal, 26(4)*, 315–330.

Herring, S. C. (1999). The rhetorical dynamics of gender harassment online. *The Information Society, 15(3),* 151–167.

Hindelang, M. J., Gottfredson M. R., & Garofalo, J. (1978). *Victims of personal crime: An empirical foundation for a theory of personal victimization.* Cambridge, MA: Ballinger Publishing Company.

Holt, T. J., & Bossler, A. M. (2009). Examining the applicability of lifestyle-routine activities theory for cybercrime victimization. *Deviant Behavior, 30(1),* 1–25.

Holt, T. J., & Bossler, A. M. (2014). An assessment of the current state of cybercrime scholarship. *Deviant Behavior, 35(1),* 20–40.

Jensen, G. F., & Brownfield, D. (1986). Gender, lifestyles, and victimization: Beyond routine activity. *Violence and Victims, 1(2),* 85–99.

LaGrange, T. C., & Silverman, R. A. (1999). Low self-control and opportunity: Testing the general theory of crime as an explanation for gender differences in delinquency. *Criminology, 37(1),* 41–72.

Lauritsen, J. L., Sampson, R. J., & Laub, J. H. (1991). The link between offending and victimization among adolescents. *Criminology, 29(2),* 265–292.

Lenhart, A., & Madden, M. (2007). *Teens, Privacy, and Online Social Networks.* Pew Internet and American Life Project. Retrieved from http://www.pewinternet.org/Reports/2007/Teens-Privacy-and-Online-Social-Networks.aspx.

Lenhart, A., Purcell, K., Smith, A., & Zickuhr, K. (2010). *Social Media and Young Adults.* Pew Internet and American Life Project. Retrieved from http://www.pewinternet.org/Reports/2010/Social-Media-and-Young-Adults.aspx.

Marcum, C. D., Ricketts, M. L., & Higgins, G. E. (2010). Assessing sex experiences of online victimization: An examination of adolescent online behaviors using routine activity theory. *Criminal Justice Review, 35(4),* 412–437.

Miethe, T. D., Stafford, M. C., & Long, J. S. (1987). Social differentiation in criminal victimization: A test of routine activities/lifestyle theories. *American Sociological Review, 52(2),* 184–194.

Mustaine, E. E., & Tewksbury, R. (1998). Victimization risks at leisure: A gender-specific analysis. *Violence and Victims, 13(3),* 231–249.

Navarro, J. N., & Jasinski, J. L. (2012). Going cyber: Using routine activities theory to predict cyberbullying experiences. *Sociological Spectrum, 32(1),* 81–94.

Navarro, J. N., & Jasinski, J. L. (2013). Why girls? Using routine activities theory to predict cyberbullying experiences between boys and girls. *Women and Criminal Justice, 23(4),* 286–303.

Popp, A. M., & Peguero, A. A. (2011). Routine activities and victimization at school: The significance of gender. *Journal of Interpersonal Violence, 26(12),* 2413–2436.

Pratt, T. C., & Cullen, F. T. (2000). The empirical status of Gottfredson and Hirschi's general theory of crime: A meta-analysis. *Criminology, 38(3),* 931–964.

Pratt, T. C., Holtfreter, K., & Reisig, M. D. (2010). Routine online activity and Internet fraud targeting: Extending the generality of routine activity theory. *Journal of Research in Crime and Delinquency, 47(3),* 267–296.

Pratt, T. C., Turanovic, J. J., Fox, K. A., & Wright, K. A. (2014). Self-control and victimization: A meta-analysis. *Criminology, 52(1),* 87–116.

Reyns, B. W., Burek, M. W., Henson, B., & Fisher, B. S. (2013). The unintended consequences of digital technology: Exploring the relationship between sexting and cybervictimization. *Journal of Crime and Justice, 36(1),* 1–17.

Reyns, B. W., Henson, B., & Fisher, B. S. (2011). Being pursued online: Applying cyberlifestyle-routine activities theory to cyberstalking victimization. *Criminal Justice and Behavior, 38(11),* 1149–1169.

Reyns, B. W., Henson, B., & Fisher, B. S. (2012). Stalking in the twilight zone: Extent of cyberstalking victimization and offending among college students. *Deviant Behavior, 33(1),* 1–25.

Reyns, B. W., Henson, B., & Fisher, B. S. (2014). Digital deviance: Low self-control and opportunity as explanations of sexting among college students. *Sociological Spectrum, 34(3),* 273–292.

Schreck, C. J. (1999). Criminal victimization and low self-control: An extension and test of a general theory of crime. *Justice Quarterly, 16(3),* 633–654.

Schwartz, M. D., & Pitts, V. L. (1995). Exploring a feminist routine activities approach to explaining sexual assault. *Justice Quarterly, 12(1),* 9–31.

Tillyer, M. S., Wilcox, P., & Gialopsos, B. M. (2010). Adolescent school-based sexual victimization: Exploring the role of opportunity in a gender-specific multilevel analysis. *Journal of Criminal Justice, 38(5),* 1071–1081.

Tokunaga, R. S. (2010). Following you home from school: A critical review and synthesis of research on cyberbullying victimization. *Computers in Human Behavior, 26(3),* 277–287.

Van Wilsem, J. (2013). Hacking and harassment—Do they have something in common? Comparing risk factors for online victimization. *Journal of Contemporary Criminal Justice, 29(4),* 437–453.

Wilcox, P., Sullivan, C. J., Jones, S., & Van Gelder, J. L. (2014). Personality and opportunity: An integrated approach to offending and victimization. *Criminal Justice and Behavior, 41(7),* 880–901.

Wilcox, P., Tillyer, M. S., & Fisher, B. S. (2009). Gendered opportunity? School-based adolescent victimization. *Journal of Research in Crime and Delinquency, 46(2),* 245–269.

Yar, M. (2005). The novelty of 'cybercrime': An assessment in light of routine activity theory. *European Journal of Criminology, 2(4),* 407–427.

Chapter Five

The Rise of the "Virtual Predator": Technology and the Expanding Reach of Intimate Partner Abuse

Denise N. Crisafi, Alyssa R. Mullins, and Jana L. Jasinski

Introduction

Particularly within the past decade, the breadth of technological outlets available for individuals to communicate and connect with others has grown substantially. According to the PEW Research Internet Project (2014), approximately three-quarters of adults use social networking sites, 90% of adults own a cellular phone, 81% of cell phone owners regularly send and receive text messages, and just under half of adults frequently post their own photos and videos online. While these innovations have certainly created the opportunity for individuals to maintain social ties, access time-sensitive material more efficiently, become creators of knowledge, and remain informed on political and social issues (PEW, 2014), there has been growing evidence that an increasing reliance on information communication technologies (ICTs) and other devices, such as geographic information systems and tracking software, has fostered a broader and more convenient platform for stalking, harassment, and coercion to occur (Southworth, Finn, Dawson, Fraser, & Ducker, 2007; Spitzberg & Hoobler, 2002; Woodlock, 2014).

While these types of imprudent and criminal acts have the potential to affect individuals across age, gender, and relationship status, national statistics indicate the risk of cyberstalking, cyberharassment, and sexual victimization through online media to be greatest among intimate partners; that more men than women use these methods to control their current or estranged partners; and that men and women between the ages of 18 and 29 are most likely to encounter these forms of abuse (Black et al., 2011). While the federal government and all U.S. states and territories have adopted anti-stalking and anti-harassment legislation that recognize these recent types of virtual predation (Baum et al., 2009), the ubiquity of the "online world" necessitates a comprehensive understanding of cybercrime in the context of intimate partner abuse, as well as continued investigations into the ways that perpetrators of intimate partner abuse are using technology to control their victims, and the effects of both offline and online intimate partner abuse on victims' livelihood. Since intimate partner abuse in an online environment is a relatively recent area of research inquiry, presenting the trends that are known is prudent to informing policy and practice on what will undoubtedly continue to be an ever-growing phenomenon.

In order to frame the current state of knowledge about intimate partner abuse in both offline and online settings, this chapter will begin by presenting comprehensive definitions of intimate partner abuse and the prevalence rates of both violent and nonviolent forms of victimization. The concept of coercive control (Dutton & Goodman, 2005; Stark, 2007) will also be incorporated into this chapter to contextualize the gendered patterns of intimate partner abuse that have been at the center of historical and contemporary discussions of prevention and policy, and to highlight the impact that psychologically and emotionally driven forms of abuse have had on survivors especially since emerging technologies have enabled abusers to engage in an even greater degree of coercive control through surveillance of their intimate partners. Next, Johnson's (2005; 2010) concept of intimate partner terrorism is introduced as a means of theoretically orienting the myriad cyberabuses that have been documented within the intimate partner abuse literature and to clarify the relationships between perpetrators and survivors when online abuse is an exclusive control tactic versus when it is used in combination with offline stalking. The chapter concludes with implications for policy, advocacy, and intervention strategies that consider the magnitude of virtual intimate partner abuse on victims' ability to leave abusive relationships, access appropriate resources, and move toward violence-free lives.

Changing Landscapes: How Technology Has Reinforced and Shifted Our Knowledge of Intimate Partner Abuse

Defining Intimate Partner Abuse

Knowledge of intimate partner abuse perpetration and victimization has undoubtedly grown over the past several decades. Initial efforts, such as the Domestic Abuse Intervention Project (DAIP) (1980), served as the impetus for a more coordinated approach between individual communities and the criminal justice system when addressing violence against women and also provided the Duluth Model which has generated a more complete understanding of the power and control tactics underlying the perpetration of intimate partner abuse (Pence & Paymar, 1990; Pence & Shephard, 1999). Legislation such as the Violence Against Women Act (1994; 2000; 2005; 2013) has also expanded the availability of protections to survivors, secured grant funding to incentivize prevention and intervention initiatives, and imposed greater prohibitions and penalties for perpetrators (Seghetti & Bjelopera, 2012). Indeed, the development and widespread availability of the internet, smartphones, and social media have made issues surrounding intimate partner abuse more apparent as organizations such as the National Coalition Against Domestic Violence (NCADV),[1] the National Network to End Domestic Violence (NNEDV),[2] and the U.S. Department of Justice Office on Violence Against Women[3] have incorporated Facebook, Twitter, and online blogs as central components of their efforts to raise awareness, share survivors' stories, dispel myths about those who are victimized, and impassion others to become active agents within these campaigns. Furthermore, news stories and policy briefs about stalking, homi-

---

1. "This month, RAINN will be sharing stories of survivors of sexual assault who have experienced running away from home. If you or someone you know needs support, you can call the National Runaway Safeline at 1-800-RUNAWAY. You are not alone. #NRPM2014." Published on Facebook and Twitter by the National Coalition Against Domestic Violence (NCADV) on November 5, 2014.

2. "Today—the International Day for the Elimination of Violence Against Women—kicks off #16Days of Activism! We will be sharing 16 ways to get involved starting with an easy one: change your profile picture or cover photo on social media to show your support for ending violence against women and girls." Published on Facebook and Twitter by the National Network to End Domestic Violence on November 25, 2014.

3. "VAWA 2013 Nondiscrimination Provision: Making Programs Accessible to all Victims of Domestic Violence, Sexual Assault, Dating Violence, and Stalking." Published April 9, 2014 by the Office on Violence Against Women at http://www.justice.gov/ovw.

cide, and sexual assault among intimate partners have become readily publicized and accessible through national and local news websites. Collectively, these advancements have helped to frame intimate partner abuse as a more serious and visible social problem and, as a result, have broadened the ways in which intimate partner abuse is conceptualized in both the legal and public health arenas.

The National Institute of Justice (NIJ) (2007) classifies intimate partner abuse as a pattern of physical, sexual, emotional, economic, or psychological behaviors or threats of actions that is used by one partner to maintain power and control over another intimate partner. In a similar fashion, the Centers for Disease Control and Prevention (CDC) (2014) defines intimate partner abuse as involving threats or acts of physical, sexual, and psychological harm by either a current or former partner or spouse. Both entities acknowledge that physical abuse involves both minor (e.g., kicking, biting) as well as severe (e.g., burning, use of a weapon) forms of physical violence; that sexual abuse includes marital rape, the use of physical force to complete a sexual act against another's will, and an attempted or completed sexual act on an individual who is incapable of consent; and that behaviors such as constant criticism and name-calling, restricting access to finances or employment, and intimidation and isolation comprise emotional, financial, and psychological forms of intimate partner abuse. More recently, stalking has also become a widely recognized category of intimate partner abuse that involves physical surveillance, unwanted communication, property damage, and "proxy stalking" (i.e., using others to spy on the victim) as a means of controlling and frightening the intended victim (CDC, 2014). Overall, these convergent descriptions of intimate partner abuse underscore the breadth and profound nature of both nonviolent and violent methods that are used by abusers with the purpose of threatening, intimidating, and harming their victims.

Although the rate of intimate partner abuse has been steadily declining over the past twenty years, both fatal and nonfatal cases of intimate partner abuse nonetheless remain pervasive and experiences of victimization and perpetration are largely demarcated by gender. Large-scale, nationally representative surveys have consistently found that women are more likely to experience physical and sexual violence within their intimate relationships, to be stalked by an intimate partner, and to be killed by an intimate partner (Black et al., 2011; Catalano, 2013; Tjaden & Thoennes, 2000). For instance, the CDC's National Intimate Partner and Sexual Violence Survey (NISVS), which was conducted by Black and colleagues (2011) on a sample of 16,507 adults, evidenced that the lifetime prevalence rate of intimate partner violence is approximately 36 percent for women compared to 29 percent for men; that 17 percent of women and 8 percent of men have experienced sexual violence perpetrated by an intimate partner; and that 24 percent of women and 14 percent of men have been severely physically assaulted by an intimate partner. The National Violence Against Women Survey (NVAWS) (Tjaden & Thoennes, 2000) also reified this gender pattern, demonstrating that women were 22.5 times more likely to be raped, 2.9 times more likely to be physically assaulted, and 8.2 times more likely to be stalked by a current or former marital or cohabiting partner in comparison to men. This same study also specifically reported that 8 percent of women have been stalked during their lifetime compared to 2 percent of men, and that 4.8 percent of women and 0.5 percent of men knew their stalkers to be current or estranged intimate partners. The NISVS (Black et al., 2011) determined that the rates of stalking were greater than those presented from the NVAWS (Tjaden & Thoennes, 2000). Here, approximately 16 percent of women and 5 percent of men are estimated to have lifetime prevalence rates of stalking while two-thirds of women compared to 40 percent of men have been stalked by a current or former intimate partner. Lastly, data from the Bureau of Justice Statistics (Catalano, 2013) shows that 39 percent of the 3,032 homicides in 2010 involving female victims were committed by an intimate partner, while 3 percent of the 10,878 homicides in 2010 involving male victims were committed by an intimate partner.

Coercive Control in an Offline Environment

Consistent with empirical data that demonstrate differential experiences of intimate partner abuse for men and women, the motivations underlying the perpetration of abuse are in many instances divided among gendered lines. Although variations exist and debates have waged as to whether men and women perpetrate intimate partner abuse at equivalent or disparate rates (Straus, 2011; Straus, Gelles, & Steinmetz, 2006), women's use of violence against intimate partners is often a defensive or retaliatory response while men's use of violence is more apt to be associated with maintaining power and control or reaffirming their sexual propriety and masculinity (Busch & Rosenberg, 2004; Hamberger & Guse, 2005; Miller, 2001). These particular gendered dynamics are best understood as a function of *coercive controlling violence* (Kelly & Johnson, 2008) or *coercive control* (Stark, 2007), which has been identified by scholars as a pattern of violence, intimidation, isolation, and control that is largely used by men to subjugate their female partners and regulate their partners' everyday activities.

Within this framework, abusers ensure their victims' compliance through surveillance and the threatened or actual use of physical and/or sexual violence

(Goodman & Dutton, 2005; Kelly & Johnson, 2008; Stark, 2007). Studies have exceedingly documented the central elements and effects of coercive control within abusive relationships (Beck & Raghavan, 2010; Glass, Manganello, & Campbell, 2004; Goodman & Dutton, 2005). In their endeavor to create a measure of coercion within intimate relationships, Goodman and Dutton (2005) identified multiple domains of control in intimate relationships, including but not limited to personal appearance/activities (e.g., mandating that the victim dress a certain way), legal (e.g., forcing the victim to engage in illegal activities), health (e.g., preventing victim from obtaining medical treatment), and children (e.g., threatening to call child services on the victim). Three-quarters of women in Brewster's (2003) qualitative study revealed that their abusers often resorted to shame, guilt, isolation, and jealousy in combination with physical and sexual violence in order to prevent or persuade them from leaving, and that coercively controlling tactics continued to actualize through stalking and harassment following the termination of those relationships. Furthermore, while Tanha, Beck, Figueredo, and Raghavan's (2010) findings from 762 couples indicate that both men and women engage in coercive control within their abusive relationships, women were more likely than men to encounter psychological abuse, threats of escalated physical violence, sexual assault, intimidation, and coercion. Coercive control also served as a motivator or causal factor for women's experiences with sexual assault, intimidation, and physical abuse. These studies signify that nonviolent, controlling methods of abuse are both common and preferred among abusers. What is also of great concern here are the mechanisms that abusers are using to achieve their desire or need to coerce and impair their victims, and the rapidity with which new technologies have developed and integrated into the social milieu has once again begun to change how intimate partner abuse is understood.

Coercive Control in an Online Environment

While the violent and nonviolent tactics of intimate partner abusers in a non-virtual, real-world environment have been well-documented, the growing availability and capacity of information and communication technologies (ICTs) has presented a host of new techniques and forums for abusers to monitor, intimidate, and coercively control their victims. ICTs include a variety of implements, such as computers, the Internet, social networking sites, e-mail and instant messages, spyware and keystroke logging software, cellular phones, downloadable applications (apps), global positioning systems (GPS), digital cameras, and recording devices (Logan, 2010; Southworth et al., 2007). While ICTs have improved women's capacity to learn about various resources and contact service providers (Finn & Atkinson, 2009), these devices have also paradoxically placed women at a heightened risk, for instance, of being geographically located without their consent, blackmailed by abusers who have sensitive recordings or photographs of them, and cyberstalking (Finn & Banach, 2000; Silverstein, 2004). Cyberstalking, or the use of technological media to pursue and harass victims, has become a focal point among intimate partner abuse research in recent years (Belknap, Chu, & DePrince, 2012; Southworth et al., 2007; Spitzberg & Hoobler, 2002) and is designated by an abuser's use of the Internet and email to gather physical information about their victim's location and personal life, send unwanted images or messages, or assume the identity of their victim to spread false and damaging information (NIJ, 1999).

Although cyberstalking is not necessarily a new phenomenon, our knowledge of this type of abuse among intimate partners is still in its early stages. A subset of studies on the subject of cyberstalking have communicated prevalence estimates of 6 percent to 41 percent depending upon sample size (Baum, Catalano, Rand, & Rose, 2009; Dressing, Anders, Gallas, & Bailer, 2011; Reyns, Henson, & Fisher, 2012; Sheridan & Grant, 2007; Spitzburg & Hoobler, 2002) and an even smaller group of studies are beginning to document gender patterns of female victimization and male perpetration that are similar to offline stalking (Working to Halt Online Abuse, 2013; Reyns et al., 2012). Statistics from 256 incidences of cyberstalking gathered by the volunteer organization Working to Halt Online Abuse (WHOA, 2013) affirmed that over half of victims of cyberstalking were female, 40 percent of harassers were male, and just over half of the victims had maintained a previous romantic relationship with their online perpetrator. Among a sample of 974 college students, Reyns et al. (2012) discovered that significantly more women than men had been cyberstalked, harassed online, repeatedly contacted by the perpetrator after requesting that they cease communication, and received repeated unwanted sexual advances, and that more men than women were cyberstalking offenders. Among the men and women who reported online forms of victimization (n=438), 12.1 percent indicated that their perpetrators were current or ex-boyfriends while 3.6 percent were current or former girlfriends.

Of additional note, the coercion and psychological abuse that underlies cyberstalking is evidenced to occur in connection with "offline" stalking (Alexy, Burgess, Baker, & Smoyak, 2005; Lee, 1998; Sheridan & Grant, 2007). In the aforementioned surveys by Working to Halt Online Abuse (2013), one-quarter of victims indicated that their harassers threatened physical violence against them. Another study by Sheridan and Grant (2007) compared stalking between the real and virtual worlds across a sample of 1,051 individuals representing North America, the United Kingdom, and Australia. These authors created four distinct categories to measure stalking victimization: purely online, which comprised 4 percent of their population whose experiences were exclusive to an online environment; the crossover group (5%), which included individuals who were stalked online for at least four weeks followed by offline stalking; the proximal with online stalking group (39%) with those who were primarily stalked offline, but methods of online stalking were occasionally used by the perpetrator; and purely offline (54%), which consisted of those who were exclusively stalked offline and were not pursued through online mediums. From their analyses, Sheridan and Grant (2007) concluded that the processes and impact of stalking across these four categories share more similarities than differences, but that those in the crossover group expressed the greatest risk for extreme stalking and physical violence. Additionally, Korchmaros, Ybarra, Langhinrichsen-Rohling, Boyd, and Lenhart (2013) used longitudinal data collected through the national Growing Up with Media study to examine the perpetration of psychological teen dating violence through long-standing modes of communication (LSMC; e.g., in-person and telephone conversations) and computer-mediated communication (CMC; e.g., text messaging, social network websites). Young people in this study who used both methods of communication perpetrated psychological abuse more frequently, but more of these respondents did use LSMC, leading the authors to conclude that nondigital communication provides the context for perpetration through CMC to occur.

As technology continues to burgeon and the potential of new devices to erode the boundaries of personal space and privacy becomes a growing reality, measures are being taken to clarify the ways in which abusers are using digital tools to coercively control and terrorize their intimate partners, to determine whether the processes of cyberstalking are fundamentally different than offline stalking, and to create various categories and theories of cybercrime and cyberabuse to better measure perpetration and victimization. As our society continues to rely upon technology in their personal and professional lives, remaining informed about the possible misuse of these devices is of utmost importance to ensuring that cyberabuses are easily identifiable to victims and advocates and treated as serious offenses by the criminal justice system.

Exploring the Current State of Cyberabuses and Intimate Partner Violence Perpetration

Theoretical Constructs for Understanding Online Intimate Partner Abuse

Nearly twenty years ago, Michael Johnson (1995) published his influential article *Patriarchal Terrorism and Common Couple Violence: Two Forms of Violence Against Women*, which theorized that "common (or situational) couple violence" is a product of specific arguments that escalate to violence but show no evidence of an attempt for either partner to exert control, and that "patriarchal (or intimate) partner terrorism" involves frequent and escalating abuse and coercion perpetrated by men in order to control women in what is commonly refer to as domestic violence. Later publications by Johnson (Kelly & Johnson, 2008; Johnson, 2010) witnessed the addition of two other theoretical categories of violence: "violent resistance," where victims violently respond to the abuse of their intimate terrorists either immediately or over time, and "mutual violent control," where each partner engages in a violent attempt to control the relationship. In essence, these classifications were created as a means of clarifying extremely disparate findings from feminist scholars whose reports highlighted that women were the majority of survivors of intimate partner abuse (DeKeseredy & Schwartz, 1998; Dobash & Dobash, 1979; Dobash, Dobash, Cavanaugh, & Lewis, 1998; Loseke & Kurz, 2005) and those who are a part of the popularly termed "family conflict studies" that reported men and women to perpetrate violence at equivalent rates (DeMaris, 1992; Dutton & Corvo, 2006; Straus, 1979, 2005). Johnson's typologies have been applied in myriad circumstances, from understanding abused women's help-seeking (Leone, Johnson, & Cohan, 2007), implications for child custody proceedings (Ver Steegh, 2004) and violence perpetrated between cohabiting partners (Brownridge, 2010). While Johnson's concept of intimate partner terrorism is largely focused on women as recipients of violence since they constitute the majority of survivors, other studies that have employed this theoretical construct have shown that men are also likely to experience intimate terrorism from their female partners (Straus & Gozjolko, 2014), albeit with less severe health and economic outcomes than women who experience intimate partner terrorism (Jasinski, Blumenstein, & Morgan, 2014; Johnson & Leone, 2005).

Johnson's typology of intimate partner terrorism underscores the specific importance of highlighting gender as an important component within the discussion of intimate partner abuse and coercive control. Within the scope of intimate partner cyberstalking and other cyberabuses that are either partially or fully relegated to the online realm, women are theorized to be central objects of the "male gaze." In her essay *Visual Pleasure and Narrative Cinema*, Laura Mulvey (1975) states that, "In a world ordered by sexual imbalance, pleasure in looking has been split between active/male and passive/female. The determining male gaze projects its phantasy [sic] on to the female form which is styled accordingly. In their traditional exhibitionist role women are simultaneously looked at and displayed, with their appearance coded for strong visual and erotic impact so that they can be said to connote to-be-looked-at-ness." Here, Mulvey is arguing that women are constructed within film as a digital medium as erotic objects intended to signify male desire, both for characters within the narrative as well as for the spectator who is viewing the film. Importantly as well, Mulvey states that the narrative is imbued with a sexual division of labor that provides the male protagonist with control and possession and the female figure subjected to the protagonist alone. It is through this power dynamic, Mulvey states, that the spectator, through identification with the protagonist, can also possess the female figure with his own gaze. In a similar vein to the concept of the male gaze, feminist theories have long examined why the female body is also subject to violence and oppression (MacKinnon, 1989; Millett, 1970). For instance, within her text *Toward a Feminist Theory of the State* (1989), Catharine MacKinnon writes extensively about coercion and rape of women and women's sexual objectification through pornography:

> Possession and use of women through the sexualization of intimate intrusion and access to them is a central feature of women's social definition as inferior and feminine. Visual and verbal intrusion, access, possession, and use is predicated upon and produces physical and psychic intrusion, access, possession, and use. In contemporary industrial society, pornography is an industry that mass produces sexual intrusion on, access to, possession and use of women by and for men for profit. It exploits women's sexual and economic inequality for gain. It sells women to men as and for sex. It is a technologically sophisticated traffic in women (p. 195).

MacKinnon's statement is poignant in the respect that intimate abusers have been known to exploit technology to humiliate their partners through the distribution of sexual imagery and recordings that were coerced or taken without consent (Citron & Franks, 2014; Franks, 2014). Moreover, while the "male gaze" was originally imparted into film as a means of understanding power hierarchies within a particular fictional narrative, this concept can be extended to the many technologies that intimate abusers utilize to observe their partners in the present day. Intimate abusers, for instance, can easily check their partners' Facebook profile, determine who their partner contacted, record them without their consent, locate their whereabouts, and assume false identities to harass their victims (Southworth et al., 2007).

Taken together, mounting evidence suggests that the aforementioned theories of intimate partner terrorism and the objectification of women are appropriate to understand intimate partner cyberabuse. Indeed, mounting research suggests that intimate partners and abusers who stalk their victims tend to be far more dangerous and persistent in their pursuits when compared to intimate partners and abusers who do not stalk their victims (James & Farnham, 2003; Logan & Cole, 2011; Melton, 2007; Mohandie, Meloy, McGowan, & Williams, 2006) and that intimate partner stalkers use a *broad array of tactics* to pursue their victims more frequently and intently (Johnson & Kercher, 2009; Palarea, Zona, Lane, Langhinrichsen-Rohling, 1999). Melton (2007) also asked survivors to share their perspectives of what they felt motivated their perpetrators to stalk them, and the most common responses were that their stalkers wanted to control them, or were acting out of anger or jealousy. The rapid transgression of technology has indeed provided "the intimate terrorist enhanced capacity to threaten, intimidate, and monitor his victim" (Dunlap, 2010, p. 17), and with ICTs growing in form and fashion, the following section covers the breadth of available devices that intimate partner abusers have used from the inception of the world-wide web to satellite-based tracking devices.

Social Networking Sites

The use of social networking websites, including Facebook, Twitter, Instagram, Pinterest, and LinkedIn is incredibly widespread. The PEW Research Internet Project (2014) estimates that 71 percent of online adults use Facebook, 19 percent use Twitter, 17 percent are on Instagram, 21 percent on Pinterest, and 22 percent on LinkedIn. Intimate abusers have been known to utilize social networking websites to defame and harass their victims or gain information regarding their whereabouts. At this time, the majority of empirical data about motivations for pursuing current or ex-partners come from studies that focus on Facebook as the social networking forum. For instance, Lyndon, Bonds-Raacke, and Cratty (2011) found that over two-thirds of their sample (n=411) indicated having used covert provocation against an ex-partner through Facebook (e.g., wrote a post on their Facebook wall to provoke ex-partner, posted poetry or music lyrics on ex-partner's Facebook wall to taunt ex-partner or in an attempt to repair the relationship), 18 percent publicly harassed their ex-partners (e.g., created a fake Facebook profile of ex-partner to cause them problems, posted embarrassing photos of ex-partner), and 18 percent vented about their ex-partners (e.g., wrote inappropriate comments about their ex-partner on a friend's Facebook wall, posted an inappropriate comment on ex-partners Facebook photo). Also, those who engaged in Cyber Obsessional Pursuit (COP), which is understood as cyberstalking with the intent to harass or demand intimacy from another person, or Obsessive Relational Intrusion (ORI), which is the repeated pursuit of ineunwanted intimacy through the violation of physical or symbolic privacy, were significantly more likely to perpetrate covert provocation, public harassment, and venting through social media. Others have pinpointed a correlation between romantic jealousy and those who have an excessive attachment to social networking websites (Elphinston & Noller, 2011; Muise, Christofides, & Desmarais, 2009). Specifically, Elphinston and Noller (2011) state that "Facebook intrusion may threaten romantic relationships, given that it provides an easily accessible interpersonal communication medium, with an infinite number of potential third-party threats and may even involve monitoring one's partner's activities on Facebook. Hence, Facebook intrusion may translate into hypervigilance for relationship threats, jealousy-related suspicions, and surveillance behaviors in a person's romantic relationship" (p. 632). Results of these authors' study confirmed the linkage between Facebook intrusion and relationship dissatisfaction through experiences of jealousy and surveillance of partners, and that these feelings disrupted romantic relationships both online and offline. Lastly, women interviewed by Dimond, Fiesler, and Bruckman (2011) described how their abuse continued through Facebook and other social networking websites following the dissolution of the relationship. Not only did abusers continue to harass and threaten both their victims as well as family members of the victim through Facebook, but one survivor's account told of menacing behavior by her husband's new lover.

Non-empirical works that have looked at trends with social media and violence against women have also illuminated trends that may incite intimate abusers to pursue their partners through online fora by using indirect threats or even portray an abusive situation to in many ways seem acceptable. For example, Aumiller (2011) discusses a topic that trended on Twitter—indicating that it was a widely discussed topic on that particular day—that was all about reasons to beat your girlfriend. Specifically, Aumiller (2011) wrote that "The tag '*#reasonstobeatyourgirlfriend*' continued to gain steam, with many people giving reasons (like '*#becauseshedidntmakeyouasandwich*'), along with other people calling for the topic to be removed, and other's trying to take away the violent meaning of the topic by saying things like '*#reasonstobeatyourgirlfriend* to the door ... So you can open it for her.' While others said that it was never OK, and a petition was created for Twitter to see how this topic needed to be removed." While a specific petition was circulating for Twitter to remove this offensive topic (Aumiller, 2011), Twitter's policy to date only allows for the removal of content if an individual attempts to impersonate another with the goal of deception, posts private information (social security number, street address), or directly threatens violence against another person but otherwise states that "we respect the ownership of the content that users share and each user is responsible for the content he or she provides. Because of these principles, we do not actively monitor and will not censor user content" (Twitter, 2014). As Perry (2012) suggests, "You can never make social networks 'safe' for victims to use, you can only make them 'safer.' Ideally, a victim would deactivate their account to reduce their risks. However, social networks do offer support and reduce isolation so many victims are reluctant to leave their account. They must be given advice to minimise [sic] the risk, including how to improve privacy settings" (p. 27).

Case Study 5.1

In Washington State on November 10, 2014, Ian Martin Elias murdered his ex-wife, Nicollette Naomi Elias, and then turned the gun on himself following what is described as long and bitter divorce and custody disputes. According to reports, Nicollette Elias had been physically and sexually abused by Ian Elias during their marital relationship, and Ian's repeated abuses, alcoholism, and obsession with firearms prompted Nicollette to obtain a restraining order in January 2014 and their family court judge to terminate Ian's visitation rights in April 2014. Days following the termination of his visitation rights, Ian began to use YouTube and Facebook as fora to post derogatory comments about Nicollette and to allege that she has physically and mentally abused him. Shortly before the murder-suicide, Ian Elias also posted multiple messages on his Twitter account blasting the judge who ordered him away from his children, using hashtags *#parentalalienation* and *#fathersrights* (Bernstein, 2014).

This particular case illuminates the extent to which social media can become an outlet for intimate abusers to harass and humiliate their partners, but also raises questions as to whose responsibility it is to police social media websites. If direct threats of violence are not made but disparaging comments and false accusations abound, when does social media become a tool of stalking and harassment versus a lesser form of venting or practicing a first amendment right to free speech? Also, should responsibility be placed upon the victim to protect themselves by increasing their security settings or deactivating their accounts, or do social media-based companies have a greater responsibility in this digital age to amend how they regulate the dissemination of insinuated or actual threats?

Spyware and Global Positioning Systems

One of the most dangerous times for women who are abused is when they attempt to terminate their relationship with their intimate partners (Fleury, Sullivan, & Bybee, 2000; Johnson & Hotton, 2003). While technology has provided a space for women to conveniently access information about the nearest domestic violence shelter,[4] domestic violence emergency hotlines,[5] and safety plans,[6] abusers have resorted to spyware—illegal software that can be installed on victims' smartphones, tablets, or computers in order to track online activities and personal information, eavesdrop on personal conversations—and GPS technology—tracking devices that can be attached to smartphones or vehicles and use satellites to access real-time location—that may reveal what types of resources their victims were accessing, where their victims intend to flee, and even where their victims might be following their departure (Southworth & Tucker, 2007). National Public Radio (NPR) recently surveyed 70 domestic violence shelters located in both large urban centers and small towns, and found that 85 percent of these shelters were working with women whose abusers had attempted to track them their location through GPS, 75 percent had encountered women in their shelters whose abusers had used hidden mobile apps to eavesdrop on their phone conversations, and half of these shelters prohibit the use of Facebook at the shelters in order to protect survivors from being located (Shahani, 2014).

Much of what is understood about the use of spyware and GPS comes from national estimates and anecdotal evidence. According the data collected by the CDC, nearly half (49.7 percent) of female stalking victims and 32 percent of male stalking victims reported being watched, followed, or spied upon through the use of a listening device, camera, or GPS device (Black et al., 2011). Among 5.2 million cases of stalking and harassment gathered by the U.S. Department of Justice, 44.1 percent involved computer spyware, 40.3 percent video or dig-

---

4. See www.domesticshelters.org as a resource that offers a listing of women's shelters by city, language spoken, and types of services provided.
5. The National Domestic Violence Hotline (www.thehotline.org).
6. See the National Coalition Against Domestic Violence (http://www.ncadv.org/protectyourself/SafetyPlan.php) and the National Domestic Violence Hotline (www.thehotline.org) for examples of domestic violence safety plans.

ital cameras, 35.8 percent listening devices, and 9.7 percent GPS monitoring (Baum et al., 2009). Woodlock (2014) surveyed 46 survivors about the types of technology that their abusers used to control them with; 17 percent stated that they had been tracked with a GPS device or through a downloadable spyware app, over half indicated that their abuser had used mobile technology to locate them, and 17 percent had abusers that demanded their electronic passwords. Media reports have also brought the issues of GPS monitoring and stalking to light. The most infamous publicized case of GPS use in an intimate abusive relationship is that of Jackie Wisniewski who, two months prior to her murder, discovered that her estranged boyfriend, Timothy Jorden, had installed a GPS tracking device on her vehicle to stalk and track her movements (Hirtzel, 2014). Although Wisniewski filed a complaint with law enforcement, Jorden could not be prosecuted since New York did not identify GPS devices as prohibited under the state's stalking statute. Two months following the discovery of the GPS device, Wisniewski was shot and killed by Jorden. This incident has prompted the creation and passage of *Jackie's Law*, which allows law enforcement to charge and prosecute offenders who use GPS to stalk their victims (Hirtzel, 2014). Another instance comes from *The Wall Street Journal* (Scheck, 2010) which publicized an instance where an assailant (Andre Leteve) installed a GPS tracking device on his estranged wife's cell phone because he was worried that she was going to take their children to another state; Leteve ultimately killed their two children and attempted to commit suicide in an act of revenge.

Case Study 5.2

Widely available cell phone spyware apps and global positioning systems (GPS) for modern smartphones have given perpetrators a new technique to monitor, harass, and locate victims with ease (Southworth et al., 2005). Most of these mobile spy apps are marketed as legal means to monitor behaviors of children or employees; however, domestic violence advocates report growing numbers of clients stalked and harassed via these affordable and effective means (Gross, 2014). With these tools enabled, abusers can use GPS tracking and app data to identify the real time location of victims, and may even lead these abusers to safe houses or shelters (Shahani, 2014).

At this time, stalking apps are legal although efforts are being made to create and pass legislation to protect users from this abuse. One example of proposed legislation is the Location Privacy Protection Act, led by Senator Al Franken (Gross, 2014), banning the development and sale of spying apps while also regulating the collection of geolocation information in non-emergency circumstances. However, this bill is not without critics and opposition (Gross, 2014), and its enactment is not guaranteed. Thus, while companies continue to profit from mobile spy apps, these tools may also put lives at risk by granting perpetrators an easy and effective means to monitor and harass victims. The rapid pace at which these technological tools become available for use often conflicts with the much slower speed of legislative action. Who should be responsible for preventing this misuse of location-based data? Additionally, how can legislation keep up with the speed of technological advancements to protect users from this evolving type of abuse?

Nonconsensual Pornography

Nonconsensual pornography, which is often referred to as revenge pornography, cyber rape, or involuntary pornography, involves the distribution of sexually explicit images of individuals without their consent (Franks, 2014). According to Citron and Franks (2014), this method of coercion consists of publishing images and recordings of sexual encounters that are covertly obtained as well as exacting revenge by circulating images that were originally obtained with consent but with the expectation that they remain confidential or private. Few studies to date quantified this particular phenomenon as experienced through technology by adults in marital or estranged relationships. However, some studies that have focused on "sexting," which describes the creation and dissemination of sexual images by minors and young adults through instant messaging, email, and social networking websites, have provided a snapshot of how many individuals are engaging in this type of behavior. A survey on technology use and sexting of 1,280 teens and young adults between the ages of 13 and 26 commissioned by The National Campaign to Prevent Teen and Unplanned Pregnancy (2008) found that 20 percent of teens and 33 percent of young adults have sent or posted nude or semi-nude images of themselves, and these sexual images were being sent to current partners in 75 percent of cases. Furthermore, 15 percent of this population had forwarded a nude or semi-nude image to an unintended third party while 30 percent had been exposed to this type of sexual image that was originally intended for someone else, and young men constitute a greater proportion of those that had seen sexual images intended for another person. According to Dir, Coskunpinar, Steiner, and Cyders' (2013) study on sexting, approximately 47 percent of undergraduates had sent "sext" pictures while 64 percent received this content. Within this sample, women reported strong negative expectancies (e.g., embarrassment or discomfort) of receiving sexts while men reported positive expectancies (e.g., feeling sexy or excited), and sexts were also most common among those who were dating, in a serious relationship, or cohabiting. McAfee Security's (2013) *Love, Relationships, and Technology Survey* found that 1 in 10 ex-partners threatened to share risqué pictures of their former partners online, and 60 percent of those threats were carried out, yet women in this study were more likely than men to threaten to post and follow through with these threats. The timeliest data specifically on revenge porn comes from an internal evaluation of 1,244 individuals by the Cyber Civil Rights Initiative (CCRI) (2011) which indicates that "over 50% of victims reported that their naked photos appeared next to their full name and social network profile; over 20% of victims reported that their e-mail addresses and telephone numbers appeared next to their naked photos ... and over 80% of revenge porn victims experience severe emotional distress and anxiety" (Citron & Franks, pp. 350–351). This study also revealed that 90 percent of revenge porn victims were women, and ex-boyfriends were responsible for publishing revenge porn content in 57 percent of cases (Franks, 2014). Revenge porn websites are also on the rise, providing anonymous forums for perpetrators to publish photographs, videos, and contact information of their former friends or partners with minimal risk of legal repercussion (Najdowski and Hildegrand, 2014).

The results of the aforementioned studies are informative, yet disquieting in the respect that the prevalence of nonconsensual sex through the use of ICTs is pervasive but also likely to be underreported. What is even more concerning is that rates of perpetration appear to be equivocal due to the use of different populations and definitions between revenge porn and sexting. Indeed, *Time* magazine recently published a commentary that questions the extent to which revenge porn and other types of cyberabuses are predominant to women (Young, 2014) as well as another op-ed that highlighted women's disproportionate victimization through revenge porn, cyberharassment, and cyberstalking along with women's overrepresentation in rape videos and online human trafficking to be entrenched in our society's historically misogynistic treatment of women (Chemaly, 2014). The latter position taken by Chemaly (2014) has merit in the respect that prior research has thoroughly identified nonconsensual sex and pornography as tools used by abusers to coerce their partners (Bergen, 1998; Shope, 2004). Indeed, Henry and Powell (2014) describe their interviews with women's support workers who recounted cases where abusers had recorded sexual assaults against their intimate partners, coerced their intimate partners into taking intimate photos where saying "no" was likely an unsafe option for the victim, and threatened to show sexual recordings or images to the couple's children or family if the victim pursued legal action for the abuse.

Telephones and Texting

Hand, Chung, and Peters (2007) note that "the surveillance of women in situations of domestic violence often involves checking with whom the woman is having contact: family and friends, work colleagues, and so on" (p. 6). A range of telephone technologies are at the disposal of intimate partner abusers, such as caller identification, fax machines, calling cards, TTY and TTD (technologies used by the hearing impaired which can be misused to impersonate others), and cellular phones which include downloadable apps and texting capabilities (Logan, 2010). Due to the long-standing availability of telephones—from landlines to cordless and cellular phones—it follows that telephones and texting are two of the most common ways that abusers have stalked and harassed their partners (Dimond et al., 2011; Woodlock, 2014). Nearly two-thirds of individuals in the U.S. Department of Justice's report on stalking victimization received unwanted phone calls or messages, the largest overall experienced form of stalking and harassment among this sample (Baum et al., 2009). Over three-quarters of women in Woodlock's (2014) sample had an abuser who used text messages and phone calls to harass and disparage them, more than half were made fearful of what would happen if they did not respond to a phone call or text from their abuser, 47 percent were with abusers who had checked their text messages without permission, and 44 percent were threatened over text, email, or through social media. Personal accounts from individuals in Melander's (2010) interviews highlighted the use of texting and phone calls to coercively control within relationships classified as intimate terrorism, with respondents mentioning tactics where an abuser would control which contacts could be listed in his partners telephone and another spoke of an instance where constant texting was used to check on an intimate partner. When telephones are used to harass the intended target, the perpetrator may call and hang up, remain silent once the phone is answered, engage in conversation, or become verbally abusive (Sheridan, Davies, & Boon, 2001).

Online Abuse vs. Offline Abuse: Fundamental Similarities or Differences?

The aforementioned studies have exemplified how the extent of available technologies has provided a more unregulated space that allows abusers to terrorize their intimate partners and exert a power and control in ways that were inconceivable twenty years ago. What's more, the selected case studies illustrated the challenges of anti-stalking legislation to keep pace with the online and offline exploits of abusers. Research on cyberstalking and other cyberabuses has recently demonstrated valuable to informing possible legislative reform (Franks, 2014; Southworth, 2014), yet there are also conceptual issues within cyberstalking studies that also need to be rectified. One primary issue is that there remains no consensus as to whether cyberstalking is a modified form of offline stalking or a distinct crime that has emerged alongside new technologies (Cavezza & McEwan, 2014; Nobles, Reyns, Fox, & Fisher, 2014; Sheridan & Grant, 2007). Although researchers have applied operational definitions to cyberstalking and offline stalking as a means of differentiating prevalence, pursuit, and impact (Nobles et al., 2014; Spitzberg & Hoobler, 2002), these conceptual definitions are often discordant with the legal criteria used to prosecute stalking cases (Tjaden, 2009). While state-level statutes vary in their legal definition of what constitutes stalking, the common requirements are that (1) there be an unwanted or obsessive pattern of behavior; (2) the course of conduct causes the victim to reasonably fear for his or her safety or the safety of others; and (3) the course of conduct causes the victim to suffer substantial emotional distress (18 U.S. Code § 2261A). ICTs also cover a wide-range of possibilities for cyberabuse, and some of these devices have become antiquated while others undoubtedly remain undiscovered. Lastly, the self-protective behaviors of victims of cyberstalking in relation to offline stalking are relatively unknown (Nobles et al., 2014). These problems certainly have complicated our understanding of cyberstalking, yet at the same time these inconsistencies are also inspiring more thorough investigations.

The available evidence nonetheless infers that intimate partner abuse in the online and offline worlds share similar characteristics, particularly if intimate partner terrorism is used as a guiding theoretical principle. First, the previous sections of this chapter presented evidence that victimization and perpetration are highly polarized by gender: women are more likely to endure sexual assault within their intimate relationships and be the targets of online sexual abuses, and men are more likely to be offenders of intimate partner abuse and cyberabuse (Baum et al., 2009; Black et al., 2011; Cintron & Franks, 2014). Earlier research published by Bocij (2003) demonstrated that cyberstalking victimization was typically shorter in duration than offline stalking, and victims of cyberstalking were less likely to know their assailants, leading this author to conclude that cyberstalking was indeed a new form of deviant behavior distinguishable from offline abuse. Yet, more recent inquiries where the population of study are exclusively survivors of intimate partner abuse—those who are known to each other through a current or past relationship—emphasize that perpetrators use technology to stalk their partners during the relationship and following the termination of the relationship (Brewster, 2000; Dimond et al., 2011; Melander, 2010; Woodlock, 2014). While other studies using variable samples, from college students and national data to self-identified stalking victims, have largely gathered support for the notion that there are indeed few differences between stalking and cyberstalking (Cavezza & McEwan, 2014; Nobles et al., 2014; Sheridan & Grant, 2007), there is an ever-increasing importance for future studies to explicitly consider and compare the differences between intimate partner abusers who may utilize technology as a means of terrorization, dating or cohabiting partners where situational circumstances may incite cyberstalking and cyberabuse, and among strangers who are arguably afforded the greatest degree of anonymity in cyberspace. Investigating offender motivations and relationship to the victim may provide us with evidence that cyberstalking is perhaps not a "new" crime, but that technologies have created spaces where some exclusively offend under the guise of anonymity while others blatantly use these technologies to openly continue their assaults on their victims.

Conclusion

Information Communication Technologies (ICTs) have revolutionized the possibilities for individuals to exchange information and connect around the globe. The latest technology, such as iPhone and iCloud are intended to create conveniences for individuals to access and synchronize information, and social media such as Facebook was created to connect individuals with friends and those who work, live, and study around them. The largest percentage of the population that is using smartphones and social networking websites are between the ages of 18 and 29 (PEW, 2014), thus illuminating a trend whereby younger generations will come to rely upon technology and digital devices as a part of their daily milieus. As such, there is an ever-increasing need to not only ascertain the benefits that technology provides our society but also the potential for others to corrupt and misuse these devices. Fifteen years ago, then U.S. Attorney General Janet Reno (1999) stated before the Senate Judiciary Committee that "Our Nation has become so reliant on new technology that the national and economic security of the United States now depends largely on the rapid, consistent, secure, and reliable movement and storage of data. As a result, without proper safeguards, we are potentially vulnerable to hackers, cyberterrorists, and other criminals who would use their computers for illegal intrusion into, and exploitation of, America's major information and communications networks." While various types of cybercrimes that often breach the security of large groups of individuals has come to be known within the current digital age, so have highly personal attacks ensued through cyberbullying, cyberharassment, and cyberstalking.

The personal intrusions that technological forums have fostered are undoubtedly coupled with tangible threats of violence, and this has become particularly evident among intimate partners. Previous studies have linked intimate partner stalking with a woman's increased risk of severe physical violence and femicide (McFarlane et al., 1999) as well as sexual assault (Logan & Cole, 2010). When cyberstalking of intimate partners becomes a facet of an already violent relationship, the omnipresence of threats, degrading remarks, and public humiliation undoubtedly heighten women's emotional distress and fear (Woodlock, 2014). As intimate partners comprise the largest group of known cyberstalking offenders (WHOA, 2013) and media reports linking cyberstalking and online surveillance to intimate partner homicides become more common (Bernstein, 2014; Kennedy, 2014), it is imperative that future studies identify the digital methods that appeal to abusers in their pursuit to coerce and harm their intimate partners, and it is equally necessary for legal authorities, politicians, practitioners, and activists to acknowledge the magnitude of cyberstalking and cyberabuse on the physical and emotional well-being of survivors. Southworth et al. (2007) recommend that advocates focus on survivors' needs, incorporate the topic of cyberstalking into survivor support groups, educate survivors about technological risks and safety, and ensure that their respective organization's website is accessible and has updated safety information for survivors who may be seeking support online. These authors also recommend that advocates coordinate with local law enforcement, prosecutors, and computer crime specialists in order to create a plan whereby evidence of cyberabuse can be documented and processed, identify state laws that could apply to emerging technology, and foster an open dialogue between prosecutors, law enforcement officers, and survivors as to how pressing charges might impact their lives. In many ways, the work of Southworth and colleagues (2007) brings this discussion full circle in the context of intimate partner abuse prevention: their recommendation for advocates and the legal system to coordinate is reminiscent of the Domestic Abuse Intervention Project (Pence & Paymar, 1986) that brought the issues of intimate partner abuse to the public fore, just as similar efforts are now needed to address intimate partner cyberabuse in the digital world and determine answers to the question of "Who is the virtual intimate terrorist?"

References

Alexy, E. M., Burgess, A. W., Baker, T., & Smoyak, S. A. (2005). Perceptions of cyberstalking among college students. *Brief Treatment and Crisis Intervention, 5*(3), 279–289.

Aumiller, S. (1 August, 2011). *Why is Twitter promoting violence against women?* Retrieved from https://givehopeavoice.wordpress.com/2011/08/01/why-is-twitter-promoting-violence-against-women/.

Baum, K., Catalano, S., Rand, M., & Rose, K. (2009). Stalking victimization in the United States. United States Department of Justice.

Beck, C. J., & Raghavan, C. (2010). Intimate partner abuse screening in custody mediation: The importance of assessing coercive control. *Family Court Review, 48*(3), 555–565.

Belknap, J., Chu, A. T., & DePrince, A. P. (2011). Roles of phones and computers in threatening and abusing women victims of male intimate partner abuse, *The Duke Journal of Gender, Law, and Policy, 19*, 373.

Bergen, R. K. (1996). *Wife rape: Understanding the response of survivors and service providers.* Thousand Oaks, CA: Sage.

Bernstein, M. (2014, November 10). Portland man faced restraining and stalking orders for escalating threats before he killed ex-wife, then himself. *The Oregonian.* Retrieved from http://www.oregonlive.com/portland/index.ssf/2014/11/portland_man_faced_restraining.html.

Black, M. C., et al. (2011). The national intimate partner and sexual violence survey (NISVS): 2010 summary report. Atlanta, GA: National Center for Injury Prevention and Control, Centers for Disease Control and Prevention. Retrieved from http://www.cdc.gov/violenceprevention/nisvs/summary_reports.html.

Bocij, P. (2003). Victims of cyberstalking: An exploratory study of harassment perpetrated via the internet. *First Monday, 8*(10), (October). Retrieved from http://firstmonday.org/ojs/index.php/fm/article/view/1086/1006.

Brewster, M. P. (2000). Stalking by former intimates: Verbal threats and other predictors of physical violence. *Violence and Victims, 15*(1), 41–54.

Brewster, M. P. (2003). Power and control dynamics in prestalking and stalking situations. *Journal of Family Violence, 18*(4), 207–217.

Brownridge, D. A. (2010). Does the situational couple violence-intimate terrorism typology explain cohabitors' high risk of intimate partner violence?. *Journal of Interpersonal Violence, 25*(7), 1264–1283.

Busch, A. L., & Rosenberg, M. S. (2004). Comparing women and men arrested for domestic violence: A preliminary report. *Journal of Family Violence, 19*(1), 49–57.

Catalano, S. (2013). Intimate partner violence: Attributes of victimization, 1993–2011. Bureau of Justice Statistics. Retrieved from http://www.bjs.gov/content/pub/pdf/ipvav9311.pdf.

Cavezza, C., & McEwan T. E. (2014). Cyberstalking versus off-line stalking in a forensic sample. *Psychology, Crime & Law, 20*(10), 955–970.

Centers for Disease Control and Prevention (2014). Intimate partner violence: Definitions. Retrieved from http://www.cdc.gov/violenceprevention/intimatepartnerviolence/definitions.html.

Chemaly, S. (2014, September 9). There's no comparing male and female harassment online. *Time*. Retrieved from http://time.com/3305466/male-female-harassment-online/.

Citron, D. K., & Franks, M. A. (2014). Criminalizing revenge porn. *Wake Forest Law Review, 49*, 345–391.

Cooper, A., & Griffin-Shelley, E. (2002, 2002). A quick tour of online sexuality: Part 1. *Annals of the American Psychotherapy Association, 5*, 11–13.

DeKeseredy, W. S., & Schwartz, M. D. (1998). Measuring the extent of woman abuse in intimate heterosexual relationships: A critique of the Conflict Tactics Scales. *U.S. Department of Justice Violence Against Women Grants Office Electronic Resources*. Retrieved from http://stoprelationshipabuse.org/wp-content/uploads/2013/06/A-Critique-of-the-Conflict-Tactics-Scales.pdf.

DeMaris, A. Male versus female initiation of aggression: The case of courtship violence. In Viano, E. C. (Ed.), *Intimate violence: Interdisciplinary perspectives* (pp. 111–120). Hemisphere Publishing Corporation.

Dimond, J. P., Fiesler, C., & Bruckman, A. S. (2011). Domestic violence and information communication technologies. *Interacting with Computers, 23*(5), 413–421.

Dir, A. L., Coskunpinar, A., Steiner, J. L., & Cyders, M. A. (2013). Understanding differences in sexting behaviors across gender, relationship status, and sexual identity, and the role of expectancies in sexting. *Cyberpsychology, Behavior, and Social Networking, 16*(8), 568–574.

Dobash, R. E., & Dobash, R. (1979). *Violence against wives: A case against the patriarchy*. New York: Free Press.

Dobash, R. P., Dobash, R. E., Cavanagh, K., & Lewis, R. (1998). Separate and intersecting realities: A Comparison of men's and women's accounts of violence against women. *Violence Against Women, 4*(4), 382–414.

Dressing, H., Anders, A., Gallas, C., & Bailer, J. (2011). Cyberstalking: prevalence and impact on victims. *Psychiatrische Praxis, 38*(7), 336–341.

Dunlap, J. A. (2012). Intimate terrorism and technology: There's an app for that. *University of Massachusetts Law Review, 7*(10), 10–38.

Dutton, M. A., & Goodman, L. A. (2005). Coercion in intimate partner violence: Toward a new conceptualization. *Sex Roles, 52*(11–12), 743–756.

Elphinston, R. A., & Noller, P. (2011). Time to face it! Facebook intrusion and the implications for romantic jealousy and relationship satisfaction. *Cyberpsychology, Behavior, and Social Networking, 14*(11), 631–635.

Federal Statute on Domestic Violence and Stalking, 18 U.S. Code §2261A.

Finn, J., & Atkinson, T. (2009). Promoting the safe and strategic use of technology for victims of intimate partner violence: evaluation of the technology safety project. *Journal of Family Violence, 24*(1), 53–59.

Finn, J., & Banach, M. (2000). Victimization online: The downside of seeking human services for women on the Internet. *CyberPsychology & Behavior, 3*(5), 785–796.

Fleury, R. E., Sullivan, C. M., & Bybee, D. I. (2000). When ending the relationship does not end the violence women's experiences of violence by former partners. *Violence Against Women, 6*(12), 1363–1383.

Franks, M. A. (2014). Drafting an effective 'revenge porn' law: A guide for legislators. Retrieved from http://papers.ssrn.com/sol3/papers.cfm?abstract_id=2468823.

Gross, G. (2014, June 4). Mobile spying apps fuel domestic violence, U.S. senator says. *PC World*. Retrieved from http://www.pcworld.com/article/2360060/mobile-spying-apps-fuel-domestic-violence-us-senator-says.html.

Hamberger, L. K., & Guse, C. (2005). Typology of reactions to intimate partner violence among men and women arrested for partner violence. *Violence and Victims, 20*(3), 303–317.

Hand, T., Chung, D., & Peters, M. (2009). *The use of information and communication technologies to coerce and control in domestic violence and following separation.* Australian Domestic and Family Violence Clearinghouse, UNSW.

Henry, N., & Powell, A. (2014). Beyond the 'sext': Technology-facilitated sexual violence and harassment against adult women. *Australian & New Zealand Journal of Criminology*, 0004865814524218.

Hirtzel, A. (2014, July 23). Governor signs 'Jackie's Law' to prevent GPS stalking. Buffalo's NPR News Station. Retrieved from http://news.wbfo.org/post/governor-signs-jackies-lawprevent-gps-stalking.

Glass, N., Manganello, J., & Campbell, J. C. (2004). Risk for intimate partner femicide in violent relationships. *Domestic Violence Report 9, 2*(12), 30–33.

Jacobs, H. (2013). A message from our founder, Dr. Holly Jacobs. Cyber Civil Rights Initiative. Retrieved from http://www.cybercivilrights.org/a_message_from_our_founder_dr_holly_jacobs.

James, D. V., & Farnham, F. R. (2003). Stalking and serious violence. *Journal of the American Academy of Psychiatry and the Law Online, 31*(4), 432–439.

Jasinski, J., Blumenstein, L., & Morgan, R. (2014). Testing Johnson's typology: is there gender symmetry in intimate terrorism?. *Violence and Victims, 29*(1), 73–88.

Johnson, M. P. (1995). Patriarchal terrorism and common couple violence: Two forms of violence against women. *Journal of Marriage and the Family, 57*(2), 283–294.

Johnson. M. P. (2010). *A typology of domestic violence: Intimate terrorism, violent resistance, and situational couple violence.* Lebanon, New Hampshire: University Press of New England.

Johnson, H., & Hotton, T. (2003). Losing control homicide risk in estranged and intact intimate relationships. *Homicide Studies, 7*(1), 58–84.

Johnson, M., & Kercher, G. (2009). Identifying predictors of negative psychological reactions to stalking victimization. *Journal of Interpersonal Violence, 24*(5), 886–882.

Johnson, M. P., & Leone, J. M. (2005). The differential effects of intimate terrorism and situational couple violence findings from the national violence against women survey. *Journal of Family Issues, 26*(3), 322–349.

Kelly, J. B., & Johnson, M. P. (2008). Differentiation among types of intimate partner violence Research update and implications for interventions. *Family Court Review, 46*(3), 476–499.

Korchmaros, J. D., Ybarra, M. L., Langhinrichsen-Rohling, J., Boyd, D., & Lenhart, A. (2013). Perpetration of teen dating violence in a networked society. *Cyberpsychology, Behavior, and Social Networking, 16*(8), 561–567.

Lee, R. K. (1998). Romantic and electronic stalking in a college context. *William & Mary Journal of Women and the Law, 4*(2), 373–466.

Leone, J. M., Johnson, M. P., & Cohan, C. L. (2007). Victim help seeking: Differences between intimate terrorism and situational couple violence. *Family Relations, 56*(5), 427–439.

Logan, T. K. (2010). Research on partner stalking: Putting the pieces together. Lexington, KY: University of Kentucky, Department of Behavioral Science & Center on Drug and Alcohol Research.

Logan, T. K., & Cole, J. (2011). Exploring the intersection of partner stalking and sexual abuse. *Violence Against Women, 17*(7), 904–924.

Loseke, D. R., & Kurz, D. (2005). Men's violence toward women is the serious social problem. In Loseke, D. R., Gelles, R. J., & Cavanaugh, M. M. (Eds.) *Current controversies on family violence* (pp. 79–95). Thousand Oaks, CA: Sage.

Lyndon, A., Bonds-Raacke, J., & Cratty, A. D. (2011). College students' Facebook stalking of ex-partners. *Cyberpsychology, Behavior, and Social Networking, 14*(12), 711–716.

MacKinnon, C. A. (1989). *Toward a feminist theory of the state.* Harvard University Press.

McAfee (2013). Love, relationships, and technology survey. Retrieved from http://www.mcafee.com/us/about/news/2013/q1/20130204-01.aspx.

McFarlane, J. M., Campbell, J. C., Wilt, S., Sachs, C. J., Ulrich, Y., & Xu, X. (1999). Stalking and intimate partner femicide. *Homicide Studies, 3*(4), 300–316.

Melander, L. A. (2010). College students' perceptions of intimate partner cyber harassment. *Cyberpsychology, Behavior, and Social Networking, 13*(3), 263–268.

Melton, H. C. (2007). Predicting the occurrence of stalking in relationships characterized by domestic violence. *Journal of Interpersonal Violence, 22*(1), 3–25.

Miller, S. L. (2001). The paradox of women arrested for domestic violence criminal justice: Professionals and service providers respond. *Violence Against Women, 7*(12), 1339–1376.

Millett, K. (1977). *Sexual politics. 1970.* London: Virago.

Mohandie, K., Meloy, J. R., McGowan, M. G., & Williams, J. (2006). The RECON typology of stalking: Reliability and validity based upon a large sample of North American stalkers. *Journal of Forensic Sciences, 51*(1), 147–155.

Muise, A., Christofides, E., & Desmarais, S. (2009). More information than you ever wanted: Does Facebook bring out the green-eyed monster of jealousy?. *CyberPsychology & Behavior, 12*(4), 441–444.

Mulvey, L. (1975). Visual pleasure and narrative cinema. *Screen, 16*(3), 6–18.

Najdowski, C. J., & Hildegrand, M. M. (2014). The criminalization of 'revenge porn.' American Psychological Association. Retrieved from http://www.apa.org/monitor/2014/01/jn.aspx.

The National Campaign to Prevent Teen and Unplanned Pregnancy (2008). *Sex and Tech: Results from a Survey of Teens and Young Adults.* Retrieved from http://thenationalcampaign.org/resource/sex-and-tech.

National Institute of Justice (1999). Stalking. Retrieved from http://www.nij.gov/topics/crime/stalking/Pages/welcome.aspx.

National Institute of Justice (2007). Intimate partner violence. Retrieved from http://www.nij.gov/topics/crime/intimate-partner-violence/Pages/welcome.aspx.

Nobles, M. R., Reyns, B. W., Fox, K. A., & Fisher, B. S. (2014). Protection against pursuit: A conceptual and empirical comparison of cyberstalking and stalking victimization among a national sample. *Justice Quarterly, 31*(6), 986–1014.

Palarea, R. E., Zona, M. A., Lane, J. C., & Langhinrichsen-Rohling, J. (1999). The dangerous nature of intimate relationship stalking: Threats, violence, and associated risk factors. *Behavioral Sciences & the Law, 17*(3), 269–283.

Pence, E., & Paymar, M. (1990). *Power and control: Tactics of men who batter: An educational curriculum.* Minnesota Program Development Incorporated.

Pence, E., & Shepard, M. F. (1999). An introduction: Developing a coordinated community response. In Shepard, M. F., & Pence, E. L. (Eds.) *Co-*

ordinating community responses to domestic violence: Lessons from Duluth and beyond (pp. 3–24). Sage Publications.

Perry, J. (2012). A guide to technology risks for victims. Network for Surviving Stalking and Women's Aid Federation of England.

PEW Research Internet Project (2014). Mobile technology fact sheet. Retrieved from http://www.pewinternet.org/fact-sheets/mobile-technology-fact-sheet/.

PEW Research Internet Project (2014). Social networking fact sheet. Retrieved from http://www.pewinternet.org/fact-sheets/social-networking-fact-sheet/.

Reno, J. (1999, May 5). Committee on the judiciary United States senate concerning Justice Department oversight. Retrieved from http://www.justice.gov/archive/ag/testimony/1999/agjudic050599.htm.

Reyns, B. W., Henson, B., & Fisher, B. S. (2012). Stalking in the twilight zone: Extent of cyberstalking victimization and offending among college students. *Deviant Behavior, 33*(1), 1–25.

Seghetti, L. M., & Bjelopera, J. P. (2012, May 10). The Violence Against Women Act: Overview, legislation, and federal funding. Congressional Research Service. Retrieved from http://fas.org/sgp/crs/misc/R42499.pdf.

Scheck, J. (2010, August 3). Stalkers exploit cellphone GPS. *The Wall Street Journal*. Retrieved from http://online.wsj.com/articles/SB10001424052748703467304575383522318244234.

Shahani, A. (2014, September 15). Smartphones used to stalk, control domestic violence victims. *National Public Radio*. Retrieved from http://www.npr.org/blogs/alltechconsidered/2014/09/15/346149979/smartphones-are-used-to-stalk-control-domestic-abuse-victims.

Sheridan, L., Davies, G., & Boon, J. (2001). The course and nature of stalking: A victim perspective. *The Howard Journal of Criminal Justice, 40*(3), 215–234.

Sheridan, L. P., & Grant, T. (2007). Is cyberstalking different?. *Psychology, Crime & Law, 13*(6), 627–640.

Shope, J. H. (2004). When words are not enough: The search for the effect of pornography on abused women. *Violence Against Women, 10*(1), 56–72.

Silverstein, L. (2004). Double edged sword: An examination of the global positioning system, enhanced 911, and the internet and their relationships to the lives of domestic violence victims and their abusers, *The Buffalo Women's Law Journal, 13*, 97.

Southworth, C., Dawson, S., Fraser, C., & Tucker, S. (2005). A high-tech twist on abuse: Technology, intimate partner stalking, and advocacy. Retrieved from http://www.mincava.umn.edu/documents/commissioned/stalkingandtech/stalkingandtech.pdf.

Southworth, C., Finn, J., Dawson, S., Fraser, C., & Tucker, S. (2007). Intimate partner violence, technology, and stalking. *Violence Against Women*, 13(8), 842–856.

Southworth, C., & Tucker, S. (2006). Technology, Stalking and Domestic Violence Victims. *Mississippi Law Journal*, 76, 667–676.

Southworth, C. (2014, June 4). Hearing of the Senate Judiciary Committee, Subcommittee on Privacy, Technology and the Law, United States Senate Location Privacy Protection Act of 2014. Retrieved from http://www.judiciary.senate.gov/imo/media/doc/06-04-14SouthworthTestimony.pdf.

Spitzberg, B. H., & Hoobler, G. (2002). Cyberstalking and the technologies of interpersonal terrorism. *New Media & Society*, 4(1), 71–92.

Stark, E. (2007). *Coercive control: How men entrap women in personal life.* Oxford University Press.

Straus, M. A. (1979). Measuring intrafamily conflict and violence: The conflict tactics (CT) scales. *Journal of Marriage and the Family* 41(1), 75–88.

Straus, M. A. (2005). Women's violence towards men is a serious social problem. In Loseke, D. R., Gelles, R. J., & Cavanaugh, M. M. (Eds.) *Current controversies on family violence* (pp. 79–95). Thousand Oaks, CA: Sage.

Straus, M. A. (2011). Gender symmetry and mutuality in perpetration of clinical-level partner violence: Empirical evidence and implications for prevention and treatment. *Aggression and Violent Behavior*, 16(4), 279–288.

Straus, M. A., Gelles, R. J., & Steinmetz, S. K. (2006). *Behind closed doors: Violence in the American family*. New Brunswick, N.J: Transaction Publishers.

Straus, M. A., & Gozjolko, K. L. (2014). "Intimate terrorism" and gender differences in injury of dating partners by male and female university students. *Journal of Family Violence*, 29(1), 51–65.

Tanha, M., Beck, C. J., Figueredo, A. J., & Raghavan, C. (2010). Sex differences in intimate partner violence and the use of coercive control as a motivational factor for intimate partner violence. *Journal of Interpersonal Violence*, 25(10), 1836–1854.

Tjaden, P. G. (2009). Stalking policies and research in the United States: A twenty-year retrospective. *European Journal on Criminal Policy and Research*, 15(3), 261–278.

Tjaden, P., & Thoennes, N. (2000). Full report of the prevalence, incidence, and consequences of violence against women: findings from the National Violence Against Women Survey. *Washington, DC: United States Department of Justice*.

Ver Steegh, N. (2004). Differentiating types of domestic violence: Implications for child custody. *Louisiana Law Review*, 65(4), 1379–1431.

Violence Against Women Act (VAWA, P.L. 103-322) (1994).

Violence Against Women Act of 2000: http://www.gpo.gov/fdsys/pkg/BILLS106hr3244enr/pdf/BILLS-106hr3244enr.pdf.

Violence Against Women and Department of Justice Reauthorization Act (2005): http://www.gpo.gov/fdsys/pkg/BILLS-109hr3402enr/pdf/BILLS-109hr3402enr.pdf.

Violence Against Women Reauthorization Act (2013): https://www.govtrack.us/congress/bills/113/s47/text.

Woodlock, D. (2014) Technology-facilitated stalking: findings and resources from the SmartSafe project Domestic Violence Resource Centre Victoria, Collingwood. Retrieved from http://www.researchgate.net/publication/267928015_Technology-facilitated_stalking_findings_and_resources_from_the_SmartSafe_project.

Working to Halt Online Abuse (2013). Online harassment/cyberstalking statistics. Retrieved from http://www.haltabuse.org/resources/stats/.

Young, C. (2014, November 4). Online harassment effects men too. *Time*. Retrieved from http://time.com/3546044/online-harassment-affects-men-too/.

Chapter Six

Cyberabuse and Cyberstalking

Jordana N. Navarro

Introduction

The rapid advancement of technology has produced substantial benefits for society, such as how individuals communicate with each other and how they organize in communities (Fox & Rainie, 2014). However, the rapid advancement of technology has arguably also produced new methods by which individuals can cyberabuse others (Navarro & Jasinski, 2012, 2013, 2014). While scholars have begun to call attention to the malicious uses of technology, one area of research ripe for investigation is how technology is being utilized by perpetrators of intimate partner abuse[1] (IPA) to engage in the cyberabuse and cyberstalking of survivors.[2] In order to call attention to the intersection between IPA, technology, and cybercrime, this chapter presents an overview of the limited research conducted to date on cyberabuse and cyberstalking occurring within the context of domestic abuse—including the tactics frequently utilized by perpetrators. Taking into account the limited research in this area, anecdotal case studies will be included to supplement the text.

Abuse and Coercive Control[3]

The National Violence against Women (NVAW) survey indicates that " ... 1.3 million women and approximately 835,000 men are physically assaulted

---

1. The terms "intimate partner abuse" and "domestic abuse" will be used interchangeably.

2. "Survivor" is used instead of "victim" to indicate agency of those who experienced or are experiencing IPA.

3. For a more expansive review of IPA, readers should reference Chapter Two of this text.

by an intimate partner annually in the United States" (Tjaden & Thoennes, 2000, p. 26). Similar—and equally alarming—results were also found in the National Intimate Partner and Sexual Violence Survey (NISVS), which indicates that more than 33 percent of women have experienced IPA at some point in their lifetime (Black, Basile, Breiding, Smith, Walters, Merrick, Chen, et al., 2011). Unfortunately, this social problem is not isolated to adults as research has also found that a substantial proportion of youth (between 9 percent to 34 percent) experience dating abuse as well (Khubchandani et al., 2012). Moreover, these problems are not restricted to the United States of America; indeed, the severity and persistence of IPA as a *global* social problem continues to be documented (Ely, Dulmus, & Wodarski, 2004; El-Mouelhy, 2004).

Research has found IPA can include several forms of abuse, such as physical abuse, emotional abuse, and sexual abuse (El-Mouelhy, 2004). Additionally, research has also documented that abuse occurs online in the forms of cyber dating abuse, cyberharassment, and cyberstalking (Belknap, Chu, & DePrince, 2011; Dimond, Fiesler, & Bruckman, 2011; Hand, Chung, & Peters, 2009; Hinduja & Patchin, 2011; Stonard, Bowen, Lawrence, & Price, 2014; Zweig, Dank, Lachman, & Yahner, 2013). Even cyberbullying, which is typically discussed in comparison to "offline bullying," also has a nexus to domestic abuse (Hinduja & Patchin, 2011; Zweig et al., 2013) yet this connection remains largely unexplored (Alvarez, 2012). To understand the ramifications of these forms of virtual abuse on the IPA survivor, and why they should not be underestimated, it is important to briefly discuss Evan Stark's concept *coercive control* (Stark, 2007).

According to Stark (2007, pg. 21), coercive control is defined as " ... a strategic course of self-interested behavior designed to secure and expand gender-based privilege by establishing a regime of *domination* in personal life" (emphasis added). Physical violence is only one tactic of coercion, or "the use of force or threats to compel or dispel a particular response"; others include intimidation, isolation, and control (Stark, 2007, p. 22). Of specific interest for the purposes of this chapter is the tactic of "intimidation," which is typically accomplished through the utilization of threats, *surveillance*, and degradation (Stark, 2007). As will be documented in the following sections, the advancement of technology has provided perpetrators of IPA new methods by which they can *intimidate* and further enact coercive control over survivors—particularly through increased surveillance methods.

Case Study 6.1

In early 2012, a pregnant teenager was beaten and held against her will by a jealous boyfriend who was enraged after finding a text message from another man on her cell phone (Tracy, 2012). In addition to the assaults perpetrated by the boyfriend, a friend of his also participated in the assaults and assisted in the restraint of the teenager (Tracy, 2012). Aside from beating her, the boyfriend also threatened the teenager with a knife, burned her with a lighter, and strangled her at one point (Tracy, 2012). Ultimately, the boyfriend allowed the teenager to leave after she suffered nine days of abuse (Tracy, 2012).

In this case, the perpetrator read the survivor's text messages arguably as a method of surveillance to ultimately exert control over who she interacted with. Although this example illustrates a relatively "low tech" method by which a perpetrator monitored a survivor, a repertoire of more sophisticated technological methods/software also exists (e.g., GPS monitoring software, keyloggers, etc.). The existence of the latter leads one to question whether companies that produce such monitoring software and tools (e.g., GPS software, keyloggers, screenloggers, etc.) have an ethical responsibility to prevent the malicious use of their software by IPA perpetrators.

Methods and Tactics Utilized by Perpetrators to Engage in Cyberabuse and Cyberstalking

Low-Tech Methods

The Internet has been referred to as the "Triple-A-Engine," meaning it is accessible, affordable, and largely anonymous (Cooper & Griffin-Shelley, 2002)— an attractive resource for IPA perpetrators and, at the same time, a devastating combination for survivors entrapped within and/or fleeing destructive relationships (Bocij & McFarlane, 2003). In addition to the Internet, telephones, particularly since the rise of the "smartphone," have also become resources by which offenders abuse, harass, and stalk survivors of IPA (Belknap et al., 2011; Burke, Wallen, Vail-Smith, & Knox, 2011; Dimond et al., 2011; Hand et al., 2009; Hinduja & Patchin, 2011; Southworth, Dawson, Fraser, & Tucker, 2005). The importance of the Internet and technology to perpetrators of IPA should not be surprising given that the supervision of the partner is essential to maintaining power and control (Belknap et al., 2011).

In reviewing the methods specifically utilized by perpetrators to control and monitor survivors, one tactic frequently reported across studies is the monitoring of phone calls—a method that does not necessitate any advanced technological knowledge (i.e., a "low-tech" method) (Belknap et al., 2011; Burke et al., 2011; Dimond et al., 2011; Hand et al., 2009; Hinduja & Patchin, 2011; Southworth et al., 2005). This monitoring not only includes the supervision of actual phone calls, but also the utilization of caller ID to screen calls to the survivor (Southworth et al., 2005). Perhaps even more alarming, IPA perpetrators have even used information contained within fax headers (e.g., sender's phone number, location of fax) to locate survivors in hiding (Southworth et al., 2005). Aside from utilizing telephones, other commonly used "low-tech" tactics include: utilizing email to communicate threats, insults, or to harass survivors; impersonating the survivor online to damage his/her financial or personal reputation; and using public information sites to compile information about survivors in order to engage in subsequent harassment (i.e., electronic dumpster diving) (Burke et al., 2011; Cavezza & McEwan, 2014; Melander, 2010; Southworth et al., 2005; Spence-Diehl, 2003).

High-Tech Methods

In contrast to the "low-tech" methods previously noted, perpetrators of IPA also utilize "high-tech" methods available to them in order to control and monitor survivors. One of the most dangerous methods is the installation of "spyware" on survivors' computers and phones, which could include keyloggers or screenloggers (Southworth et al., 2005; Southworth, Finn, Dawson, Fraser, & Tucker, 2007). As the names imply, keyloggers record a target's keystrokes without his/her knowledge and send the information back to the perpetrator, while screenloggers capture information on computer screens and send the information back to the perpetrator (Southworth et al., 2005; Southworth et al., 2007). Other methods utilized by perpetrators include tracking survivors through GPS chips installed in cell phones and installing cameras in unsuspecting locations (e.g., smoke detectors, children's lamps) (Southworth et al., 2005; Southworth et al., 2007). While the aforementioned is not an exhaustive list of all the different tactics perpetrators engage in to monitor and control survivors, it does demonstrate how the concept of "feeling safe" is no longer tied to geographic distance (Hand et al., 2009). Unfortunately, the cyberabuse and cyberstalking that is now possible with the advancement of technology has sufficiently destroyed the concept of safety (Hand et al., 2009). Despite the aforementioned, there remains a dearth of information on cyberabuse and cyberstalking although research is steadily increasing. In the following sections, overviews of cyberabuse and cyberstalking are provided utilizing the research that is available today.

Case Study 6.2

In the summer of 2009, an IPA perpetrator threw his then-wife to the floor of their bedroom (Scheck, 2010). After escaping to a friend's house, the wife was shocked when her husband suddenly showed up, attacked her again, and stole her car (Scheck, 2010). In an interview later, the husband disclosed he had activated a tracking service through his cell phone company to monitor his wife's movements (Scheck, 2010). Although the cell phone company had alerted the wife that the tracking had been activated via text message, she (at that point) could not refuse to be tracked by the account holder (Scheck, 2010).

The aforementioned case illustrates how technological innovations, although designed with a noble purpose, can have serious consequences as well. Indeed, even though the tracking utilized in this case was for malicious purposes, cell phone tracking was originally created to help rescue lost drivers or children and to assist parents in monitoring adolescents (Scheck, 2010). Taking into account the extent to which technology permeates social life (e.g., we use it to communicate, to accomplish daily tasks such as banking, and to acquire resources such as food and shelter through check/credit cards), imagine how you would escape a dangerous relationship. How would you escape knowing that your bank/credit cards, cell phone, and movements were possibly being tracked by the perpetrator? What would you do?

Cyberabuse as a Form of Coercive Control

Although there is no universally accepted definition of cyberbullying, these actions are typically defined as the " ... willful and repeated harm inflicted through the use of computers, cell phones, and other electronic devices" (Patchin & Hinduja, 2006, p.152). Similarly, "cyberharassment refers to acts such as harassing messages, threats, photo manipulation, posting of personal information, and impersonation that are conducted online and harass an individual or group" (Dimond et al., 2011, p.2). Taking into account these similarities, the two actions (i.e., cyberbullying and cyberharassment) are referred to as "cyberabuse" in this section—a term utilized in previous work on similar online abuses (Mishna, McLuckie, & Saini, 2009). Aside from their obvious similarities, these behaviors also overlap in the sense that they are all unwanted and can cause recipients to experience fear or distress (Cavezza & McEwan, 2014).

Cyberabuse (i.e., cyberbullying/cyberharassment) and IPA share several additional similarities: (1) both actions typically involve persons known to each other, (2) both actions result in specific psychosocial consequences, and (3) the goal of both actions is to exert *power* and *control* (Hinduja & Patchin, 2011). Although cyberbullying is distinguishable from IPA in that the former typically involves two individuals who do not like each other, that characteristic should not overshadow research that also indicates cyberbullying does occur within the context of IPA as well (Alvarez, 2012; Hinduja & Patchin, 2011). Indeed, the need to investigate cyberbullying within the context of IPA is particularly important given the accessibility and affordability of various (potentially harmful) technological tools on the Internet, the relatively unguarded and unsupervised nature of the Internet, and the capability to expose the victimization to a wide audience—which makes the ramifications of these actions on survivors that much more severe (Alvarez, 2012; Hinduja & Patchin, 2011). In contrast to the dearth of information on cyberbullying occurring within the context of IPA, studies have investigated cyberharassment (within the context of IPA) and cyber dating abuse (Burke et al., 2011; Dimond et al., 2011; Hand et al., 2009; Melander, 2010; Schnurr, Mahatmya, & Basche III, 2013; Zweig et al., 2013) although additional research is sorely needed in this area as well (Melander, 2010).

Given the nascent stage of the literature and the methodological variation across studies, research on cyber dating abuse have found prevalence rates ranging from 12 percent to 26 percent (Hinduja & Patchin, 2011; Zweig et al., 2013). Additionally, although some studies have found females were particularly vulnerable to cyberabuse (Burke et al., 2011; Zweig et al., 2013), other studies found largely no difference in victimization rates by gender (Hinduja & Patchin, 2011). Conflicting results are also apparent when reviewing information on whom typically perpetrates cyberabuse.

Indeed, in a study conducted by Burke et al. (2011), females were significantly more likely to report that they had checked their partners' call and email histories and had made an excessive number of phone calls to their partners. The aforementioned finding aligns with research studies that found females perpetrated more non-sexual cyber dating abuse compared to males (Zweig et al., 2013) or that females and males utilized cyber aggression against their partners in comparable amounts (Hinduja & Patchin, 2011). In terms of the utilization of particularly invasive forms of technology or perpetration of sexual cyber dating abuse, however, males were significantly more likely to have utilized GPS monitoring and hidden cameras (Burke et al., 2011) and to have engaged in sexual cyber dating abuse against their partner (Zweig et al., 2013). Although the role of gender as a risk factor for perpetrating or experiencing cyberabuse remains unclear, cutting-edge research has begun investigating whether these differences may stem from the *type* of IPA relationship occurring.

Since recognition of IPA as a serious social problem began in the 1970s (Gelles, 1985), research has greatly expanded our collective understanding of domestic abuse. Specifically, research has documented that IPA encompasses four different types and patterns of relationships: (1) intimate terrorism (IT), (2) violent resistance (VR), (3) situational couple violence (SCV), and (4) mutual violent control (MVC) (Johnson, 1995, 2006). In an IT relationship, an individual who is violent and controlling is involved with a partner who is not (Johnson, 2006). In a VR relationship, a violent individual is involved with a partner whom is violent *and* controlling (Johnson, 2006). In a SCV relationship, individuals may act out violently, but neither is normally violent or controlling (Johnson, 2006). Finally, in a MVC relationship, both individuals involved are violent and controlling towards each other (Johnson, 2006). The aforementioned types of IPA arose in the mid-1990s as the family violence field was grappling with conflicting research that showed IPA was largely a male-to-female perpetrated social problem (Dobash, Dobash, Wilson, & Daly, 1992) versus findings that showed that men and women utilized violence within relationships at comparable amounts (Straus, 1999). Although the current status of that debate is outside the scope of this chapter, recent studies on cyberharassment have sought to investigate whether these patterns apply to IPA perpetrated through technology as well (Melander, 2010).

To date, only one study has investigated whether Johnson's IPA typology is applicable to understanding cyberabuse between intimate partners (to the best of knowledge of this author). In Melander's (2010) study, which included five focus group interviews involving undergraduate students, six themes emerged through the analyses that ultimately supported Johnson's patterns of IPA. According to Melander (2010), situation couple violence (SCV) emerged as a theme in cases where technology was the trigger of the resulting conflict as illustrated in the following example:

> My friend, his girlfriend, she was—she was terrible in the fact that she would—she always wanted to see his phone because she liked to read the text messages and stuff.... He told me that they got in a fight because he went to the bathroom and his phone was there, and she, like, went through all of his text messages. And if there was just like one girl, like, "Hey, what's up?" Even if they were just friends, she would just flip out. And it was—their relationship, that's kind of why it didn't really work is because she didn't want—wouldn't let him see her phone, but she wanted to see his (pg. 264).

Interestingly, the role of technology as not only a "tool" for engaging in abuse, but also as "trigger" for violence has also been highlighted in other studies of cyberharassment (Belknap et al., 2011).

The most extreme form of IPA identified by Johnson—intimate terrorism—was also seen in Melander's (2010) research as a couple of respondents noted that their partners utilized electronic monitoring devices to track their physical locations. In addition, other tactics utilized by perpetrators included monitoring the survivors' online activities, online social networking sites, and constantly communicating with them in order to foster and maintain a sense of control as noted in the following example:

> Or like if you're out with friends one night and someone is just, like, constantly texting you, like, "Where are you at?" "What are you doing?" "Who are you with?" "I know you're with someone else." Like, it's just, like, being controlling, you know, like, they're trying to act like they care about you, but it's still, like, they're being controlling over the situation (Melander, 2010, p. 264).

Similar results indicative of IT were also found in a study conducted by Dimond and colleagues (2011), which focused on how information communication technologies impacted the life of IPA survivors residing in a shelter. Respondents in their study also reported that perpetrators utilized GPS and other technologies to monitor their movements (Dimond et al., 2011). Moreover, perpetrators also sent death threats and engaged in various other forms of unwanted communication with survivors (Dimond et al., 2011).

Mutual violent control (MVC), which is similar to IT, was seen in Melander's (2010) research through the comments of some respondents regarding how they used technology to exert control over their partners, and vice-versa, as indicated by the following:

> Boyfriends and girlfriends can probably keep a lot better tab on each other with Facebook and MySpace nowadays than they ever could before, unless they're literally with them all the time. But now, I mean, you've got a time thing that says exactly what time you talked to who and whatever (p. 265).

Finally, respondents also noted ways in which technology was utilized as a tool of self-defense or as a tool to confront their abuser—similar in nature to cases of violent resistance (VR)—as illustrated by the following:

> I know a couple of girls who have been in bad relationships and they used Facebook to be like, I don't want to see you anymore. And, like,

it sounds so sixth grade, but they just couldn't bring themselves to do it in person, and they didn't know what else to do (Melander, 2010, p. 265).

Aside from the aforementioned findings, Melander (2010, p. 266) also found that cyberabuse differed from offline abuse in that respondents perceived cyberharassment as "easier" and "a quicker method" for perpetrators intent on attacking the survivor. Finally, respondents in Melander's (2010) study also noted how perpetrators utilized the Internet to embarrass and harass their partners, which were particularly impactful given these actions exposed what was occurring to a wide audience. In order to combat these occurrences and spur prevention/intervention programs, in addition to highlighting *how* and *why* cyberabuse occurs, scholars have also worked towards identifying survivor and perpetrator risk factors across studies.

Case Study 6.3

In April of 2007, a 19-year-old female and her 22-year-old male friend were killed by an ex-boyfriend of the female (Stutzman, 2008). According to reports, the ex-boyfriend had begun cyberstalking his ex-girlfriend after she broke up with him (Stutzman, 2008). In addition, the ex-boyfriend also utilized the Internet to cyberabuse her by gaining access to her bank account, masquerading as her online, and sending threatening messages noting his intention to kill her male friend (Stutzman, 2008). In fact, eight hours before the shooting, the victims had approached law enforcement to ask the ex-boyfriend be arrested, but their request was denied due to lack of evidence (Stutzman, 2008). After pleading guilty, the ex-boyfriend was sentenced to death and is currently sitting on Florida's Death Row (Stutzman, 2008).

As the aforementioned case gained traction in local news media, the law enforcement officer who denied taking action merely eight hours before the incident was heavily criticized. In reflecting on this case, is it possible that the seriousness of the cyberabuse and cyberstalking was underestimated compared to offline abuse and offline stalking? Given the details of the case provided, do you believe this event could have been avoided?

Cyberstalking

Although public awareness of stalking as a serious social problem has increased greatly since the 1990s, the cyberstalking literature remains largely in its infancy and much of what is known is based on information from victims (Cavezza & McEwan, 2014; Reyns, Henson, & Fisher, 2012; Spence-Diehl, 2003). Cyberstalking typically refers to the utilization of information and communication technologies to harass and/or stalk another person (Gregorie, 2001). Although there is an on-going debate regarding whether cyberstalking is truly different and distinct from offline stalking (McFarlane & Bocij, 2003; Sheridan & Grant, 2007), the two behaviors do share two important similarities: (1) a relatively consistent finding across studies is that many cyberstalkers are former intimate partners (Alexy, Burgess, Baker, & Smoyak, 2005; Cavezza & McEwan, 2014; Dreßing, Bailer, Anders, Wagner, & Gallas, 2014), and (2) both behaviors consist of repeated actions over time which invade a survivor's sense of privacy and result in feelings of being threatened (Spitzberg & Hoobler, 2002).

Scholars who contend cyberstalking is a unique form of cyberdeviance (compared to offline stalking), point out that online stalking differs in the following ways: (1) cyberstalking does not require a prior relationship between the victim and perpetrator, (2) cyberstalking is not restricted by geographic or spatial constraints, (3) prior research has found cyberstalkers are driven by various motivations aside from exerting power and control over the target (Bocij & McFarlane, 2003). Indeed, according to Cyberangels, a non-profit organization dedicated to only safety education, there are four basic motivations for cyberstalking: (1) sexual harassment, (2) love obsession, (3) hate/revenge vendettas, and (4) power/ego trips (as cited in Deirmenjian, 1999). Recent research by Cavezza and McEwan (2014) comparing cyberstalking offenders with offline offenders also addresses this debate.

In a study that compared 36 cyberstalking offenders with matched offline stalkers (through gender and age), Cavezza and McEwan (2014) found few between group differences. For example, cyberstalkers were typically ex-intimate partners of the survivor and were less likely to approach the survivor (Cavezza & McEwan, 2014). However, cyberstalkers were not restricted to online activities and did utilize offline stalking tactics as well (Cavezza & McEwan, 2014). As far as similarities, both groups (i.e., cyberstalkers and offline stalkers) targeted females for the purposes of rekindling a relationship or to obtain retribution for a rejection (Cavezza & McEwan, 2014). Ultimately, although there were a few differences between the two groups, the results led Cavezza and McEwan (2014) to conclude that the Internet is likely just another medium by which stalking occurs.

Although the debate surrounding whether cyberstalking and offline stalking are distinct social problems continues, several studies have established that cyberstalking does impact a substantial proportion of the population (Alexy et al., 2005; Baum, Catalano, Rand, & Rose, 2009; Finn, 2004; Fisher, Cullen, & Turner, 2002; Spitzberg & Hoobler, 2002). Indeed, in a national-level study, 21.5 percent and 7.8 percent of stalking victims also experienced cyberstalking and/or electronic monitoring, respectively (Baum et al., 2009). Similar to information found in studies on cyberabuse, respondents noted that cyberstalking perpetrators utilized email (82.5%), instant messaging (35.1%), blogs/bulletin boards (12.3%), Internet sites about the victim (9.4%), and chatrooms (4.4%) to harass and instill fear in the survivors (Baum et al., 2009). Of the methods utilized by perpetrators to monitor the stalking victims, 33.6 percent noted utilizing computer spyware, while more than 40 percent reported using video/digital cameras and/or listening devices/bugs (Baum et al., 2009). While many of the studies on cyberstalking utilize college student samples, these investigations also provide evidence of the existence of the problem.

A study conducted by Fisher et al. (2002) found similar results to the aforementioned study in that nearly 25 percent of respondents who were stalked also experienced cyberstalking victimization. In several other studies, the prevalence of cyberstalking ranged from one percent to more than 30 percent depending on the methodology utilized (Alexy et al., 2005; Finn, 2004; Spitzberg & Hobbler, 2002). In a more recent study utilizing college students, results indicated that slightly over 40 percent of respondents had experienced cyberstalking (Reyns et al., 2012). In contrast, a study focused on social network users found that just over six percent had experienced cyberstalking—although the percentage varied greatly depending on the definition utilized (from 40% to 6.3%) (Dreßing et al., 2014). Aside from prevalence estimates, the results of these studies have begun to highlight patterns in perpetrator and survivor characteristics.

In reviewing risk factors across studies, available evidence largely indicates that females are more at risk of experiencing cyberstalking compared to males (Cavezza & McEwan, 2014; Dreßing et al., 2014; Reyns et al., 2012; Sheridan & Grant, 2007; Vasiu & Vasiu, 2013), although some research has found the inverse: that males were more likely to be cyberstalked (Alexy et al., 2005). As far as perpetration of cyberstalking behavior, most studies have found that males were more likely to engage in this behavior (Cavezza & McEwan, 2014; Dreßing et al., 2014; Reyns et al., 2012). Aside from gender, several other demographic and background characteristics have been identified across studies.

According to research conducted by McFarlane and Bocij (2003), a majority of individuals who experienced cyberstalking were Caucasian, educated at the high school level or beyond, employed, single, and were moderately skilled with technology. Overall, comparable information was found when reviewing information on individuals who engaged in cyberstalking. A majority of offenders were also Caucasian, educated at the college level or beyond, employed, single, and moderately skilled with technology (McFarlane & Bocij, 2003). However, there is some contention whether engaging in cyberstalking, by the nature of the crime, indicates an underlying mental health disorder (McFarlane & Bocij, 2003). Indeed, although some research has identified a relationship between the presence of a mental illness and engagement in cyberstalking behavior (Meloy, 1998 as cited in Bocij & McFarlane, 2003), others contend that research also indicates cyberstalkers can be motivated towards very specific goals (e.g., financial gain) which is not rooted in an underlying mental illness (Bocij & McFarlane, 2003). Although findings from studies on cyberstalking continue to vary—likely as a result of the relative newness of the field—it is clear from the available research that a proportion of cyberstalking does occur within the context of an IPA relationship and that technology has provided perpetrators new methods by which to control and monitor survivors.

Conclusion

This chapter provided an overview of cyberabuse and cyberstalking that occurred within the context of IPA. Although research on the topic is sparse, several cutting-edge studies provide evidence to support further investigation into the problem. Indeed, as technology continues to advance, it is likely that perpetrators of IPA will have *more tools* at their disposal to exert power and control over survivors of IPA. Thus, the onus is on researchers to investigate the prevalence of the problem as well as the tools perpetrators utilize to exert a "virtual coercive control" over survivors. Then, these results can be utilized in prevention and intervention programs to combat the problem and provide some measure of safety to survivors of IPA.

References

Alexy, E. M., Burgess, A. W., Baker, T., & Smoyak, S. A. (2005). Perceptions of cyberstalking among college students. *Brief Treatment and Crisis Intervention, 5*(3), 279.

Alvarez, A. R. (2012). "IH8U": Confronting Cyberbullying and Exploring the Use of Cybertools in Teen Dating Relationships. *Journal of Clinical Psychology, 68*(11), 1205–1215.

Baum, K., Catalano, S., Rand, M., & Rose, K. (2009) Stalking Victimization in the United States. U.S. Department of Justice. Bureau of Justice Statistics Special Report.

Belknap, J., Chu, A. T., & DePrince, A. P. (2011). Roles of Phones and Computers in Threatening and Abusing Women Victims of Male Intimate Partner Abuse, The. *Duke J. Gender L. & Pol'y, 19*, 373.

Black, M. C., Basile, K. C., Brieding, M. J., Smith, S. G., Walters, M. L., Merrick, M. T., Chen, J., and Stevens, M. R. (2011). *The National Intimate Partner and Sexual Violence Survey (NISVS): 2010 Summary Report.* Atlanta, GA: National Center for Injury Prevention and Control, Centers for Disease Control and Prevention. Retrieved from: http://www.cdc.gov/violenceprevention/pdf/nisvs_executive_summary-a.pdf.

Bocij, P., & McFarlane, L. (2003). Cyberstalking: The technology of hate. *The Police Journal, 76*(3), 204–221.

Burke, S. C., Wallen, M., Vail-Smith, K., & Knox, D. (2011). Using technology to control intimate partners: An exploratory study of college undergraduates. *Computers in Human Behavior, 27*(3), 1162–1167.

Cavezza, C., & McEwan, T. E. (2014). Cyberstalking versus off-line stalking in a forensic sample. *Psychology, Crime & Law* (ahead-of-print), 1–16.

Deirmenjian, J. M. (1999). Stalking in cyberspace. *Journal of the American Academy of Psychiatry and the Law Online, 27*(3), 407–413.

Dimond, J. P., Fiesler, C., & Bruckman, A. S. (2011). Domestic violence and information communication technologies. *Interacting with Computers, 23*(5), 413–421.

Dreßing, H., Bailer, J., Anders, A., Wagner, H., & Gallas, C. (2014). Cyberstalking in a Large Sample of Social Network Users: Prevalence, Characteristics, and Impact Upon Victims. *Cyberpsychology, Behavior, and Social Networking, 17*(2), 61–67.

El-Mouelhy, M. (2004). Violence against women: A public health problem. *The Journal of Primary Prevention, 25*(2), 289–303.

Ely, G. E., Dulmus, C. N., & Wodarski, J. S. (2004). Domestic violence: A literature review reflecting an international crisis. *Stress, Trauma, and Crisis, 7*(2), 77–91.

Finn, J. (2004). A survey of online harassment at a university campus. *Journal of Interpersonal Violence, 19*(4), 468–483.

Fisher, B. S., Cullen, F. T., & Turner, M. G. (2002). Being pursued: Stalking victimization in a national study of college women. *Criminology & Public Policy, 1*, 257–308.

Fox, S., & Rainie, L. (2014). The Web at 25 in the US. *Pew Research Center's Internet & American Life Project*, 5. Retrieved from: http://www.pewinternet.org/2014/02/27/the-web-at-25-in-the-u-s/.

Gelles, R. J. (1985). Family violence. *Annual Review of Sociology, 11*, 347–367.

Gregorie, T. M. (2001). Cyberstalking: Dangers on the information superhighway. *National Center for Victims of Crime.*

Hand, T., Chung, D., & Peters, M. (2009). *The use of information and communication technologies to coerce and control in domestic violence and following separation*: Australian Domestic and Family Violence Clearinghouse, UNSW.

Hinduja, S., & Patchin, J. (2011). Electronic dating violence: A brief guide for educators and parents. *Cyberbullying Research Center. Retrieved March, 1,* 2011.

Johnson, M. P. (1995). Patriarchal terrorism and common couple violence: Two forms of violence against women. *Journal of Marriage and the Family,* 283–294.

Johnson, M. P. (2006). Conflict and control gender symmetry and asymmetry in domestic violence. *Violence Against Women, 12*(11), 1003–1018.

Khubchandani, J., Price, J. H., Thompson, A., Dake, J. A., Wiblishauser, M., & Telljohann, S. K. (2012). Adolescent dating violence: A national assessment of school counselors' perceptions and practices. *Pediatrics, 130*(2), 202–210.

McFarlane, L., & Bocij, P. (2003). An exploration of predatory behaviour in cyberspace: Towards a typology of cyberstalkers. *First Monday, 8*(9).

Melander, L. A. (2010). College students' perceptions of intimate partner cyber harassment. *Cyberpsychology, Behavior, and Social Networking, 13*(3), 263–268.

Mishna, F., McLuckie, A., & Saini, M. (2009). Real-world dangers in an online reality: A qualitative study examining online relationships and cyber abuse. *Social Work Research, 33*(2), 107–118.

Navarro, J. N., & Jasinski, J. L. (2012). Going cyber: Using routine activities theory to predict cyberbullying experiences. *Sociological Spectrum, 32,* 81–94.

Navarro, J. N., & Jasinski, J. L. (2013). Why girls? Using routine activities theory to predict cyberbullying experiences between girls and boys. *Women & Criminal Justice, 23,* 286–303.

Navarro, J. N., & Jasinski, J. L. (2014). Identity Theft and Social Networks. In C.D. Marcum & G.E. Higgins (Eds.), *Social Networking as a Criminal Enterprise,* 69–90. Boca Raton, FL: CRC Press.

Patchin, J. W., & Hinduja, S. (2006) Bullies move beyond the schoolyard a preliminary look at cyberbullying. *Youth Violence and Juvenile Justice* 4: 148–169.

Reyns, B. W., Henson, B., & Fisher, B. S. (2012). Stalking in the twilight zone: Extent of cyberstalking victimization and offending among college students. *Deviant Behavior, 33*(1), 1–25.

Scheck, J. (2010, August 3). Stalkers exploit cellphone GPS. *The Wall Street Journal.* Retrieved from: http://www.wsj.com/articles/SB10001424052748 703467304575383522318244234.

Schnurr, M. P., Mahatmya, D., & Basche III, R. A. (2013). The role of dominance, cyber aggression perpetration, and gender on emerging adults' perpetration of intimate partner violence. *Psychology of Violence, 3*(1), 70.

Sheridan, L. P., & Grant, T. (2007). Is cyberstalking different? *Psychology, Crime & Law, 13*(6), 627–640.

Southworth, C., Dawson, S., Fraser, C., & Tucker, S. (2005). *A high-tech twist on abuse: Technology, intimate partner stalking, and advocacy*: Violence Against Women Online Resources.

Southworth, C., Finn, J., Dawson, S., Fraser, C., & Tucker, S. (2007). Intimate partner violence, technology, and stalking. *Violence Against Women, 13*(8), 842–856.

Spence-Diehl, E. (2003). Stalking and technology: The double-edged sword. *Journal of Technology in Human Services, 22*(1), 5–18.

Spitzberg, B. H., & Hoobler, G. (2002). Cyberstalking and the technologies of interpersonal terrorism. *New Media & Society, 4*(1), 71–92.

Stark, E. (2009). *Coercive Control. The Entrapment of Women in Personal Life.* New York, NY: Oxford University Press.

Stonard, K., Bowen, E., Lawrence, T., and Price, S. A. (2014) The relevance of technology to the nature, prevalence and impact of Adolescent Dating Violence and Abuse: A research synthesis. *Aggression and Violent Behavior, 19*(4), 390–417.

Straus, M. A. (1999). The controversy over domestic violence by women: A methodological, theoretical, and sociology of science analysis. In X. Arriaga & S. Oskamp (Eds.), *Violence in Intimate Relationships* (pp. 17–44). Thousand Oaks, CA: Sage.

Tjaden, P., & Thoennes, N. (2000). Full report of the prevalence, incidence, and consequences of violence against women: Findings from the National Violence Against Women Survey. Washington, DC: United States Department of Justice.

Tracy, E. (2012, February 28). Pregnant teen held captive, tortured for more than week, Ceres police say. *The Modesto Bee.* Retrieved from: http://www.modbee.com/news/local/crime/article3141197.html.

Vasiu, I., & Vasiu, L. (2013). Cyberstalking Nature and Response Recommendations. *Academic Journal of Interdisciplinary Studies, 2*(9), 229.

Zweig, J. M., Dank, M., Lachman, P., & Yahner, J. (2013). Technology, Teen Dating Violence and Abuse, and Bullying: The Urban Institute.

Chapter Seven

Sexting, Sextortion, and Other Internet Sexual Offenses

Reneè D. Lamphere and Kweilin T. Pikciunas

Introduction

The advancement of communication technologies such as the Internet, cell phones, and social networking sites has given individuals the tools to help establish and maintain interpersonal relationships (Hertlein & Ancheta, 2014). In addition to expediting communication between friends and family, these advancements in technology have also allowed for increased accessibility and communication with individuals one may have romantic interests in. While this increased means of romantic communication is certainly more convenient than ever before, it has also created an opportunity for new types of behaviors, including sexual and aggressive acts (Marganski & Fauth, 2013).

The purpose of this chapter is to discuss sexual offenses on the Internet (and other related technologies) involving intimate partners. In particular, it will describe the offenses of sexting, revenge pornography, sextortion, online romantic/dating frauds, and catfishing. A history, discussion of relevant literature, and current issues are included for each of the mentioned offenses. Specific focus will be given to the victimization aspect of these offenses, as it is important to understand the unique circumstance that Internet-based victims face.

Sexting

What Is Sexting?

While the term can have many meanings, in general, sexting refers to the sharing of sexually explicit content via mobile phone or device (Weins, 2014).

The characterizations of this behavior are vast. Sexting has been described as an outlet for youth to explore and express their sexuality (Brown, Keller, & Stern, 2009). However, it has also been viewed as the production, possession, and distribution of child pornography (Wastler, 2010). There are serious consequences for both offenders and victims of this offense. While definitions of this term vary, *The Oxford Dictionaries* define a "sext" as "a sexually explicit photograph or message sent via cell phone" ("Sext", n. d.). The primary means of transmission of a sext-message (hereafter, sext, and sexting) is via cellular telephone (Boucek, 2009; Dilberto & Mattey, 2009; Shafron-Perez, 2009; Weins, 2014). While some definitions of this term focus specifically on nude or semi-nude photographs and videos (Boucek, 2009; Hinduja & Patchin, 2010; Shafron-Perez, 2009), others have expanded the definition to include sexually suggestive text-only messages as a form of sexting (Dilberto & Mattey, 2009; Jaishankar, 2009). While there are certainly adults who engage in sexting, it is most often discussed in reference to participation by adolescents and youth (Jaishankar, 2009).

The earliest known citation for sexting dates back to 2004 to an article in the Canadian publication, *The Globe and Mail*, which published a report about sexually explicit text messages shared between professional soccer player David Beckham and his assistant (Rosenberg, 2011). Despite this early publication appearance, the term "sext" did not gain in popularity in mainstream culture until 2009 when a story about sexting was headlined by *The New York Post* (Cahalan, 2009). Sexting and similar terms began to trend, with stories appearing in notable publications and news outlets such as the *New York Times*, the *Chicago Tribune*, CBS, NPR, and NBC, among others (Rosenber, 2011).

One can argue that sexting dates back at least as far as the use of the Polaroid camera (Brown et al., 2009). There is one key factor that separates the images of the past from the images produced today: technology. As discussed by Fox & Potocki (2014), the fact that sexting occurs on a cellular phone makes the shared information both highly portable and widely accessible. While one may intend for a sext to only be seen by a particular party, the originator of the message often has no control over the destination of the message once it leaves his or her telephone. This can lead to "downward distribution" of these messages to parties other than the intended receiver (Wastler, 2010). A number of stories have garnered media attention as underage youth sharing nude and sexually suggestive text messages via cell phone have had the messages shared with unintended viewers (Comartin, Kernsmith, & Kernsmith, 2013; Shafron-Perez, 2009). It is important to note that while there is evidence that some youth are sexting, there is no reason to believe that this is a wide-spread epidemic among today's youth (Salter, Crofts, & Lee, 2013). The cases that receive media attention are those where youth, particularly those who create the sext message, are bullied or harassed by peers as a result of uncontrolled downstream distribution of the material (Temple, Le, Peskin, Marcum, & Tortolero, 2014). This can be a great source of embarrassment for the youth who created the message, and can pose seriously legal consequences for all parties involved.

Prevalence of Youth Sexting

While the research on sexting among youth has grown significantly in recent years, the results have varied significantly. One of the earliest and most commonly cited studies on youth sexting was done in 2008 by *The National Campaign to Prevent Teen and Unplanned Pregnancy* (NCPTUP). A non-probability sample of 1,280 teenagers and young adults ages 13 to 26 completed an online survey about their participation in sexting. A reported 20 percent of participants admitted to electronically submitting nude or semi-nude pictures or videos of themselves to others (NCPTUP, 2008). Other early inquiry by the Associated Press with a similar sample and research design found that 10 percent of the 1,247 online respondents age 14 to 24 reported sending nude/semi-nude images. In addition, 17 percent reported forwarding the messages to unintended recipients (Associated Press, 2009).

Inquiry with teenage-only participants yielded slightly lower levels of sexting. A survey of teens age 13 to 18 was conducted by Cox Communication in 2009. Of the 655 online survey respondents, 19 percent reported sexting in general, with 9 percent sending nude or nearly-nude photos specifically (Cox Communication, 2009). Similar research by Lenhart and the Pew Internet & American Life Project (2009) found even lower rates of sexting among their sample of 800 adolescents and teens age 12 to 17. This telephone survey, which required parental consent to participate, resulted in 4 percent of youth admitting to sending nude or nearly-nude photographs or videos of themselves to another person (Lenhart, 2009).

The results of the early Internet and telephone-based surveys helped to gain a general understanding of this behavior. However, some of the inherent methodological issues associated with these research designs may have affected the validity of these studies (Lamphere, 2014). For example, while Internet research is a relatively easy and cost-effective means of obtaining information, problems such as low response rate and coverage error (i.e., populations excluded because of lack of access to the Internet) will alter the composition of the study sample. There are also inherent limitations in the use of telephone-based research. For example, a recent study by Mitchell and colleagues (2012) garnered media attention due to the relatively low rates of sexting that were discovered. Of the 1,560 youth participants, only 39 (2.5%) reported sending a nude or semi-nude image (Mitchell, Finkelhor, Jones, & Wolak, 2012). This led some to conclude that sexting is not problematic behavior among youth (Lamphere, 2014).

More recent research has used other research design techniques in an attempt to obtain more accurate results on youth sexting. In 2010, Hinduja & Patchin furthered the sexting literature by surveying 4,400 students ages 11 to 18 in a large public school district. The results showed that 12.9 percent reported receiving a naked or semi-naked image and 7.7 percent reported sending such images (Hinduja & Patchin, 2010). Dake and colleagues' (2012) school-based research involved 1,289 middle and high school participants from 35 school districts in a Midwestern state. Of these participants, 17 percent reported sending or receiving sext messages (Dake, Price, Maziarz, & Ward, 2012).

Current research on sexting is looking to expand beyond prevalence rates alone to examine the correlates and motivational factors for sexting. For example, Martinez-Prather & Vandiver (2014) recently examined sexting under the framework of Cohen & Felson's (1979) routine activities theory, testing for the three major elements of the theory: motivated offender, suitable target, and absence of capable guardian. Approximately one-third of the 378 college freshman respondents reported sending a nude or semi-nude photo to someone else while in high school. Also, spending time with friends in an unsupervised setting (i.e., absence of capable guardian) resulted in youth being significantly more likely to report sexting (Martinez-Prather & Vandiver, 2014). Reyns and colleagues (2014) explored the relationship between self-control and opportunity. Drawing on elements of routine activities theory (Felson & Cohen, 1979) and the general theory of crime (Gottfredson & Hirschi, 1990), 1,929 college-age sophomores, juniors, and seniors were surveyed via Internet survey about their participation in sexting under theses theoretical perspectives. Of the 5 percent who reported sending nude or semi-nude images it was found that low self-control is significantly and positively related to sexting behavior, and lifestyles and routine activities had a moderate mediating effect on self-control (Reyns, Henson, & Fisher, 2014). It is suggested that future research should move beyond exploring prevalence rates alone and explore sexting and its correlates from a variety of theoretical frameworks (Benotsch, Snipes, Martin, & Bull, 2013; Lounsbury, Mitchell, & Finkelhor, 2011).

Female vs. Male Sexting

In addition to the variations between studies, there is also variation within studies regarding the prevalence of sexting in reference to the gender of the study participant. A number of studies reveal no significant gender differences in terms of frequency of sexting (Benotsch et al., 2013; Dake et al., 2012; Lenhart et al., 2009; NCPTUP, 2008). Of the studies that do find a gender effect, the results indicate that females are more likely than males to be the sender of sext messages (Associated Press, 2009; Cox Communication, 2009; Englander, 2012; Reyns et al., 2014). For example, the Cox Communication (2009) study found that girls were more likely to be sext senders than boys (65% girls vs. 35% boys). Recent research by Reyns and colleagues (2014) found that females were 5 times more likely to be the sender of a sext message.

In looking for an explanation for the difference between gender and the rate of sending a sext message, Englander (2012) further explored this relationship. This study looked at sext-senders from two perspectives, those who sent a message of their own free will, and those who were coerced or pressured into doing so. The gendered difference is only found in the case of coercive sexting, as females were more likely to report feeling pressured to send a sext message. In fact, coercion to sext is twice as common among girls as it is boys, with over half of all female sexting attributed to coercion or pressure from another party (Englander, 2012). Given the varied nature of these results it is apparent that more inquiry is necessary to understand the relationship between gender and sexting.

The Legal Consequences of Sexting

Prior to discussing the potential legal consequences of sexting, it is important to note that the actual act of sexting is not illegal in and of itself. Using sexual communication to express intimacy is a common practice among adults (Shafron-Perez, 2009). Despite arguments that it may be viewed as an obscene act, it is nonetheless a protected act by the First Amendment of the United States Constitution (Wastler, 2010). It is the age of the person who creates, possesses, and distributes a sext that makes the action illegal (Halloran-McLaughlin, 2014). While there are many potential avenues for responding to youth sexting, the chosen response is often formal sanctioning via the criminal justice system (Willis & Hedward, 2014).

One of the central debates surrounding youth participation in sexting is whether these images fall within the realm of current child pornography statutes (Wastler, 2010). Beginning with the enactment of *The Protection of Children against Sexual Exploitation Act* in 1977, and continuing with many laws passed since, specific behaviors such as possessing, selling, receiving, sending, or transmission of child pornography have been deemed illegal (Richards & Calvert, 2009). Child pornography statutes are intended to prevent children from being sexually exploited, violated, and manipulated by adults (Corbett, 2009; Wastler, 2010). However, in the circumstances of youth sexting, the persons who are creating, possessing, and disseminating the messages are often those with whom the laws were intended to protect (Comartin, et al., 2013; Richards & Calvert, 2009). This predicament has been a catalyst for much debate over whether criminalizing youth sexting under existing child pornography statutes is the most appropriate course of action.

Complicating this debate is the fact that the statutes governing responses to youth sexting are not standardized. The criminal justice response is often dependent on jurisdiction in which a teen resides, and his or her role in the production, possession, or distribution of the message. As of September 2014, 20 states have passed laws specific to youth sexting (Hinduja & Patchin, 2014). Although it should be noted that prosecutors may initially charge a teen that sexts with child pornography offenses, most youth end up with phone confiscation and community service (Eraker, 2010).

In addition to the general hardships faced by those travelling through the criminal justice system, in many states a conviction for sexting under child pornography laws may require sex offender registration for the offender (Comartin, et al., 2013). In addition to deterring future offenses, sex offender registries were created to increase public awareness of offenders living in a particular community (Farkas & Stichman, 2002). Registration as a sex offender can result in long-term consequences, such as loss of employment opportunities, inability to find housing, harassment, and social isolation, among others (Comartin, et al., 2013; Craun & Kernsmith; Tewskbury, 2005; Tewskbury & Lees, 2006).

The serious legal implications of youth sexting are illustrated in the case of Phillip Alpert, who faced and continues to face the consequences of sex offender registration. Phillip Alpert and his girlfriend were high school sweethearts who had been dating for over two years. In 2008, following a heated argument with his then 16-year-old girlfriend, Alpert, who had turned 18 just twenty days prior, sent a nude photo of his girlfriend to her closest friends and family without her permission. Days later, Alpert was arrested and faced 72 criminal charges, including lewd and lascivious battery, possession of child pornography, and distribution of child pornography. Alpert submitted a plea of no-contest and was subsequently found guilty and sentenced to five years of probation. He was also required by Florida law to register as a sex offender. He will remain on the registry for a minimum of 25 years, meaning he will be on the list until age 43 (Fayerick & Steffen, 2009; Jolicoeur & Zedlewski, 2010; Mabrey & Perozzi, 2010; Potter, 2011; Rybak, 2013). Alpert was reportedly tortured and harassed by other students following his conviction. He has faced numerous challenges obtaining employment, and was even expelled from Valencia Community College in Orlando, Florida, once his status as a registered sex offender was discovered (Potter, 2011). The story of Phillip Alpert is just one of hundreds of reports of youth facing the very real consequences of their digital communication decisions.

Case Study 7.1

The grave consequences of what can happen when private sext messages are shared with people other than the intended recipient can clearly be seen in the highly publicized case of Jessica Logan (Celizic, 2009). Logan, a high school student from Ohio, sent nude pictures of herself to her boyfriend in 2008. Shortly after the couple broke up, Logan's then ex-boyfriend sent the nude pictures intended for him to other students from the high school. Some reports suggest that the nude images of Logan were sent to 100 students attending four different schools (Kazdin & Ibanga, 2009).

After the dissemination of Logan's images, she endured harsh treatment by other peers and classmates (Kazdin & Ibanga, 2009). In an interview with a Cincinnati television station in May 2008, Jessica Logan reported being harassed by the female students, and called names like "slut" and "whore." Despite alleged efforts by Logan and her family to contact school officials to end the harassment, she continued to endure what she described as "torture." She was reportedly taunted through social media networks and text message. In July of 2008, at the age of 18, Jessica Logan hanged herself in her bedroom (Celizic, 2009).

Cynthia Logan, Jessica Logan's mother (who also discovered her daughter's body), has made it a personal mission to educate young people about the potential dangers of sexting (Kazdin & Ibanga, 2009). In January 2012, the *Jessica Logan Act* was signed into law in the state of Ohio. It requires schools to change their anti-bullying policies to reflect cyberbullying and harassment. It also increases anti-bullying training for teachers and gives school districts the authority to suspend student who harass, intimidate, or bully other students via text or internet (Wilson, 2012). In October 2012, Logan's family was awarded $154,000 as part of a settlement with her high school (Wells, 2012).

Revenge Porn

There are over 3,000 pornographic websites that have a "revenge" genre for viewers and, due to a rapid advancement of technology and growth of media outlets, this number too will inevitably continue to grow (*The Economist*, 2014). There is no universal definition of revenge porn. However, it has been conceptualized as encompassing any sexually explicit media that is shared with the public online without the consent of the pictured individual (Arnold, 2014). Revenge porn has also been defined as "a form of sexual assault that involves the distribution of nude/sexually explicit photos and/or videos of an individual without their consent" (Webb, 2014). Pornographic websites that serve this purpose often feature "explicit photos by ex-boyfriends, ex-husbands and ex-lovers, often accompanied by disparaging descriptions and identifying details" (Goode, 2013; Peterson, 2013). Research indicates that a large majority of the revenge pornography sites feature "selfies" or amateur photos taken by the victims themselves. That is, often images are taken voluntarily by the victim but are forwarded to revenge porn sites by disgruntled ex-lovers or former sexual partners who did not seek consent from the victim to do so (Goode, 2013).

In a study recently published by the *Cyber Civil Rights Initiative,* researchers found that a large majority (90%) of victims in revenge porn cases were women. Most victims (93%) reported that they had experienced a significant amount of emotional distress because of their victimization. Moreover, half of the victims (49%) reported that they were harassed or stalked by people who followed the pornographic site that they were featured on (Webb, 2014).

History of Revenge Porn

Websites and blogs dedicated to the revenge porn genre began to appear on the Internet as early as 2000. Around the same time, Sergio Messina was credited for first introducing the *realcore pornography* genre, which was the sharing of photos and/or videos of ex-girlfriends in shared online groups. Several years later, more pornographic websites that featured user-submitted images emerged, including *XTube, realexgirlfriends.com,* and *iknowthatgirl.com* (Tsoulis-Reay, 2013). In 2010, revenge porn gained national media attention following the creation of *IsAnyoneUp.com.* This website boasted the use of pornography for spiteful purposes, principally revenge porn. The creator, Hunter Moore, a 25-year-old man from Sacramento, California, began the website which featured sexually explicit photos, a link to the person in the photo's Facebook, Twitter, and/or Tumblr, as well as personal information about the person. The site allowed anonymous submissions of photos of any person to its database, and at one point it had reached a rate of over 30 million views per month (Gold, 2011; Zelmer, 2011).

In April of 2011 the web address for *Is Anyone Up?* was sold to an anti-bullying charity *BullyVille* (Neil, 2014; Vaas, 2014). Moore was eventually indicted on charges of conspiracy, email hacking, and aggravated identity theft (Neil, 2014; Tsoulis-Reay, 2013). Unfortunately, other websites much like Moore's still exist on the Internet today. Much like Moore's sentiment that victims are deserving of the abuse, other moderators have excused their websites, stating that they serve only as "entertainment" (Peterson, 2013).

Criminalization of Revenge Porn

Revenge porn has become hugely problematic in the past few years, and victims are not often protected by legislation (Stebnar, 2013). There are currently 13 states in the U.S. that have passed laws against revenge porn (Arizona, California, Colorado, Delaware, Georgia, Hawaii, Idaho, Maryland, New York, Pennsylvania, Utah, Vermont, and Wisconsin). Other states are close behind. This year, revenge porn bills were introduced or are pending in at least 28 states, the District of Columbia, and Puerto Rico (National Conference of State Legislatures, 2014). Victims are becoming involved as well and have been petitioning against revenge porn, using avenues such as *EndRevengePorn.org*, an initiative that was first introduced by Dr. Holly Jacobs, a victim of revenge porn (End Revenge Porn, 2014).

Revenge porn can be seen as a form of misogynistic abuse that is "normalized in the online space" (Edwards, 2014), and there is a link between domestic partner violence and revenge porn. *Cyber Civil Rights* (2014) estimates that 1 in 10 ex-partners have made threats that they would expose photos of their ex online, with 60 percent actually carrying through with the behavior (Webb, 2014). Revenge porn can cut across same-sex, as well as heterosexual, couples, and can be done by the female to the male as much as the other way round. However, research indicates that victims of revenge porn are mostly women (Edwards, 2014; Webb, 2014).

Eliminating sexually explicit material that is posted on the Internet poses challenges and, because of the proliferation of means to communicate, the amount of damage the victim can experience is significant. The process of criminalizing revenge porn is slow-moving and legalities are often found to hinder the process further, yet victims are still vehemently demanding change (Marcotte, 2014). Revenge porn has devastating consequences for those who are targeted.

Sextortion

Another new crime that has emerged from the increase in technology that characterizes today's society is *Sextortion*. This is a form of sexual exploitation in which non-physical intimidation is used in the coercion of sexual favors from victims. There is no universal definition for sextortion, but the term has been applied to cybercrimes that involve the posting of sexually explicit material on the Internet to blackmail former intimate partners. Sextortion involves the stealing of photos or videos, usually by hacking an individual's computer, phone or webcam, and then demands some form of payment not to distribute them online (Gregg, 2014). Often, perpetrators will use guilt, power, or knowledge of secretive information against the victim and will pressure them to perform sexual acts or will take pornographic photos. The crime itself is exclusive to the digital age (Bello, 2014).

The individuals who are responsible for making threats and harassing individuals are known as *sextortionists*. Victims of sextortion may know the perpetrator, or they could be targeted by strangers who hack into their webcam (Ramasastry, 2010). Typically, sextortion begins when someone, unsuspecting and vulnerable, meets an unknown individual online through a social networking/chat site. Once trust is established, the predator will make convincing attempts to get the victim to send them an explicit image. That image will then be used to blackmail the victim. If they do not do what is asked of them, the pornography will be leaked to the public (McClam, 2014).

Because there are no laws to date that specifically prosecute sextortion, the behavior often falls under an array of different statutes and is not an easy crime to prosecute (Anderson, 2013). Sextortion is still a fairly new crime, so there are not yet any national statistics to inform us of its prevalence. However, authorities know that predators are targeting teenagers. Many experts believe that they are often targeted because they are at an age where they experiment with sexuality and take risks (Bello, 2013). *USA Today* reported that the number of complaints that were made to the *Internet Crimes Against Children Task Force* about sextortion grew from 5,300 in 2010 to 7,000 in 2013 (Bello, 2014). However, it must be noted that this is not a true representation of actual perpetration of this crime, as there are surely more survivors who have not reported.

While blackmail is nothing new, incidents of sextortion manifested from the arrival of the camera phone and soon thereafter, webcams for computers (McLaren, 2002). Recently, the FBI published information about sextortion for Internet users, warning them of social networking schemes and the use of fake identities. They also highlighted the scheme that was orchestrated by Christopher Gunn. Gunn, a 31-year-old from Alabama, was accused of searching social media websites to extort demands from hundreds of young female victims. He created a fake Facebook page that gave off the appearance that he was a "new kid" in the area. He also pretended to be pop star Justin Bieber to employ his tactics. After befriending victims, Gunn would then make threats to leak the images to parents, friends, and school officials unless the victims complied with his demands to exchange sexually explicit pictures or videos. According to the FBI report, girls, ages 9 to 16 years old, would comply with Gunn's demands because they would do whatever they could to protect their reputation. Gunn was sentenced to 35 years in prison for producing child pornography through his online sextortion scheme (Federal Bureau of Investigation, 2014; Liebowitz, 2012).

In another high-profile sextortion case, Miss Teen USA Cassidy Wolf had fallen victim to a sextortionist who had targeted her four months before she had been crowned. After Cassidy received a message from Facebook notifying her that someone from another state had tried to access her account, she received an email from a stranger who told her that he had nude photos of her from the webcam she had in her bedroom. Cassidy was unaware that her computer was hacked, noting that the light on her webcam had never come on. Wolf said that the hacker had tried to extort her and threatened to make the photos public (Blankstein, 2013; Newcomb, 2013). Following an FBI investigation, Jared James Abrahams, 19, was charged with extortion. The hacker used malicious software to control the victim's webcams and masked his identity when sending emails threatening to publish the photos.

In 2010, Canadian teenager Amanda Todd befriended a man on a video chat and impulsively showed her breasts, not knowing that he had taken a photo. Soon after, Amanda was sent multiple harassing messages and told that if she did not post more images of herself, the photo of her would be posted online. The man later followed through with his threat, and the images of Amanda were sent to all of her Facebook friends. After the video had gone viral, Amanda was teased and harassed relentlessly. She soon became depressed and anxious and eventually committed suicide. The sextortionist, Aydin Coban, was arrested for extorting Amanda, as well as other girls and adult men in the United States, Canada, Britain, and the Netherlands (White, 2014).

Criminalizing Sextortion

As with many different cybercrimes, authorities were slow to address the problem of sextortion and various criminal statues were used as a way of prosecuting sextortion cases. Sextortion is often charged under such crimes as: bribery, extortion, break of trust, sexual assault, child pornography, sexual exploitation, computer hacking, corruption, and wiretapping (Associated Press, 2013; CNN Wire Staff, 2011; Glogowski, 2014). Over the past five years, efforts to address the issue of sextortion have become more prevalent. This is largely due to the scope of online communications and the number of potential online offenders (Gross & Arkin, 2013). In 2009, *The International Association of Women Judges,* in a partnered, government-funded attempt, launched *Stopping the Abuse of Power through Sexual Exploitation: Naming, Shaming, and Ending Sextortion.* This three-year program examined sextortion as a form of sexually coercive abuse of power. From a law enforcement perspective, the FBI has become extremely proactive in searching for predators, having recently arrested over 250 predators that engaged in online sexual abuse and possessed, produced, or traded pornography (Gross & Arkin, 2014). However, ultimately, more research will need to be done in this area regarding the prevalence and frequency of sextortion. Further, legislation that addresses the specific crime of sextortion may be of use in the future, as much of this behavior is not illegal by current standards.

Online Dating/Romance Scams

The Internet has now made it possible for a person to date without ever leaving their home. The use of internet dating sites, social networking sites, and dating applications has enabled humans to date 24 hours a day, 7 days a week, 365 days a year (Rege, 2009). With the growth in popularity of online dating in the past twenty years has come a growth in both the numbers and revenues of online dating websites (Close & Zinkhan, 2004). There are over 1,400 dating site in North America alone (Rege, 2009), which are estimated to generate $2 to $4 billion in revenue annually (Hamm, 2014; Rogers, 2013). Popular sites such as Match.com, eHarmony.com, Chemistry.com, and OKCupid.com make it easy for individuals to meet potential online matches (Rege, 2009). Online dating is not limited to dating sites only, as social networking sites such as Facebook, Instagram, and Twitter have generated a new method of connecting with others who may share similar interests (Wortham, 2014).

Recent research by Smith & Duggan (2014) in conjunction with the Pew Research Internet Project echoes the trend towards online dating, with 1 in 10 Americans reporting using online dating sites or mobile dating applications. In regard to social networking sites (SNS), 31 percent of respondents reported using these sites to check up on someone they used to date or be in a relationship with and 15 percent asked someone out on a date using an SNS (Smith & Duggan, 2014). While the majority of people who go online to date do not experience major difficulties, it is an industry that has faced a number of problems, particularly the emergence of dating/romance scams (Rege, 2009).

While the exact origin of online dating/romance scams is unknown, its roots can be traced back to the mid-2000s (Whitty & Buchanan, 2012). Although these scams can manifest in a number of ways, there are commonalities among them. The typical anatomy of an online dating/romance scam goes as follows: the criminal (scammer) often initiates contact with their victim through a dating or social networking site (Buchanan & Whitty, 2014; Rege, 2009). The offender, whose profile is often created with stolen photographs, will declare their affection and/or love for the victim at an early stage and will seek to move the communication from the dating site or SNS to other forms of communication (Whitty, 2013). The communication between the scammer and the victim is described as being both frequent and intense and builds over a period of weeks, months, or even years (Buchanan & Whitty, 2014).

After a trusting relationship is established, the scammer will begin with requests for small amounts of money or gifts. Buchanan and Whitty (2014) refer to this as a "testing-the-water" strategy, where the scammer is looking to see if the victim grants their request. The small requests often quickly accelerate into requests for larger sums of money. The scammer may bring in a third party to assist in the scam to make the monetary appeals more realistic. For example, a third party may contact the victim and explain that the scammer is "ill" or has been in an "accident" and requires money to make payment on a hospital bill, capitalizing on the feelings of empathy the victim has developed for the scammer (Rege, 2009; Whitty & Buchanan, 2012). For most victims, the online dating/romance scam ends when the victim both realizes and accepts that he or she has been scammed and refuses to pay the scammer (Whitty, 2013). Unfortunately for many victims, when they do decide to come forward there is often little room for recourse regarding these actions (Rege, 2009). While the FBI does offer warning about online dating/romance scams (FBI, 2012), beyond this there is little assistance for victims of this crime (Rege, 2009).

To date, there is little information regarding the typical characteristics of victims for these types of scams (Buchanan & Whitty, 2014). Rege (2009) asserts that romance scams are gender neutral in that males and females are targeted equally. While there are no reported differences between male and female victimization, it is believed that the most common targets for online dating/romance scammers are women over the age of 40 who are divorced, widowed, and/or disabled (Federal Bureau of Investigation, 2012). Buchanan and Whitty (2014) hypothesize that there may be feelings and characteristics that are common among victims. For example, those who experience extreme feelings of loneliness may tend to form strong attachments and relationships on the Internet, increasing their chance of victimization. Another hypothesis is that those individuals who are high sensation seekers looking for new, complex, intense sensations may be willing to risk their financial and emotional well-being to achieve these sensations (Buchanan & Whitty, 2014).

Whitty (2013) interviewed twenty individuals who had been victims of online dating/romance scams. The sample consisted of 14 heterosexual women, 4 heterosexual men, and 2 homosexual men. Many of these victims had been scammed for money, one person repeatedly (over 40 times). One of the themes that emerged was that many victims felt the person who scammed them portrayed themselves as an "ideal romantic partner" (p. 673). Others described feeling addicted to the relationship, and found it difficult to exit the relationship even when they learned the true intentions of the person they were speaking with. Under what is referred to as the *elaboration likelihood model*, some individuals were so motivated to find a romantic relationship that they would ignore cognitive cues that they were being scammed (Whitty, 2013).

Part of the difficulty in determining who the typical online dating/romance scam victim is, is due to the lack of reliable victimization statistics, as most victims do not report their victimization to law enforcement officials. An individual may not report because he or she is embarrassed, feels the police cannot help them, or simply does not know he or she is a victim (King & Thomas, 2009; Rege, 2009). Online dating scams can result in huge financial loss for its victims. Conservative estimates are that online dating/romance scams cost victims more than $50 million annually (Rogers, 2013). Losses can range from a few hundred dollars to upwards of six figures or more. For example, in 2013, it was reported that a Vancouver, Canada man lost $500,000 (CAD) to online dating/romance scammers (Rankin & Uda, 2013). In addition to being a potential source of financial victimization, online romance scam victims also suffer emotional harm, which can erode a person's senses of self and trust in others (Berg, 2009). Emotions such as fear, anxiety, anger, and depression are often reported. A victim often feels embarrassed that he or she fell for an online dating scam and can affect a person's overall online experiences (Rege, 2009).

"Catfishing": The New Face of the Online Dating/Romance Scam

Not all online romantic scams have a financial basis. Recent attention has been brought to the online dating/romance scam known as "catfishing." According to *Merriam-Webster Dictionary*, a catfish is "a person who sets up a false personal profile on a social networking site for fraudulent or deceptive purposes" ("Catfish," n.d.). Catfishes differ from other types of online dating/romance scams primarily because these scams take place primarily via SNS and not online dating sites, and while there may be financial aspects involved, catfishing scammers often commit their acts for personally motivated, non-financial reasons (Warner, 2012). Rothman (2013) suggests several themes that emerge as potential explanations for reasons why a person would engage in catfishing behavior. The first is revenge against someone you dislike as way of getting back at them. It may also be loneliness, in which a person feels ostracized from their community. A person may also engage in a catfish scam due to sexual identity anxiety in which posing as a person of another sex can be a means of helping one gain confidence in his/her own gender identity. It may also be low self-esteem in which catfishing boosts a person's own self-esteem (Rothman, 2013).

Case Study 7.2

The popular MTV show "Catfish: The TV Show" was inspired by the documentary of the same name (*Catfish: The Movie*), which was based on the real-life story of Nev Schulman, a 24-year-old New York City photographer (Warner, 2012). Schulman's story began when he was contacted on the popular social media website Myspace by an 8-year-old girl named "Abby," a budding artist from Michigan. Abby contacted Schulman to request permission to paint a photograph he had taken that was published in a newspaper months before. Flattered by the young girl's request, and with the blessing of Abby's mother, "Angela," Schulman began an online correspondence with Abby, which eventually developed into a friendship with her and her entire family (Berman & Deutsch, 2010; Jarecki, Smerling, Joost, & Schulman, 2010). Schulman's relationship particularly blossomed with "Megan," Abby's 19-year-old half-sister, whom Schulman described as "very attractive" and his "dream woman" (Berman, Deutsch, & Sher, 2010). After seven months of flirtatious correspondence with Megan, Schulman set off to Michigan to meet Megan and her family (with his brother and a friend documenting the trip with a video camera) (Warner, 2012).

Upon arriving in Michigan, Schulman and his crew were met by a woman named Angela Wesselman. It was quickly revealed that Wesselman had been posing as both 8-year-old Abby and 19-year-old Megan. Wesselman, a married women in her 40s who claims to be a diagnosed schizophrenic, explained that "Megan" and "Abby" were characters in a complex fantasy world she had developed (Berman, et al., 2010). While some may view this as an unforgivable betrayal, Schulman instead has chosen to view it as a learning experience. He still keeps in regular contact with Angela and admits that he does not hold anger or grudges towards her (Solon, 2010).

Conclusions

This chapter discussed the sexual offenses on the Internet and other related technologies that involve intimate partners. In particular, the offenses of sexting, revenge pornography, sextortion, online dating scams and catfishing were presented providing, details of both the offenders and victims of these sexually based offenses. Technology allows for an overabundance of means in which individuals, particularly intimate partners, can be victimized. Technology will continue to evolve, allowing for more ways to communicate and send images to one another. For this reason, it is suggested that Internet users be aware of what they are doing online. Further, it is suggested that youth and adults protect themselves by avoiding sending explicit images to others via technology and making sure that they know who they are conversing with online. Additional research on the cyber-victimization and perpetration of the crimes discussed in this chapter is needed. Future efforts should consider cybercrime as it relates to males as well as females, and should attempt to examine the long-term effects of online victimization.

References

Anderson, L. (2013, December 3). 'Sextortion': An old form of corruption gets new attention. *Thomas Reuters Foundation.* Retrieved from http://www.trust.org/item/20131202171549-yeq1d/?source=spotlight.

Arnold, M. (2014, July 21). A disturbing picture: Revenge porn is a vicious new way to smear someone's professional reputation. *HRMagazine, 59*(8), 58–58. Retrieved from http://www.shrm.org/publications/hrmagazine/editorialcontent/2014/0814/pages/0814-revenge-porn.aspx.

The Associated Press (2013, June 26). Indiana's 'sextortionist' gets 40-year sentence. *USA Today.* Retrieved from http://www.usatoday.com/story/news/nation/2013/06/26/indiana-sextortionist/2461487/.

The Associated Press. (2009). A thin line: 2009 AP-MTV digital abuse study. Retrieved from http://www.athinline.org/MTV-AP_Digital_Abuse_Study_Executive_Summary.pdf.

Bartow, A. (2012). Copyright law and pornography. *Organization Law Review, 91*(1), 44–46.

Bello, M. (2014, July 2). 'Sextortion' is an online 'epidemic' against children. *USA Today.* Retrieved from http://www.usatoday.com/story/news/nation/2014/07/01/sextortion-teens-online/11580633/.

Benotsch, E. G., Snipes, D. J., Martin, A. M., & Bull, S. S. (2013). Sexting, substance use, and sexual risk behavior in young adults. *Journal of Adolescent Health, 52*(3), 307–313.

Berg, S., (2009). Identity theft causes, correlates, and factors: A content analysis. In F. Schmalleger & M. Pittaro (Eds.), *Crimes of the Internet* (pp. 225–250). New Jersey: Pearson Prentice Hall.

Berman, T., & Deutsch, G. (2010, October 8). Inside 'catfish': A tale of twisted cyber-romance. Abcnews.com. Retrieved from http://abcnews.go.com/2020/catfish-movie-tale-twisted-cyber-romance/story?id=11817470.

Berman, T., Deutsch, G., & Sher, L. (2010, October 8). Exclusive: 'Catfish's' Angela Wesselman speaks out. Abcnews.com. Retrieved from http://abcnews.go.com/2020/catfish-woman-angela-wesselman-twisted-cyber-romance-abc/story?id=11831583.

Blankstein, A. (2013, September 26). FBI arrests suspect in Miss Teen USA 'sextortion' case. *NBC News*. Retrieved from http://www.nbcnews.com/news/other/fbi-arrests-suspect-miss-teen-usa-sextortion-case-f8C11267183.

Blankstein, A. (2013, August 14). FBI investigating 'sextortion' case targeting Miss Teen USA. *Los Angeles Times*. Retrieved from http://articles.latimes.com/2013/aug/14/local/la-me-ln-fbi-investigating-sextortion-case-targeting-miss-teen-usa-20130814.

Bluestone, G. (2014, September 1). Everything we know about the alleged celeb nude 'trading ring' and leak. *Gawker*. Retrieved from http://gawker.com/everything-we-know-about-the-alleged-celeb-nude-tradin-1629340923.

Boucek, S. (2009). Dealing with the nightmare of 'sexting'. *Education Digest*, 75, 10–12.

Brown, J. D., Keller, S., & Stern, S. (2009). Sex, sexuality, sexting, and sex ed: Adolescents and the media. *The Prevention Researcher*, 26, 12–16.

Buchanan, T., & Whitty, M. T. (2014). The online dating romance scam: Causes and consequences of victimhood. *Psychology, Crime & Law*, 20, 261–283.

Cadwalladr, C. (2014). Charlotte Laws' fight with Hunter Moore, the internet's revenge porn king. *The Observer* (March 29, 2014). Retrieved from http://www.theguardian.com/culture/2014/mar/30/charlotte-laws-fight-with-internet-revenge-porn-king.

Cahalan, S. (2009, January 25). Sex 'cells' for naked teenagers. *The New York Post*. Retrieved from http://nypost.com/2009/01/25/sex-cells-for-naked-teenagers/.

Calvert, C. (2014). Revenge porn and freedom of expression: Legislative pushback to an online weapon of emotional and reputational destruction. *Fordham Intellectual Property, Media & Entertainment Law Journal*, 24, 673–685.

Catfish [Def. 2]. (n.d.) In Merriam-Webster Dictionary Online. Retrieved October 10, 2014 from http://www.merriam-webster.com/dictionary/catfish.

Close, A., & Zinkhan, G. (2004). Romance and the internet: The e-mergence of e-dating. *Advances in Consumer Research*, 31, 153–157.

CNN Wire Staff. (2011, September 2). Hacker gets 6 years in prison for 'sextortion' scheme. *CNN*. Retrieved from http://www.cnn.com/2011/CRIME/09/02/california.nude.extortion/.

Cohen, L., & Felson, M. (1979). Social change and crime rate trends: A routine activity approach. *American Sociological Association*, 44(4), 588–608.

Comartin, E., Kernsmith, R., & Kernsmith, P. (2013). "Sexting" and sex offender registration: Do age, gender, and sexual orientation matter? *Deviant Behavior*, 34, 38–52.

Corbett, D. (2009). Let's talk about sext: The challenge of finding the right legal response to the teenage practice of "sexting". *Journal of Internet Law*, 13(6), 3–8.

Cox Communication (2009, May). Teen online & wireless safety survey: Cyberbullying, sexting, and parental control. Retrieved from http://www.cox.com/wcm/en/aboutus/datasheet/takecharge/2009-teen-survey.pdf.

Craun, S., & Kernsmith, P. (2006). Juvenile offenders and sex offender registries: Examining the data behind the debate. Federal Probation, 70(3), 45–49.

Dake, J. A., Price, J. H., Maziarz, L., & Ward, B. (2012). Prevalence and correlates of sexting behavior in adolescents. *American Journal of Sexuality Education*, 7, 1–15.

Dilberto, G. M., & Mattey, E. (2009). Sexting: Just how much of a danger is it and what can school nurses do about it? *NASA School Nurse*, 24, 262–267.

Dodero, C. (2012, April 4). Hunter Moore makes a living screwing you. *The Village Voice*. Retrieved from http://www.villagevoice.com/2012-04-04/news/revenge-porn-hunter-moore-is-anyone-up/.

The Economist. (2014, July 5). Misery Merchants: Revenge Porn. *The Economist*, Retrieved from http://www.economist.com/news/international/21606307-how-should-online-publication-explicit-images-without-their-subjects-consent-be.

Edgington, S. (n.d.). What Is Sextortion? *Parenting Teens*. Retrieved from http://www.sharecare.com/health/parenting-teens/what-is-sextortion.

The Editorial Board. (2013, October 12). Fighting back against revenge porn, *New York Times Editorial Board*. Retrieved from http://www.nytimes.com/2013/10/13/opinion/sunday/fighting-back-against-revenge-porn.html?_r=0.

Edwards, L. (2014, July 29). Revenge porn: Why the right to be forgotten is the right remedy. *The Guardian*. Retrieved from http://www.theguardian.com/technology/2014/jul/29/revenge-porn-right-to-be-forgotten-house-of-lords.

Englander, E. (2012, July). Low risk associated with most teenage sexting: A study of 617 18-year-olds. *Massachusetts Aggression Reduction Center*. Retrieved from http://vc.bridgew.edu/cgi/viewcontent.cgi?article=1003&context=marc_reports.

Eraker, E. C. (2010). Stemming sexting: Sensible legal approaches to teenagers' exchange of self-produced pornography. *Berkeley Technology Law Journal*, 25, 555–596.

Farkas, M., & Stichman, A. (2002). Sex offender laws: Can treatment, punishment, incapacitation, and public safety be reconciled? *Criminal Justice Review*, 27(2), 256–282.

Fayerick, D., & Steffen, S. (2009, April 8). 'Sexting' lands teen on sex offender list. *CNN.com*. Retrieved from http://www.cnn.com/2009/CRIME/04/07/sexting.busts/.

Federal Bureau of Investigation. (2013, February 5). A case of 'sextortion': Cons like 'Bieber Ruse' targeted minor girls. *Federal Bureau of Investigation*. Retrieved from http://www.fbi.gov/news/stories/2013/february/sextortion-cons-like-bieber-ruse-targeted-minor-girls/sextortion-cons-like-bieber-ruse-targeted-minor-girls.

Federal Bureau of Investigation. (2012, February 14). Looking for love? Beware of online dating scams. *U.S. Department of Justice*. Retrieved from http://www.fbi.gov/news/stories/2012/february/dating-scams_021412.

Ferguson, C. J. (2011). Sexting behaviors among young Hispanic women: Incidence and association with other high-risk sexual behaviors. *Psychiatric Quarterly*, 82, 239–243.

Fox, J., & Potocki, B. (2014). Technology & Culture. In T. Heistand & W. J. Weins (Eds.). *Sexting and youth* (pp. 95–122). Durham, NC: Carolina Academic Press.

Gold, D. (2011, November 10). The Man Who Makes Money Publishing Your Nude Pics, *THE AWL*. Retrieved from http://www.theawl.com/2011/11/the-man-who-makes-money-publishing-your-nude-pics.

Golgowski, N. (2014). California man arrested in child pornography 'sextortion' case that targeted fans of Justin Bieber: feds. *Daily News*. Retrieved from http://www.nydailynews.com/news/national/calif-man-arrested-child-sextortion-case-targeting-justin-bieber-fans-feds-article-1.1774910.

Goode, E. (2013, September 24). Once scorned, but on revenge sites, twice hurt, *New York Times*, at A11.

Gordon-Messer, D., Bauermeister, J. A., Grodzinski, A., & Zimmerman, M. Sexing among young adults. *Journal of Adolescent Health*, 52(3), 301–306.

Gottfredson, M. R., & Hirschi, T. (1990). *A general theory of crime*. Stanford, CA: Stanford University Press.

Gregg, M. (2014, July 2). Cyber-random and online extortion—5 ways you could fall victim. *Huffington Post*. Retrieved from http://www.huffingtonpost.com/michael-gregg/cyber-ransom-and-online-e_b_5548810.html.

Gross, A., & Arkin, D. (2013, July 15). Sweep snares 255 suspected child predators, rescues 61 children, officials say. *NBC News*. Retrieved from http://

www.nbcnews.com/news/other/sweep-snares-255-suspected-child-predators-rescues-61-children-officials-f6C10640100.

Hamm, N. (2014, March 28). How to make money off the online dating boom. *CNBC*. Retrieved from http://www.cnbc.com/id/101530708.

Harris, A. (2013, January 18). Who coined the term "catfish"? Slate.com. Retrieved from http://www.slate.com/blogs/browbeat/2013/01/18/catfish_meaning_and_definition_term_for_online_hoaxes_has_a_surprisingly.html.

Hertlein, K. M., & Ancheta, K. (2014). Advantages and disadvantages of technology in relationships: Findings from an open-ended survey. The *Qualitative Reporter*, 19, 1–11.

Hinduja, S., & Patchin, J. W. (2010, September 1). Sexting: A brief guide for educators and parents. *Cyberbullying Research Center*. Retrieved from http://cyberbullying.us/sexting-a-brief-guide-for-educators-and-parents-2/.

Hinduja, S., & Patchin, J. (2014, September). State sexting laws. *Cyberbullying Research Center*. Retrieved from http://www.cyberbullying.us/state_sexting_laws.pdf.

Hughs, T. (2014, May 9). States move on to ban 'revenge porn.' *USA Today*. Retrieved from http://go.galegroup.com/ps/i.do?id=GALE%7CA370318830&v=2.1&u=indi68545&it=r&p=ITOF&sw=w&asid=96d8fbeabbcf0cc1ea4de0cf52fa95ca.

Halloran-McLaughlin, J. (2014). The first amendment. In T. Heistand & W. J. Weins (Eds.). *Sexting and youth* (pp. 155–176). Durham, NC: Carolina Academic Press.

Jaishankar, K. (2009). Sexting: A new form of victimless crime? *International Journal of Cyber Criminology*, 3(1), 21–25.

Jarecki, A., Smerling, M., Joost, H., & Schulman, A. (Producers), and Joost, H., & Schulman, A. (Directors). (2010). *Catfish* [Motion picture]. United States: Universal Pictures.

Jolicoeur, M., & Zedlewski, E. (2010, June). *Much ado about sexting*. Retrieved from https://www.ncjrs.gov/pdffiles1/nij/230795.pdf.

Lamphere, R. D. (2014). Prevalence and research methodology. In T. Heistand & W. J. Weins (Eds.). *Sexting and youth* (pp. 33–62). Durham, NC: Carolina Academic Press.

Laws, C. (2013, November 22). One women's dangerous war against the most hated man on the Internet, *Jezebel*. Retrieved from http://jezebel.com/one-womans-dangerous-war-against-the-most-hated-man-on-1469240835.

Kazdin, C., & Ibanga, I. (2009, April 15). The truth about teens sexting. *Abcnews.com*. Retrieved from http://abcnews.go.com/GMA/Parenting/truth-teens-sexting/story?id=7337547.

King, A., & Thomas, J. (2009). You can't cheat an honest man: Making ($$$ and) sense of the Nigerian e-mail scams. In F. Schmalleger & M. Pittaro (Eds.) *Crimes of the Internet* (pp. 206–224). New Jersey: Pearson Prentice Hall.

Lenhart, A. (2009, December 15). Teens and sexting. *Pew Research Internet Project*. Retrieved from http://www.pewinternet.org/2009/12/15/teens-and-sexting/.

Liebowitz, M. (2012, May 3). 'Fake Justin Bieber' arrested for sextortion. *NBC News*. Retrieved from http://www.nbcnews.com/id/47286244/ns/technology_and_science-security/t/fake-justin-bieber-arrested-sextortion/#.VDxhwxb4LCs.

Lounsbury, K., Mitchell, K. J., & Finkelhor, D. (2011, April). The true prevalence of "sexting". *Crimes against Children Research Center*. Retrieved from http://www.unh.edu/ccrc/pdf/Sexting%20Fact%20Sheet%204_29_11.pdf.

Mabrey, V., & Perozzi, D. (2010, April 1). 'Sexting': Should child pornography laws apply. *Abcnews.com*. Retrieved from http://abcnews.go.com/Nightline/phillip-alpert-sexting-teen-child-porn/story?id=10252790.

Marcotte, (2014, September 9). 'The Fappening' and revenge porn culture: Jennifer Lawrence and the creepshot epidemic. *The Daily Beast*. Retrieved from http://www.thedailybeast.com/articles/2014/09/03/the-fappening-and-revenge-porn-culture-jennifer-lawrence-and-the-creepshot-epidemic.html.

Marganski, A., & Fauth, K. (2013). Socially interactive technology and contemporary dating: A cross-cultural exploration of deviant behaviors among young adults in the modern, evolving technological world. *International Criminal Justice Review*, 23(4), 357–377.

Martinez-Prather, K., & Vandiver, D. M. (2014). Sexting among teenagers in the United States: A retrospective analysis of identifying motivating factors, potential targets, and the role of a capable guardian. *International Journal of Cyber Criminology*, 8(1), 21–35.

McClam, E. (2014, July 16). Experts increasingly worried about 'sextortion' of minors online. *NBC News*. Retrieved from http://www.nbcnews.com/news/other/experts-increasingly-worried-about-sextortion-minors-online-f6C10645107.

McLaren, A. (2002). *Sexual Blackmail: A Modern History*. Cambridge, MA: Harvard University Press.

Mitchell, K. J., Finkelhor, D., Jones, L. M., & Wolak, J. (2012). Prevalence and characteristics of youth sexting: A national study. *Pediatrics*, 129, 13–20.

Morris, A. (2012, November 13). Hunter Moore: The most hated man on the Internet. *Rolling Stone*. Retrieved from http://www.rollingstone.com/culture/news/the-most-hated-man-on-the-internet-20121113.

The National Campaign to Prevent Teen and Unplanned Pregnancy. (2009). Sex and tech: Results from a survey of teens and young adults. Retrieved from http://www.thenationalcampaign.org/sextech/PDF/SexTech_Summary.pdf.

National Conference of State Legislatures (2014, October 1). State 'revenge porn' legislation. *National Council of State Legislatures.* Retrieved from http://www.ncsl.org/research/telecommunications-and-information-technology/state-revenge-porn-legislation.aspx.

Neil, M. (2014, January 24). 'Most hated man on the Internet' is charged with email hacking to get photos for revenge porn site. *ABA Journal.* Retrieved from http://www.abajournal.com/news/article/most_hated_man_on_the_internet_is_charged_with_email_hacking_to_get_photos_/?utm_source=maestro&utm_medium=email&utm_campaign=techmonthly.

Newcomb, A. (2013, August 15). FBI investigating 'sextotion' case involving Miss Teen USA Cassidy Wolf. *ABC News.* Retrieved from http://abcnews.go.com/blogs/headlines/2013/08/fbi-investigating-sextortion-case-involving-miss-teen-usa-cassidy-wolf/.

Peterson, (2013, February 5). 'It's only entertainment:' Creator of 'revenge porn' site shrugs off potential lawsuits and says his number one goal is making money. *Mail Online.* Retrieved from http://www.dailymail.co.uk/news/article-2273963/I-entertainment-Creator-revenge-porn-site-shrugs-potential-lawsuits-says-number-goal-making-money.html.

Podlas, K. (2014). Media activity and impact. In T. Heistand & W. J. Weins (Eds.). *Sexting and youth* (pp. 123–154). Durham, NC: Carolina Academic Press.

Potter, A. E. (2011). Sexting and Louisiana's punishment for the children the law intends to protect from prosecution under child pornography statutes. *Family Law Quarterly,* 45(3), 419–442.

Ramasastry, A. (2010, November 30). The FBI's alert regarding 'sextortion': Why cyber blackmail, though illegal, is difficult to stop and what computer users can do. *Find Law.* Retrieved from http://writ.news.findlaw.com/ramasastry/20101130.html.

Rankin, E., & Uda, E. (2013, September 26). Man duped $500k in online romance scam: British police arrest man in connection to international scam. *CBC News.* Retrieved from http://www.cbc.ca/news/canada/british-columbia/man-duped-500k-in-online-romance-scam-1.1870043.

Rege, A. (2009). What's love got to do with it? Exploring online dating scams and identity fraud. *International Journal of Cyber Criminology,* 3(2), 494–512.

Reyns, B. W., Henson, B., & Fisher, B. S. (2014). Digital deviance: Low self-control and opportunity as explanations of sexting among college students. *Sociological Spectrum,* 34, 273–292.

Richards, R., & Calvert, C. (2009). When sex and cell phones collide: Inside the prosecution of a teen sexting case. *Hastings Communication and Entertainment Law Journal*, 32(1), 1–39.

Rogers, A. (2013, February 6). Online dating scams cost victims more than $50 million a year. *Business Insider*. Retrieved from http://www.businessinsider.com/threatmetrix-online-dating-scam-graphic-2013-2.

Rosenberg, E. (2011, June 9). In Weiner's wake, a brief history of the word 'sexting'. *The Wire*. Retrieved from http://www.thewire.com/national/2011/06/brief-history-sexting/38668/.

Rothman, L. (2013, January 23). The anatomy of a catfish. Time Magazine Online. Retrieved from http://entertainment.time.com/2013/01/24/the-manti-teo-hoax-5-reasons-people-create-fake-girlfriends-according-to-catfish/.

Roy, J. (2012, December 2). Anonymous hunts Hunter Moore to hold him 'accountable' for his revenge porn empire. *BetaBeat*. Retrieved from http://betabeat.com/2012/12/anonymous-launches-ophunthunter-to-destroy-hunter-moore-and-his-revenge-porn-empire/.

Rybak, D (2013, July 9). "Sexting": From bad judgment to a registered sex offender. *Campbell Law Observer*. Retrieved from http://campbelllawobserver.com/2013/07/sexting-from-bad-judgment-to-a-registered-sex-offender/.

Sahagun, L. (2014, September 1). FBI joins hunt for hacker who leaked nude photos of actresses. *Los Angeles Times*. Retrieved from http://www.latimes.com/local/lanow/la-me-la-fbi-hackers-leaked-photos-actresses-lawrence-20140901-story.html.

Sext [Def. 2]. (n. d.) In Oxford Dictionaries Online, Retrieved October 1, 2014, from http://www.oxforddictionaries.com/us/definition/american_english/sext.

Shafron-Perez, S. (2009). Average teenager or sex offender? Solutions to the legal dilemma caused by sexting. *The John Marshall Journal of Computer & Information Law*, 26, 431–451.

Smith, A., & Duggan, M. (2013, October 21). Online dating & relationships. *Pew Research Internet Project*. Retrieved from http://www.pewinternet.org/2013/10/21/online-dating-relationships/.

Solon, O. (2010, December 10). Catfish review and interview with Nev Schulman. Wired. Retrieved from http://www.wired.co.uk/news/archive/2010-12/10/catfish-review-and-interview/page/2.

Stebnar, B. (2013, May 3). 'I'm tired of hiding': Revenge-porn victim speaks out over her abuse after she claims ex posted explicit photos of her online. *New York Daily News*. Retrieved from http://www.nydailynews.com/news/national/revenge-porn-victim-speaks-article-1.1334147.

Stroud, S. (2014). The dark side of the online self: A pragmatist critique of the growing plague of revenge porn. *Journal of Mass Media Ethics, 29,* 168–183.

Stump, S. (2013, August 12). Newly crowned Miss Teen USA: I was a victim of cybercrime. *Today News.* Retrieved from http://www.today.com/news/newly-crowned-miss-teen-usa-i-was-victim-cybercrime-6C10898695.

Temple, J. R., Le, V. D., Peskin, M., Markham, C., & Tortolero, S. (2014). Risky behavior and adolescent development. In T. Heistand & W. J. Weins (Eds.). *Sexting and youth* (pp. 1–32). Durham, NC: Carolina Academic Press.

Temple, J. R., Le, V. D., van der Berg, P., Ling, Y., Paul, J. A., & Temple, B. W. (2013). Brief report: Teen sexting and psychosocial health. *Journal of Adolescence, 37*(1), 33–36.

Tewksbury, R. (2005). Collateral consequences of sex offender registration. *Journal of Contemporary Criminal Justice, 21*(1), 67–81.

Tewksbury, R., & Lees, M. (2006). Perceptions of sex offender registration: Collateral consequences and community experiences. *Sociological Spectrum, 26*(3), 309–334.

Tsoulis-Reay, A. (2013, July 21). A brief history of revenge porn. *New York Magazine.* Retrieved from http://nymag.com/news/features/sex/revenge-porn-2013-7/.

Vaas, L. (2014, January 27). Revenge-porn king Hunter Moore indicted on 7 counts of aggravated identity theft). *Naked Security.* Retrieved from http://nakedsecurity.sophos.com/2014/01/27/revenge-porn-king-hunter-moore-indicted-on-7-counts-of-aggravated-identity-theft/.

Vogels, J. (2004, May 3). Textual gratification: Quill or keypad, it's all about sex. *The Globe and Mail.* Retrieved from http://www.theglobeandmail.com/technology/textual-gratification-quill-or-keypad-its-all-about-sex/article1136823/?page=all.

Warner, K. (2012, July 5). 'Catfish' MTV show brings online love stories to life. *MTV News.* Retrieved from http://www.mtv.com/news/1689098/catfish-online-love-reality-show/.

Wastler, S. (2010). The harm in sexting? Analyzing the constitutionality of child pornography statutes that prohibit the voluntary production, possession, and dissemination of sexually explicit images by teenagers. *Harvard Journal of Law & Gender, 33,* 687–702.

Webb, N. (2014, January 3). End revenge porn infographic. *Cyber Civil Right Initiative.* Retrieved from http://www.cybercivilrights.org/end_revenge_porn_infographic.

Weins, W. J. (2014). Concepts and context. In T. Heistand & W. J. Weins (Eds.). *Sexting and youth* (pp. 63–76). Durham, NC: Carolina Academic Press.

Well, C. (2012, October 9). Family of Jessica Logan, who hanged herself after nude-picture sexting led to bullying, awarded $154,000 in settlement. *The Daily News*. Retrieved from www.nydailynews.com/news/national/teen-bullying-victim-family-settlement-article-1.1178783?ref=http%3A%2F%2F.

White, P. (2014, May 31). On the trail of Amanda Todd's alleged tormentor. *The Globe and Mail*. Retrieved from http://www.theglobeandmail.com/news/world/on-the-trail-of-amanda-todds-alleged-tormentor/article18935075/?page=all.

Whitty, M. T. (2013). The scammers persuasive techniques model: Development of a stage model to explain the online dating romance scam. *British Journal of Criminology*, 53, 665–684.

Whitty, M. T., & Buchanan, T. (2012). The online dating and romance scam: A serious cybercrime. *Cyberpsychology, Behavior, and Social Networking*, 15(3), 181–183.

Wilson, R. (2012, February 14). New state law gives school districts reach to punish cyberbullying. *Springfield News-Sun*. Retrieved from http://www.springfieldnewssun.com/news/news/local/new-state-law-gives-school-districts-reach-to-pu-1/nMyqm/.

Wood v. Hustler Magazine, Inc, 744 F.2d 94 (1984).

Worthman, J. (2014, June 28). Cupid's arrows fly on social media, too. *The New York Times*. Retrieved from http://bits.blogs.nytimes.com/2014/06/28/cupids-arrows-fly-on-social-media-too/?_php=true&_type=blogs&_r=0.

Zelmer, E. (2011, February 14). Naked & famous: How a risque new website pushes boundaries and buttons, *Alternative Press*. Retrieved from http://www.altpress.com/features/entry/naked_famous_how_a_risque_new_website_pushes_boundaries_and_buttons.

Chapter Eight

Policing Initiatives and Limitations

Debarati Halder and K. Jaishankar

Introduction

Cyberspace has aided in growing human networking through hundreds of interactive sites, including emails, social media, blogs, etc. This has tremendously affected the growth in the corporate sector, whereby corporate entities (from giants to small scale entities) could connect to existing as well as new customers and gain profit from networking. Government sectors have established e-portals for better governance and through such e-portals civil society members are encouraged to report their grievances. In many instances, such interacting between the civil society members and the government has yielded good results as well (Chadwick & May, 2003). In the case of networking between private individuals, cyberspace has lived to the true meaning of "connecting and reconnecting with friends and family," which has been the motto of almost all the social networking websites of this era. However, interpersonal networking between two individuals or groups of individuals has its adversities as well.

Due to vast freedom of expression as assumed by many, and the networking tools including power to remain anonymous etc., numerous types of offensive behaviors are occurring in the Internet. As we have earlier stated, these offensive behaviors can be termed as cybercrimes and may be defined as *"offences that are committed against individuals or groups of individuals with a criminal motive to intentionally harm the reputation of the victim or cause physical or mental harm to the victim directly or indirectly, using modern telecommunication networks such as Internet (Chat rooms, emails, notice boards and groups) and mobile phones (SMS/MMS)"* (Halder & Jaishankar, 2011a, p. 15). Further, interpersonal cybercrimes can be defined as "criminal activities conducted online that take the form of an 'assault' against the individual, their integrity or reputation" (Roberts, 2008a, p. 2). Interpersonal cybercrimes may include different sorts of cybercrimes including online bullying, cyber harassment, cyber stalking (Roberts, 2008b, 2009), revenge pornography (Halder & Jaishankar, 2013; Citron, 2014), creation of *fake avatar* (Halder, 2013), identity theft, hacking etc. Interpersonal cybercrimes may include different groups of "partners" such as colleagues, siblings, student-groups, student-teacher (Halder & Jaishankar, 2013), dating partners, ex-husbands or wives, etc., and the mechanism for executing the harassment may or may not be the same in each case. The majority of such interpersonal cybercrimes has been recognized by domestic laws of many countries. However, policing such cybercrimes by the law and justice machinery is still not satisfactory.

Yar (2005) terms policing the cyberspace as "social guardianship" in the net and points out that policing the cyberspace becomes highly impossible due to ease of "offender mobility." Policing the cybercrimes including economic frauds may seem a tough task in many jurisdictions due to non-awareness of the trends of the new Internet crimes by law and justice machinery including the police (Brenner, 2002). Even for crimes like card frauds, policing may not be absolutely possible due to the ever-changing profile of the fraudsters (Yip, Whepper, Shadbolt, 2013). According to Roberts (2008b), the major challenges for policing interpersonal crime like cyber stalking may lie in the fact that the individual behaviors of the stalker which may constitute stalking may not form criminal offence individually. Roberts (2008b) further highlights that in many cases the onus lies on the victim to produce evidence of stalking since there is no universal profiling of stalker and no one can predict when a stalker can become violent and how he/she may execute the violence. Further, when the cyber stalking involves cross-jurisdictional exchange of communication, the police may face problems in proceeding with the investigation in foreign jurisdictions as well as deportation.

The same concern was presented by Chang (2013), who showed that in spite of the cybercrime conventions (which urge for international bilateral cooperation for mutual assistance to prevent cybercrimes), enmity or a hostile relationship between two countries may make policing cross-jurisdictional cybercrimes almost impossible. However, policing the cyberspace, or rather providing "guardianship" to the cyberspace irrespective of the nature of the crime, has been made possible to a certain extent in two particular ways: through development of software to help protect the computers and networks from cybercrimes including virus attack, Trojan attack, detecting scams, etc., and by personal guardianship whereby the user can take sufficient protection to save him/herself from computer crimes (Ngo & Paternoster, 2011). Such sorts of personal "guardianship" can be developed by constant review of literature on awareness campaigns, new trends of crime mechanism and possible solutions from them, etc. But again, state-funded policing or policing by criminal justice machinery may become the ultimate answer in cases of interpersonal crimes when harm is already created or there is reasonable threat to the victim. Presently social media is hugely being used to create interpersonal cybercrimes (Halder & Jaishankar, 2009, 2011).

Problems may arise due to the involvement of multiple factors when policing interpersonal cybercrimes: these may include cross–jurisdictional presence of the perpetrator, especially if the perpetrator is anonymous (Citron, 2009, 2014) as well as the server of the site which may bar the police from accessing the vital information about the perpetrator immediately (Halder & Jaishankar, 2009), and also the viral nature of the content whereby the offending content can spread rapidly in the "cyber neighborhood" (Williams, Edwards, Housely, Burnap, Rana, Avis, Morgan, & Sloan, 2013).

However, even though the data mining system in the social networking systems from the metadata provided by the users has helped the police in investigating, prosecuting and even preventing large scale social crimes like riots (Williams et. al., 2013), we argue that these systems may not be successful for policing interpersonal crimes in the cyberspace. Unlike large-scale social crimes like riots or organized crimes like terrorism or economic crimes like phishing or scamming, interpersonal crimes may involve sudden or slow eruption of hatred or animosity between two or more individuals. It may also involve execution of such hatred (which may have existed in the physical space) through the cyberspace in the forms of crimes like revenge porn (Halder & Jaishankar, 2013) or cyber bullying or hacking the accounts to create Fake Avatars (Halder, 2013), etc. Interpersonal crimes may also involve gradual formation of groups lead by one particular perpetrator to attack the victim either by way of hate crimes (Citron, 2014) or by trolling (Halder, 2013), etc. In such cases, "guardianship" by way of creation of software or by personal skill development to prevent escalation of harassment may not prove very successful since the attack would have been done by the acquaintance (perpetrator) of the victim before he/she could have actually understood that the harassment started. In this chapter we will analyze what sort of policing can be offered in such cases, what the practical limitations are, and how it can be solved.

This chapter primarily builds up its argument on the basis of the examples we received from the statistics of Working to Halt Online Abuse (WHOA), USA, and research reports of the Centre for Cyber Victim Counselling (CCVC), India, and also from the personal experiences of the authors as researchers and practitioners. The chapter also relies upon secondary data including news media reports, scholarly articles and books. This chapter is divided into two parts. The first part deals with different types of interpersonal crimes which are already recognized by law enforcement agencies in different jurisdictions and also those crimes that need recognition. For this part, we have taken up examples from selected countries from Asia, Europe, and the American continents. This part then discusses what sorts of policing are offered in these jurisdictions for such interpersonal cybercrimes and what their limitations are. The second part discusses problems of policing the cyberspace from victimological aspects. It discusses issues such as why the reporting of crimes or the rate of prosecution is less in number in some jurisdictions, what the self-policing measures are that are taken up by the victims, and whether such measures are always beneficial. The chapter ends with a conclusion, which includes suggestions.

Profiles of Interpersonal Cybercrimes and Types of Policing

Profile of Interpersonal Cybercrimes

Interpersonal cybercrimes arrived late as the interactions between individuals grew more after the advent of social networking sites. Hence, very little literature or definitions on interpersonal cybercrimes is found. "Interpersonal cyber-crimes are criminal activities conducted online that take the form of an 'assault' against the individual, their integrity or reputation. This can include acts such as cyber harassment, cyber-bullying and cyber-stalking" (Roberts, 2008a, p. 2). "Interpersonal cybercrimes refer to 'crimes where computers or ICTs are an integral part of the offence such as online fraud, identity theft' as well as online stalking and harassment" (Baxter, 2014, p. 7).

Interpersonal cybercrimes essentially involve two actors, i.e., the victim and the perpetrator, who may be known or unknown to each other both in online and offline spaces. The nature of the relationship of the perpetrator with the victim may turn victimizing when the perpetrator starts harming the victim by the use of the computer or computer resources or computer networks for any offensive motive which may be detrimental to the victim. In this context, we feel that Axelrod's (2009, p. 16) definition of interpersonal cybercrimes is more pertinent and apt. Interpersonal violence and crime on the Internet is defined as *"any threat to, or action against, personal safety, security, or property, in which a computer was used directly to interact with the victim or gain access to the victim in the physical world"* (Axelrod, 2009, p. 16).

Roberts (2008), Axelrod (2009) and Baxter (2014) give a limited view or typology of interpersonal cybercrimes. We would like to extend and expand it more. Interpersonal cybercrimes can be of two main types: *privacy-related crimes* and *content-related crimes*. Privacy-related crimes may include hacking and hacking-related crimes, cyber stalking, creating *fake avatars*, revenge pornography, etc. Content–related crimes may involve cyber bullying, trolling, resulting in online defamation, spreading of hate speech (Citron, 2014), etc., and symbolic pictorial attacks. Both of the types of interpersonal cybercrimes may overlap with each other. The brief explanation of each of these categories of crimes is given below:

Hacking and Hacking-Related Crimes. The term hacking is further defined by the National Conference of State Legislature (NCSL) website as: "Hacking is breaking into computer systems, frequently with intentions to alter or modify existing settings."[1] Researchers as well as most of the jurisdictions in the world define the term as "unauthorized access" rather than "hacking." Wall (2001) described the term as "deliberate unauthorized access to cyberspace over which rights of ownership or access have already been established, committed with the primary aim of breaching the integrated security of the computer system." The NCSL website defines the term unauthorized access in the following words: "'Unauthorized access' entails approaching, trespassing within, communicating with, storing data in, retrieving data from, or otherwise intercepting and changing computer resources without consent."[2]

Hacking or unauthorized access to computer, stored documents, computer networks, stored communication, etc. are prohibited by many domestic laws including the U.S.; prominent among such laws is the 18 U.S.C. S.2701, which in subsection (a) proscribes two types of offences, namely (i) intentionally accessing without authorization a facility through which an electronic communication service is provided; or (ii) intentionally exceeding an authorization to access that facility and thereby obtaining, altering, or preventing authorized access to a wire or electronic communication while it is in electronic storage in such system. The punishment under this provision may vary according to the motive and purpose. In India, for example, hacking is addressed as unauthorized accessing of the computer, computer files, documents, networks, etc., and can be dealt with either as a civil liability under S.43 of the Information Technology Act, 2000, (amended in 2008) or as a criminal offence under S.66. Hacking and hacking-related crimes may occur in interpersonal crimes to destroy or modify important documents, stored communications, etc., or to hamper access to electronic communication systems. Hacking in interper-

---

1. See http://www.ncsl.org/research/telecommunications-and-information-technology/computer-hacking-and-unauthorized access-laws.aspx. Accessed on 04.03.2015.
2. Ibid.

sonal crimes may involve stalking, creation of fake avatars, and revenge pornography, etc., which are explained below.

Cyber Stalking. One of the most phenomenal crimes in the arena of interpersonal cybercrimes is cyber stalking (Brenner, 2004; Baer, 2010). Cyber stalking is defined by Bocij and MacFarlane (2002, p. 32) as "a group of behaviors in which an individual, group of individuals or organization, uses information and communications technology to harass one or more individuals. Such behaviors may include, but are not limited to, the transmission of threats and false accusations, identity theft, data theft, damage to data or equipment, computer monitoring, the solicitation of minors for sexual purposes and confrontation." As stated in this definition, cyber stalking may necessarily involve unauthorized access to personal contents as well as communications stored in the electronic devices, harassment, and further Internet defamation. Even though many researchers including Brenner (2004) and Elison and Akdeniz (1998) preferred to use the term cyber stalking as quite synonymous to cyber harassment, we argue that cyber stalking should not be construed as cyber harassment. It may be a part of or a type of cyber harassment. Notably, cyber stalking has been defined and has received legal recognition in many domestic and provincial laws as "cyber harassment." The most prominent of such laws is the Protection from Harassment Act, 1997 (Ss.2–7), of the UK, which is being used to regulate cyber stalking as set of harassing behaviors. It may be noted that S.2261A of U.S.C. 18 (amended by s.114 of the "Violence Against Women and Department of Justice Reauthorization Act, 2005") in the U.S. and S.354D of the Indian Penal Code (Criminal Law Amendment Act, 2013) in India address the issue of cyber stalking especially in context of victimization of women.

Creation of Fake Avatars. Interpersonal cybercrimes may necessarily involve content moderation by the perpetrator and presenting the same in different (harassing) avatars through social networking sites to harass the victim. Halder (2013) defines a fake avatar as "*a false representation of the victim which is created by the perpetrator through digital technology with or without the visual images of the victim and which carry verbal information about the victim which may or may not be fully true and it is created and floated in the internet to intentionally malign the character of the victim and to mislead the viewers about the victim's original identity.*" It may be understood that due to the opportunities to create multiple profiles in the social networking sites by individuals, perpetrators may misuse the digital contents of the victims and/or information about the victims to produce fake avatars for large-scale harassment. The lead author, being a cybercrime victim counselor, has noticed that maximum cases of interpersonal crimes in the cyberspace may involve creation of fake avatars of the victims in the social networking sites like Facebook and also in adult entertainment sites, and this may not be limited to women victims, alone. Even though the ratio of male victims of fake avatars is comparatively less, men are also impersonated and perpetrators may create their fake avatars in different social networking sites.

Even though in some cases the concept of fake avatars may become similar to identity theft, we do not wish to term it as identity theft; however, the creation of fake avatars may also involve identity theft. The creation of fake avatars may also involve morphing of the photographs and creation of revenge pornographic materials online (Halder & Jaishankar, 2013). The creation of fake avatars has received legal attention in many jurisdictions especially when it is impersonation for financial crimes. However, in the majority of the cases of fake avatars created to harass women and men in social networking sites, laws remain silent especially if such fake avatars have restricted audience and do not fall in the categories of indecent representation of women or violent porn images or extremely damaging to reputation. It may be interesting to note that the creation of fake avatars may fall in the twilight zone of privacy infringement and content-related crimes.

Revenge Pornography. One of the recent trends of interpersonal cybercrimes is revenge pornography (Halder & Jaishankar, 2013; Citron, 2014). This may involve the creation of fake avatars in obscene and pornographic color and spreading the same through social networking sites or adult entertainment sites for large-scale harassment and defamation of the victim. Often revenge pornography may happen to women and girls (Halder & Jaishankar, 2013; Citron, 2014). The perpetrator may create the revenge porn contents with the help of the materials either supplied by the victim to him when they had been in good relationship, or with the help of the information that may have been acquired by him through various other sources. Revenge pornography is now being considered as a penal offence in the U.S.; however, in many other jurisdictions, including India or the UK, revenge porn still awaits for formal legal recognition, even though it may be addressed by existing laws that address other related issues including defamation or obscene publication, etc. (Halder & Jaishankar, 2013).

Cyberbullying. Interpersonal crimes on the Internet may also involve bullying and trolling. According to Patchin and Hinduja (2006), cyberbullying is "willful and repeated harm inflicted through the use of computers, cell phones, and other electronic devices." Jaishankar (2009, p. 30) defines cyberbullying in much broader aspect; cyberbullying is "abuse/harassment by teasing or insulting victims' body shape, intellect, family back ground, dress sense, mother tongue, place of origin, attitude, race, caste, class, name calling, using modern telecommunication networks such as mobile phones (SMS/MMS) and Internet (Chat rooms, emails, notice boards and groups)."

Trolling, on the other hand, is *"an extreme usage of freedom of speech which is exercised to disrupt the community discussions in social networking sites and which is done to deliberately insult ideologies such as feminism, secularism etc.; of the topic starter or the supporters of the topic starter"* (Halder, 2013). While bullying is most prominent among children and young adults, especially university students (Shariff & Hoff, 2007), and this may also involve sudden eruption of anger and frustration resulting in bullying or continued hatred towards the victim resulting in bullying, trolling as an interpersonal crime has not gained much attention compared to bullying. However, we argue that trolling can be an interpersonal crime especially when the harasser wishes to ridicule the victim and engages in snowballing of harassment through trolling which may or may not involve known acquaintances. Unfortunately trolling is not addressed by focused laws in any jurisdiction.

Symbolic Pictorial Attacks. With the advent of digital communication technology through emoticons, it has been noted that interpersonal crimes on the Internet may take different shape with symbolic pictorial attacks. In the 2015 research report (Halder & Jaishankar, 2015a) prepared by the Centre for Cyber Victim Counselling (CCVC), it was found that among 131 respondents, 9.9 percent had received harassing emoticons including symbols of kissing, hugging, broken hearts, etc. This may prove that online personal attacks may be expressed not only by verbal words but also by the usage of emoticons. Symbolic pictorial attack either with emoticons or with other violent images to harass and threaten the victim has been done my many perpetrators who wish to not send any written words, but to cause grave threat to the victims.[3] This may include but is not limited to sending emoticons, nude photos of women to symbolically tell the victim that her private images may be morphed and leaked into the worldwide web, violent images like mutilated bodies, etc. to give an impression to the victim that if he/she does not obey the perpetrator, he/she may also face the same fate, etc. Such pictorial attacks can be caused by posting images along with a threatening message in the "time line" of the victim in her social networking profile or tagging the victim's name with message to harass him/her, or sending such images by way of chat or mail or message. Symbolic pictorial attacks may be regulated by including it with other forms of interpersonal cybercrimes such as sending threatening mail or messages or harassment or stalking.

---

3. This has been experienced by the lead author as a cybercrime victim counselor.

What Policing May Be Offered and the Challenges Involved in It

From the above profiling of interpersonal cybercrimes, it may be understood that these can be monitored by three particular ways of policing: state-funded policing or public policing (Jewkes, 2010), corporate policing, and non-governmental policing by not-for-profit voluntary organizations. The latter two have been combined by researchers like Yar (2010) who termed it "private policing." However, for the purpose of this chapter, we would consider the types of policing in these three terms rather than restricting it to two broader terms.

Public policing or state-funded policing in cases of interpersonal crimes may necessarily mean the operation of the criminal justice machinery to prevent the crimes. Public policing in the case of interpersonal cybercrimes involves three stages: reporting by the victim, investigation by the police officers, and prosecution (Walden, 2007). There are two ways of reporting crimes in cases of interpersonal cybercrimes: manually registering crimes with the local police officials by visiting the police offices along with the documentary evidences, and digitally registering the crime through the web-portals provided by the police. While in the first case there are chances that the victim may get instant gratification by knowing whether the complaint has been received properly with cognizance or not by the registering authority, in the case of web-portals, the victim may get initial acknowledgment of the complaint and then may or may not receive further communication depending upon the subject matter of the complaint. However, it needs to be mentioned that even in the case of manually registering the complaint with the police by visiting the police and presenting the evidences, many victims have received disappointing treatment like ridiculing the victim for the type of the harassment he/she is reporting, not paying proper attention to the papers and asking the victim to come back later, etc. This has been the experience of many victims who had contacted not-for-profit organizations like Working to Halt Online Abuse or the Centre for Cyber Victim Counselling after a frustrated effort with the police.

However, the police web-portals have proved extremely beneficial for many to understand the nature of interpersonal crimes. In this context, three national-level police and crime and justice web-portals from the U.S., UK and India may be analyzed: Consider the U.S. Department of Justice Website page link,[4]

---

4. See http://www.justice.gov/criminal/cybercrime/reporting.html.

which deals with computer crimes. In this above-mentioned page, the website provides a guidance regarding the type of crime and the appropriate authorities who can be approached. The types of crimes include computer intrusion (hacking), password trafficking, counterfeiting currency, child pornography or exploitation, child exploitation and Internet fraud matters that have a mail nexus, Internet fraud and spam, etc. The web page also includes Internet harassment even though it is not defined as what may constitute the same. Given the fact that hacking, password trafficking, child pornography or exploitation, and Internet harassment may fall within the category of the interpersonal cybercrimes as per the profiling made above, our interest concentrates on these issues more. It may be seen that this webpage directs the victims or interested persons who are willing to help the victims to approach the FBI local office or the Internet crime complaint centre (IC3).

However, IC3 in its website home page[5] or in its resource page[6] does not provide details about interpersonal cybercrimes. Simultaneously, the FBI in its webpage[7] does not provide any details about types of cybercrimes that can fall within the category of interpersonal crimes. However, it does encourage victims to provide a detailed report. However, for the purpose of this chapter, we searched the Department of Justice website with the key words "domestic abuse" and "interpersonal crimes," and one of the links that came up was to the United State Attorney's office, Northern District of Georgia, which spoke about interstate stalking. This page suggested visiting the home page of the National Domestic Violence Hot Line[8] for more information regarding interpersonal stalking and domestic abuse. This website[9] also provides information about digital abuse and encourages victims to take specific safety tips or contact the hotline telephone numbers for further help.[10]

In India, provincial police departments have their own web-portals which have specific pages devoted for cybercrimes.[11] For example, Bangalore city police had taken the first step towards establishing a cybercrime cell in India, and presently almost all the cities in India have their own cybercrime cells, which devote more time for economic offences. It needs to be mentioned that by cybercrime, predominantly these sites indicate financial crimes including phish-

---

5. See http://www.ic3.gov/default.aspx.
6. See http://www.ic3.gov/preventiontips.aspx.
7. See https://tips.fbi.gov/.
8. See http://www.thehotline.org/.
9. See http://www.thehotline.org/is-this-abuse/abuse-defined/#tab-id-6.
10. See http://www.thehotline.org/help/tech-social-media-safety/.
11. See http://www.cyberpolicebangalore.nic.in/E.security.html.

ing, job scams, bank frauds, etc. Some sites, however, do speak about interpersonal crimes like cyber harassment,[12] but specific types of cybercrimes generally do not find any mention in these sites. However, most of the sites do talk about child pornography.[13] Further many of the police web-portals also provide tips to safeguard potential victims including women and children in the cyberspace. Like the FBI page, these police web-portals also have e-forms to receive complaints. They also provide phone numbers for the victims to get directly connected with police officials. Specifically, many police web-portals have a separate page for crimes against women, and in some cases these pages do include information about cyber stalking or cyberbullying or the creation of fake profiles. Other than police web-portals, the National Commission for Women and the National Commission for Protection of Children also have web-portals dedicated to cybercrimes. These sites also provide phone numbers as well as e-forms to lodge complaints. But similar to the police web-portals, the typology of interpersonal cybercrimes remains extremely restricted in these sites.

In England, Crown Prosecution Services, in their website,[14] provides information about various types of online harassment, where cyber stalking is also included, even though it is mentioned therein that the Protection of Harassment Act is the guiding regulation provision for harassment which includes cyber stalking. The Crown Prosecution Services website also provides contact details to lodge complaints digitally.

A perusal of all the criminal justice machinery websites mentioned above would suggest that none of them give clear guidance about the types of interpersonal cybercrimes, and many of them are silent about vital types such as cyber stalking or creation of fake avatars or revenge pornography. We presume that this fact may be the key factor behind secondary harassment of the victims in the hands of the police and criminal justice machinery, as police themselves may not be aware of trends and types of interpersonal cybercrimes that are emerging rapidly in the modern period. Citron (2014) showed how victims of Internet hate crimes (which necessarily included bullying, trolling and defamatory posts) had been turned back by the police because the police refused to believe that these may constitute penal offences. In our earlier researches (Halder & Jaishankar, 2011b), we have also shown how many women from the U.S., India

---

12. See http://www.cyberpolicebangalore.nic.in/pdf/Cyber%20law%20IPC.pdf. This site provides a generic view of cybercrime and legal provisions and includes some activities like publishing words, gestures, etc., harming women, etc.

13. Ibid.

14. See http://www.cps.gov.uk/legal/s_to_u/stalking_and_harassment/.

and the UK had to face secondary harassment from the police due to the same confusion.

With constant capacity building programs and police training sessions on cybercrimes, especially interpersonal cybercrimes, the scenario is changing as of now, but we argue that the scenario is still not very positive. Public policing may fail due to a victim's reluctance to report the matter to the police due to fear of society or fear of future problems especially, when children are involved. The lead author observed that many women who are in custody battles for their children do not prefer to take the cases of interpersonal cybercrimes to the police, fearing that this may hamper the custody cases. In many urban, semi-urban and rural areas in the U.S., the UK and India, victims are still refused help by the police. One of the major reasons for this is the cross-jurisdictional nature of the offence. In cases when the offender commits the offence from outside the State, the police become literally handicapped due to the absence of proper regulatory treaties and cooperation. Even though the EU convention in 2001 did mention inter-state cooperation in dealing with cybercrimes, as of now, such cooperation has been seen only in cases of cyber-aided terrorism (Halder, 2011).

Even though there are strong regulatory provisions for child porn materials, it has been seen that in many cases, victims of teen revenge porn (which may become part of child porn materials) are also denied help either due to the cross-jurisdictional viral nature of the misdeed or due to the failure to understand the nature of the offence by the police. Our argument can be supported by the cyber stalking statistics presented by WHOA for the year 2013. It may be seen that among 256 cases received by WHOA, 37 percent of the cases were referred earlier to the police by the victims. Being frustrated by police inaction, they decided to contact WHOA.

Organizations like Working to Halt Online Abuse (WHOA)[15] and the Centre for Cyber Victim Counselling (CCVC)[16] engage in private policing of the interpersonal cybercrimes through their online web-portals. Private policing by NGOs may necessarily involve three factors: (i) counseling the victims, (ii) guidance as to what to do next, and (iii) protesting on its own. Once a victim lodges a report with WHOA or CCVC, they are counseled and guided to take precautionary steps. They are also advised on how to approach Internet service providers. CCVC also additionally offers legal guidance on the legal rights of the victims, how to approach the courts directly, etc. On the basis of the

---

15. See http://www.haltabuse.org/.
16. Seehttp://www.cybervictims.org/.

nature of the cases, CCVC also approaches the police as the guiding agency for the victim. In addition, both WHOA and CCVC also monitor Internet contents and sensitive issues independently, and in a case of any offensive content being detected or a sensitive issue being observed, they report the same to the concerned ISPs or the police, or protest the same and create awareness in the form of blogs or research articles.

The best examples would be WHOA's President Jayne Hitchcock's successful attempt to create cyber stalking law in the U.S.,[17] the protest educating people about why the Supreme Court of India should not have scrapped Sec.66A of the Information Technology Act, 2000 (amended in 2008) by the lead author of this chapter, who is also the Managing Director of the CCVC (Halder, 2015), and the creation of "irrational coping theory of cybercrime victimization" by the authors (Halder & Jaishankar, 2015) which proved beneficial in creating awareness among people. It may also be noted that as part of private policing, the authors also reported the still-available private videos of the dancing of Andaman Jarawa women, which were banned by the courts in India. However, due to viral circulation of the same, it was not possible for the police to take down all the videos, and the authors wrote a scholarly article on this issue which was published in the British Journal of Criminology (Halder & Jaishankar, 2014). This research article is now being used to sensitize people as to why such viral videos may be considered "offensive" and how cyber bystanders may contribute in prohibiting further circulation of the same by reporting it to the ISP on each occasion they come across such videos and "flagging" the video.

However, it needs to be noted that private policing cannot and should not take up certain mechanisms that are possible in the public policing system: this may include hacking and tracking. Almost all the domestic laws dealing with cybercrimes, including interpersonal cybercrimes like stalking, impersonation, etc., prohibit infringing the digital privacy of any individual. However, these laws also provide an exemption for the police and criminal justice organizations in such cases. Being so empowered, the police and criminal justice machinery can track the offender, and they can also ask the service provider or search engine to remove the content. It may be important to note that as per the recent data provided by Google, it can be seen that the criminal justice machinery of the U.S., the UK and India were able to detect and notify Google and Facebook of the (number of) contents, respectively, from each country that were removed by Internet companies, subsequently. Notably, the majority of such

---

17. See http://www.haltabuse.org/jayne/index.shtml.

contents involved politically defamatory contents or religious contents. The private policing mechanism gets restricted at this point. However, the private policing by NGOs can still approach the police on behalf of the victim and convince them of the penal nature of the offence. But in such cases, the victim's cooperation and proper authorization are essentially needed. NGOs can also approach the ISPs directly.

It may further be interesting to note that NGOs can apply social reporting mechanisms whereby they may engage volunteers to report offensive content to the ISPs so that the volume of the report is large enough to attract the attention of the concerned ISP. NGOs can also use positive "Google Bombing" (Citron, 2014) mechanisms whereby they may engage volunteers to pull up positive pages about any victim in the search engines and accordingly push the negative pages down to zero viewing rates. This can happen especially when the victim would have created blogs or his/her own websites or has extremely popular social media pages, but all these were submerged due to rapid circulation of sexually explicit videos created to harass him/her, Twitter and Facebook hashtag posts created to defame and harass the victim, personal websites created specifically to harass the victim, etc.

Corporate policing or policing by Internet companies and Internet service providers could be the most effective policing mechanism when it comes to interpersonal cybercrimes. Such types of policing involve reporting the by victim him/herself, or by cyber bystanders, detecting the reported content by the ISP, judging it as per their content policies and removing the same as well as taking punitive action against the content uploader or creator by either banning the perpetrator completely from the concerned site or warning the perpetrator.[18] ISPs, in the case of social media, may also delegate responsibilities of private policing to forum moderators, administrators and forum creators whereby these people can receive the complaints from the forum/group/page/members and may decide to remove the offensive content or block and remove the offending member.[19] These Internet companies and ISPs have their own "cyber army" in the guise of "content moderators" other than their own officers in the legal or technical divisions. The "content moderators," paid on an hourly basis by the ISPs and search engines, work toward removing the offensive contents (Chaudhuri, Chatterjee & Verma, 2014). But when on contract with the ISPs and search engines, the content moderators can neither be approached individually, nor can they step into the shoes of the ISPs or search engines to remove any content they feel offensive.

---

18. See for example, https://www.facebook.com/communitystandards.
19. Ibid.

We feel such types of policing may be most effective because ISPs and Internet companies may know the source of the content, i.e., the originator as well as the I.P. address of the creator of the content. They may apply their company policies to remove the contents on the report directly submitted by the victims or concerned people. Even though such mechanisms may provide a picture that ISPs and search engines can work better and faster than the criminal justice mechanism or more effective than the NGOs, in reality, they themselves restrict such restorative actions due to First Amendment guarantees of freedom of speech and expression,[20] which is the guiding principle of all the Internet companies and ISPs created and hosted in the U.S. They judge each of the reported contents in the context of the First Amendment guarantee, their own policies and in some cases, the local laws of the place of the victim. However, as can be seen from earlier researches, the last factor is given least consideration unless the issue involves national security of the country concerned. In most cases, the ISPs require the victim to bring a government order by way of a formal content removal request from criminal justice machinery, which include court orders as well. Further, another reason for failure of policing of interpersonal crimes by way of corporate policing is the possibility of the creation of multiple accounts from different I.P. addresses by the offender. Due to the huge inflow of data, the ISPs cannot monitor each piece of content and its creator. This loophole encourages the perpetrator to put on an anonymous veil to come back through different channels and continue harassment.

Conclusion

A perusal of the above challenges in policing the cyberspace may suggest that no one group among the three groups may be always successful in policing the Internet for interpersonal cybercrimes. All three groups must be interconnected to offer help and responsibilities in understanding the nature of the offence and the need to provide a therapeutic approach to the problem. Saying this, we emphasize the execution of the laws in therapeutic[20] ways

---

20. Therapeutic jurisprudence focuses our attention on the traditionally under-appreciated area of the law's considerable impact on emotional life and psychological well-being. Its essential premise is a simple one: that the law is a social force that can produce therapeutic or antitherapeutic consequences. The law consists of legal rules, legal procedures, and the roles and behaviors of legal actors, like lawyers and judges. Therapeutic jurisprudence proposes that we use the tools of the behavioural sciences to study the therapeutic and antitherapeutic impact of the law, and that we think creatively about improving the therapeutic

(Wexler, 2003). In our earlier research (Halder & Jaishankar, 2013), we proposed the application of therapeutic jurisprudence for *"victim-aided revenge porn cases."* We propose to expand the application of therapeutic jurisprudence by the criminal justice machinery to all the above-mentioned interpersonal cybercrimes. As such, when in the case of a public policing system, the courts, instead of assigning retributive punishments alone, may also order the offender to do some correctional deeds including removing the offensive contents, erasing the contents from his own device and contacting each and every site to take down the content if it had gone viral. Once the lawmakers start making laws with punishment sections inclusive of correctional activities, the goal of therapeutic jurisprudence as well as restorative justice principles may be achieved.

Similarly, NGOs must also concentrate on sensitizing people about detrimental effects of misuse of the Internet for gratification of self-esteem, especially in cases of broken relationships. Also, profit-making corporate houses may consider taking steps through their human resource divisions to help the victims of interpersonal cybercrimes in cases where they are employees of the said companies. Perpetrators may create offensive contents describing or tagging the victim along with the name of the workplace. The corporate houses or companies, after conducting an internal enquiry with the victim to know the facts, instead of taking action against the victim, may take steps to contact the police, the courts, as well as the ISPs and search engines for safeguarding their reputation as well as that of the victim. The ISPs and search engines must also cooperate with the victims in such cases. It needs to be remembered that unless the ISPs are becoming more responsive towards the victim's genuine pleas, incidences of irrational coping (Halder & Jaishankar, 2015b) tactics may increase, which in turn may make the situation extremely difficult for policing both by public policing mechanisms as well as private and corporate policing mechanisms.

References

Axelrod, E. M. (2009). *Violence Goes to the Internet: Avoiding the Snare of the Net*. Springfield, Illinois: Charles C Thomas Publisher, Ltd.

Baer, M. (2010). CS and the Internet landscape we have constructed. *Virginia Journal of Law & Technology, 15*, 153–172.

---

functioning of the law without violating other important values, such as Gault-like due process (Wexler, 2003, p.7).

Baxter, A. (June 2014). Improving responses to cybervictimisation in South Australia. Retrieved on 15th March 2015 from http://www.victimsa.org/files/cybercrime-report-2014.pdf.

Bocij, P., & McFarlane, L. (2002). Online harassment: towards a definition of cyberstalking. *Prison Service Journal*, 139, 31–38.

Brenner, S. W. (2002). Organized Cybercrime? How cyberspace may affect the structure of criminal relationships. *North Carolina Journal of Law & Technology*, 4(1), 1–50.

Brenner, S. W. (2004). Cybercrime Metrics: Old Wine, New Bottles?. *Virginia Journal of Law & Technology*, 9(13), 1–52.

Chadwick, A., & May, C. (April 2003). Interaction between States and Citizens in the Age of the Internet: "e-Government" in the United States, Britain, and the European Union. *Governance: An International Journal of Policy, Administration, and Institutions*, 16(2), 271–300.

Chang, L. Y. C. (2013). Formal and informal modalities for policing cybercrime across the Taiwan Strait. *Policing and Society: An International Journal of Research and Policy*, 23(4), 540–555.

Chaudhuri, P., Chatterjee, A., & Verma, V. (December 7, 2014). Guardians of the Internet. *The Telegraph*. Retrieved on 20th March 2015 from http://www.telegraphindia.com/1141207/jsp/7days/story_2412.jsp.

Citron, D. K. (2009). Law's Expressive Value in Combating Cyber Gender Harassment. *Michigan Law Review*, 108, 373–415.

Citron, D. K. (2014). *Hate Crimes in Cyberspace*. Cambridge, Massachusetts: Harvard University Press.

Ellison, L., & Akdeniz, Y. (1998). Cyber-stalking: the Regulation of Harassment on the Internet. *Criminal Law Review*, December Special Edition: Crime, Criminal Justice and the Internet, 29–48.

Halder, D. (2011). Information Technology Act and Cyber Terrorism: A Critical Review. In P. Madhava Soma Sundaram, & S. Umarhathab, (Eds.), (2011). *Cyber Crime and Digital Disorder* (pp. 75–90). Tirunelveli, India: Publication Division, Manonmaniam Sundaranar University.

Halder, D. (2013). Examining the scope of Indecent Representation of Women (Prevention) Act, 1986, in the light of Cyber Victimization of Women in India. *National Law School Journal*, 11, 188–218.

Halder, D. (2015). 66A on the judgement day. 24th March, 2015. Retrieved on 25th March 2015 from http://debaraticyberspace.blogspot.in/2015/03/66a-on-judgement-day.html.

Halder, D., & Jaishankar, K. (2009) Cyber Socializing and Victimization of Women. *Temida—The journal on victimization, human rights and gender*, September 2009, 12(3), 5–26.

Halder D., & Jaishankar, K. (2011a). *Cyber crime and the Victimization of Women: Laws, Rights, and Regulations.* Hershey, PA, USA.

Halder D., & Jaishankar, K. (2011b). Cyber Gender Harassment and Secondary Victimization: A Comparative Analysis of US, UK and India. *Victims and Offenders, 6*(4), 386–398.

Halder, D., & Jaishankar, K. (2013). Revenge Porn by Teens in the United States and India: A Socio-legal Analysis. *International Annals of Criminology, 51*(1-2), 85–111.

Halder D., & Jaishankar, K. (2014). Online Victimization of Andaman Jarawa Tribal Women: An Analysis of the 'Human Safari' YouTube Videos (2012) and its Effects. *British Journal of Criminology, 54*(4), 673–688.

Halder, D., & Jaishankar, K. (2015a). *Harassment via WhatsApp in Urban and Rural India: A Baseline Survey Report (2015).* Tirunelveli, India: Centre for Cyber Victim Counselling. Retrieved on 15th March 2015 from http://cybervictims.org/CCVCresearchreport2015.pdf.

Halder, D., & Jaishankar, K. (2015b). Irrational Coping Theory and Positive Criminology: A Frame Work to Protect Victims of Cyber Crime. In N. Ronel and D. Segev (Eds.), *Positive Criminology* (pp. 276–291). Abingdon, Oxon: Routledge.

Jaishankar, K. (2009). *Cyber Bullying: Profile and Policy Guidelines.* Tirunelveli: Department of Criminology and Criminal Justice, Manonmaniam Sundaranar University.

Jewkes, Y. (2010). Public Policing and Internet Crime. In Y. Jewkes & M. Yar (Eds.), *Handbook of Internet Crime* (pp. 525–545). Cullumpton, UK: Willan Publishing.

Ngo, F. T., & Paternoster, R. (2011). Cybercrime Victimization: An examination of Individual and Situational level factors. *International Journal of Cyber Criminology, 5*(1), 773–793.

Patchin, J. W., and Hinduja, S. (2006). Bullies move beyond the schoolyard: A preliminary look at cyberbullying. *Youth Violence and Juvenile Justice, 4*(2), 148–169.

Roberts, L. (2008a). *Cyber-victimisation in Australia: Extent, impact on individuals and responses.* TILES Briefing Paper No. 6. Retrieved on 16th March 2015 from http://www.utas.edu.au/__data/assets/pdf_file/0004/293773/Briefing_Paper_No_6.pdf.

Roberts, L. (January, 2008). Jurisdictional and definitional concerns with computer-mediated interpersonal crimes: An Analysis on Cyber Stalking. *International Journal of Cyber Criminology, 2*(1), 271–285. Retrieved on 15th March 2015 from http://www.cybercrimejournal.com/lynnerobertsijccjan2008.pdf.

Roberts, L. D. (2009). Cyber-Victimization. In R. Luppicini & R. Adell (Eds.), *Handbook of Research on Technoethics* (pp. 575–592). Hershey, PA, USA: IGI Global.

Shariff, S., & Hoff, D. L. (2007). Cyber bullying: Clarifying Legal Boundaries for School Supervision in Cyberspace. *International Journal of Cyber Criminology,* 1(1), 76–118.

Walden, I. (2007). *Computer Crimes and Digital Investigations.* Oxford: Oxford University Press.

Wall, D. S. (2001). Cyber crimes and the Internet. In D. Wall (Ed.) Crime and the internet (pp. 1–17). London: Routledge.

Wexler, D. B. (2003). Introduction: Therapeutic Jurisprudence as a Theoretical Foundation for These New Judicial Approaches. In: B. J. Winick & D. B. Wexler (Eds.), *Judging in a Therapeutic Key: Therapeutic Jurisprudence and the Courts* (p. 7). Durham, North Carolina: Carolina Academic Press.

Williams, M. L., Edwards, A., Housley, W., Burnap, P., Rana, O., Avis, N., Morgan, J., & Sloan, L. (2013). Policing Cyber-Neighbourhoods: Tension Monitoring and Social Media Networks. *Policing and Society: An International Journal of Research and Policy,* 23 (4), 461–481.

Yar, M. (2005). The Novelty of 'Cybercrime': An Assessment in Light of Routine Activity Theory. *European Journal of Criminology,* 2(4), 407–427.

Yar, M. (2010). The Private Policing of Internet Crime. In Y. Jewkes & M. Yar (Eds.), *Handbook of Internet Crime* (pp. 546–561). Cullumpton, UK: Willan Publishing.

Yip, M., Webber, C., & Shadbolt, N. (2013). Trust among cybercriminals? Carding forums, uncertainty and implications for policing. *Policing and Society: An International Journal of Research and Policy,* 23(4), 516–539.

Chapter Nine

Legislative Reactions

Thaddeus Hoffmeister

Introduction

Historically, harassment between intimate partners required physical or telephonic interaction. As a result, harassers were constrained by the volume of their voice or the physical proximity of the victim. This is no longer true today as harassment, in all forms, increasingly occurs online. According to a recent study by the Pew Research Center, 41 percent of adult Internet users have experienced some form of online harassment (Drake, 2014).

With the Internet, the harasser never has to leave his house to reach the victim. In fact, the harasser doesn't have to even speak to or interact with the victim directly. He can conduct the harassment entirely online and if he so desires can involve third parties who may or may not know that they are part of a criminal enterprise. Also, in the Digital Age, the harassment does not necessarily stop because the victim moves away. In many instances, the harasser is able to easily track down the victim through her digital footprint and continue the harassment regardless of where the victim lives (Hoffmeister, 2012).

Many believe that this new method of harassment is easier to commit and more difficult to prevent than traditional harassment (Lipton, 2011). More importantly, cyber or online harassment has in certain instances led to lethal consequences for former intimate partners, which, in turn, has led some to call for newer and tougher laws on cyber harassment. This chapter will examine those proposals along with a number of statutes and criminal cases that involve online harassment between intimate partners. The focus here will be online activities that occur on social media, which has become a popular tool by which to abuse or harass a current or former intimate partner.

Due to the scope of this book and space limitations, this chapter will not examine every law or legislative response by the state and federal government to combat online harassment. Rather, this chapter will look at four broad areas: (1) impersonation; (2) threats; (3) stalking; and (4) revenge porn. Online impersonation and revenge porn will receive the most attention in this chapter because these laws are new and unique to the Internet, i.e., they lack any real offline counterpart.

Impersonation

Unlike traditional identity theft, online impersonation lacks an economic component. Instead, the defendant impersonates the victim for a non-economic reason such as to harass. According to noted cyberlaw expert Susan Brenner, most jurisdictions classify identity theft in terms of using another person's identity for financial gain (Brenner, 2010).

Online impersonations arise in a variety of different settings but generally take one of two forms. The first involves the impersonator pretending to be someone else in order to interact with or establish a relationship with one specific person who may or may not be a "victim" depending on how that term is defined. In this first category, the impersonator seeks to interact with a specific person but does not believe it will be possible unless he creates a false online persona.

This situation is apparently what occurred with Manti Te'o, the All-American linebacker from Notre Dame who was the runner-up for the Heisman Trophy in 2012 (Brady & George, 2013). Te'o claimed that he was duped into believing that he had an online relationship with a Stanford undergraduate student named Lennay Kekua. An acquaintance of Te'o's, Ronaiah Tuiasosopo, created the fictitious Lennay Kekua by using pictures of a former female high school classmate and setting up a bogus social media profile. Tuiasosopo, while masquerading as Lennay Kekua, maintained a dating relationship with Te'o for a number of months entirely through social media and the telephone. It is not entirely clear why Tuiasosopo created Lennay Kekua, but it appears he did so in order to interact with Te'o online.

The second method of impersonation involves the impersonator pretending to be someone else in order to interact with the general public. The victim in this category can be both the general public and the person impersonated. This chapter will primarily focus on this second type of online impersonation which is the one most likely to arise with respect to intimate partner abuse. By impersonating a former partner and interacting with others online, the impersonator can harass, embarrass, or harm the victim. The injury from online impersonation can range from loss of employment or friendship to physical harm carried out by a third party.

In Philadelphia, a woman created a fake Facebook page in the name of her ex-boyfriend, a narcotics police officer. While impersonating him on Facebook she wrote,

I'm a sick piece of scum with a gun

and

I'm an undercover narcotics detective that gets high every day (Bahr, 2012).

Fortunately for the police officer, this fictitious Facebook page was quickly discovered, and the woman was prosecuted and sentenced to a diversion program. It is not difficult to see, however, the potential harm that these bogus Facebook posts could have caused the police officer.

In other instances, the online impersonation has been even more malicious. Consider the case of *U.S. v. Sayer* where the criminal defendant used social media and online websites to harass his ex-girlfriend (United States v. Sayer, 2012). As will be discussed in greater detail later in this chapter, the actions of Sayer constituted not only online impersonation but also revenge porn.

In *Sayer*, the criminal defendant posted ads on Craiglist's *Casual Encounters* (section on Craigslist for meeting other people) that showed his ex-girlfriend in lingerie (prior to the break-up Sayer had taken consensual photos of his ex-girlfriend). The ad encouraged men to visit the victim at her home and included a list of sex acts that she would perform when the men arrived. As a result of the ad, strange men would routinely appear at the ex-girlfriend's house looking for sexual encounters.

In order to prevent random strangers from showing up at her house, the ex-girlfriend moved to Louisiana. However, different men again started to appear at her new home. Like before, these men claimed that they had met her online. Shortly thereafter, the ex-girlfriend discovered a sexually explicit video of her on several adult pornography sites. As with the earlier pictures, she had consented to the video prior to her break-up with Sayer. The video included the ex-girlfriend's name as well as her home address. Ultimately, Sayer was caught and successfully prosecuted.

To combat the increase in online impersonations, especially between former partners, a few states have passed laws specifically targeting online impersonators. While all states and the federal government have laws combating identity theft and harassment, only a few states have specific laws that go after online impersonators. California is one of the states that does have a law against online impersonation.

The California law (Penal Code Section 528.5) reads as follows:

a) Notwithstanding any other provision of law, any person who knowingly and without consent credibly impersonates another actual person through or on an Internet Web site or by other electronic means for purposes of harming, intimidating, threatening, or defrauding another person is guilty of a public offense punishable pursuant to subdivision (d).

(b) For purposes of this section, an impersonation is credible if another person would reasonably believe, or did reasonably believe, that the defendant was or is the person who was impersonated.

(c) For purposes of this section, "electronic means" shall include opening an e-mail account or an account or profile on a social networking Internet Web site in another person's name.

(d) A violation of subdivision (a) is punishable by a fine not exceeding one thousand dollars ($1,000), or by imprisonment in a county jail not exceeding one year, or by both that fine and imprisonment.

(e) In addition to any other civil remedy available, a person who suffers damage or loss by reason of a violation of subdivision (a) may bring a civil action against the violator for compensatory damages and injunctive relief or other equitable relief pursuant to paragraphs (1), (2), (4), and (5) of subdivision (e) and subdivision (g) of Section 502.

(f) This section shall not preclude prosecution under any other law. (Cal. Pen. Code, 2014).

One of the big questions with online impersonation laws is defining the "harm" caused by the impersonator. This is because not all online impersonations are done with the intent to cause harm. In the case of Manti Te'o, it does not appear that Ronaiah Tuiasosopo was attempting to hurt or injure Te'o or the general public when he created Lennay Kekua. Rather, Tuiasosopo merely wanted to have an online relationship or connection with Te'o.

Also, some online impersonations are done for purposes of satire or to evoke humor. For example, one online impersonator has taken on the persona of the Queen of England. This person uses the Twitter account (handle) "@Queen_UK" and sends out tweets such as:

Take the day off, people. If anyone asks, tell them the Queen said it was OK

and

It's Gin O'Clock, kids. Down Tools. (Windsor, 2014)

In defining "harm," the California statute uses terms such as "intimidating, threatening or defrauding." In applying this language to real life scenarios some believe that the harm must be more than being a "jerk." Others see it differently and believe that individuals should be prosecuted anytime they pretend to be someone else online and manifest bad intentions. Obviously, applying a lower standard to what constitutes harm will expose many more online impersonators to potential prosecution.

The reason for the varying approaches to defining harm is primarily due to two factors (Cal. Pen. Code, 2014) (Cal. Pen. Code, 2014). First, there are few cases on this particular subject matter so the law is still somewhat unsettled. Second, some jurisdictions classify this crime as a felony, e.g., Texas (Tex. Penal Code, 2013), while others view it as misdemeanor, e.g., California (Cal. Pen. Code, 2014). If charged as a felony, it is far more likely that significant harm has occurred or was intended.

The growing trend of individuals impersonating others on the Internet, especially via social media, has raised an interesting debate about how to address this problem. On one side are individuals who want to expand impersonation laws to cover fictitious people. For example, to be prosecuted under the California law one must impersonate an *actual person*. Thus, the statute could apply to Sayer who impersonated his ex-girlfriend but not to Tuiasosopo who pretended to be the fictitious Lennay Kekua. Expanding the statute would definitely catch more impersonators; however, it raises significant constitutional concerns, especially with the respect to First Amendment rights.

On the other side of the debate are individuals who question whether this activity should even be criminalized. They point to telephone impersonators and wonder why social media impersonators should be treated any differently. To counter this argument, proponents of criminalization assert that social media is unlike any other form of communication past or present; therefore, newer and tougher laws are needed. Those in favor of criminalization also point to the fact that that impersonation via social media can occur over a longer period of time and be more difficult to stop. In *Sayer*, the criminal defendant was able to use social media to repeatedly re-victimize his ex-girlfriend even when she moved out of state.

Another point of emphasis is anonymity. Those who support criminal laws targeting online impersonators argue that it is too easy to be anonymous on social media which in turn emboldens criminal defendants to victimize others. To date neither social media providers nor the government has established a cost-effective method to verify social media users. Furthermore, the Supreme Court has determined that individuals have a First Amendment right to remain anonymous (McIntyre v. Ohio Elections Comm'n, 1995).

Assuming that society does want to criminalize online impersonations, should other states emulate California and enact similar laws? Many believe that the California statute serves as the best approach because it affords both a civil and criminal remedy. Furthermore, the California law does not elevate online impersonation, which in many instances can be quite harmless, to a felony. With the growing trend of people impersonating others online, it is highly likely that in the near future more jurisdictions will enact statutes similar to California's that target online impersonators.

Threats

Another form of online harassment involves issuing threats. With respect to intimate partners, threats are used for intimidation and control (Stark, 2013). In order to prosecute someone for this crime, the threat has to go beyond merely being objectionable or offensive. The threat must communicate a serious expression of intent to commit an act of unlawful violence to a particular individual or group of individuals (Watts v. United States, 1969).

Over the past ten years, the method of communicating a threat has evolved from word of mouth to voicemails to texts to social media. Most states and the federal government have laws to address threats whether made online or offline. At the federal level, the Interstate Communications Act (ICA) makes it unlawful to "*transmit[] in interstate or foreign commerce any communication containing any threat to kidnap any person or any threat to injure the person of another*" (18 U.S.C. §875(c)). One of the limitations of the ICA is that it generally only targets overt threats to the victim not indirect threats.

To be convicted of violating the ICA, the prosecution must establish that the defendant (1) knowingly made a communication in interstate commerce that (2) a reasonable observer would construe as a true threat to another (United States v. Wheeler, 2013). The first prong of this statute has generally been a non-issue, at least with respect to cyber threats, since most if not all Internet traffic is deemed interstate commerce. However, issues have arisen with respect to the second prong. The following case study illustrates one of the challenges with proving beyond a reasonable doubt that a defendant communicated a threat to a current or former intimate partner online.

Case Study 9.1

In *U.S. v. Elonis*, the federal government charged Anthony Elonis in a five-count indictment with transmitting interstate commerce communications containing threats to injure another person, in violation of the ICA (United States v. Elonis, 2011). In the *Elonis* case, the interstate communications involved posts to Facebook where he threatened his wife, a former employer and the community as a whole. Here is a sample of what he posted:

> *That's it, I've had about enough*
> *I'm checking out and making a name for myself*
> *Enough elementary schools in a ten mile radius to initiate the most heinous school shooting ever imagined*
> *And hell hath no fury like a crazy man in a Kindergarten class*
> *The only question is ... which one?*
> ....
>
> *Fold up your PFA* [Protection from Abuse Order] *and put it in your pocket[.] Is it thick enough to stop a bullet?* [this last threat was directed to Elonis' wife].
> (United States v. Elonis, 2011)

Prior to trial, Elonis filed a motion to dismiss the charges against him arguing that his Facebook posts did not constitute a true threat. Furthermore, Elonis claimed that his prosecution violated the First Amendment because his posts contained nothing more than spontaneous and emotional language expressing frustration albeit in a crude manner (United States v. Elonis, 2011).

The court disagreed with Elonis and denied his motion. The court found that the issue of whether the Facebook posts were true threats was a question of fact and thus had to be decided by a jury. The case then proceeded to trial where the defendant testified that he never meant what he posted and that the words were taken from rap lyrics. Despite his testimony, the jury convicted Elonis on 4 of the 5 counts brought against him. Subsequent to his conviction, Elonis appealed his case to the U.S. Supreme Court (United States v. Elonis, 2011).

The question before the Supreme Court was what proof must the government put forth when prosecuting someone for making a threat. According to Elonis, the government had to demonstrate that he had the subjective intent to carry out his threats. This subjective intent standard is the law in a few jurisdictions (Ninth Circuit and the supreme courts of Massachusetts, Rhode Island, and Vermont). In contrast, the government argued that the lower court was correct and that it only has to show that a reasonable person would regard Elonis' Facebook posts as threatening. The reasonable person standard is the prevailing view in most jurisdictions. In May 2015, the Supreme Court returned with a reversal decision for the *Elonis* case, stating that the general intent standard applied to the case was insufficient.

Since the Supreme Court sided with Elonis and required the government to prove the defendant's subjective intent, it will now become more challenging to both prevent abuse between intimate partners and to safeguard victims of domestic violence. This is because, with a heightened standard, it will be more difficult to not only prosecute individuals for issuing threats, but also for victims to obtain orders of protection. Before the ruling was released, the Domestic Violence Legal Empowerment and Appeals Project, in an Amicus Curiae (friend of the court) brief filed in *Elonis v. U.S.*, stated that:

> [i]mposing a constitutional requirement of a subjective intent to threaten in criminal cases could have far-reaching and deleterious effects on civil protection orders, which are critical to deterring and limiting recurring domestic violence. Most civil protection order cases involve conduct that is also criminal, and many states require proof of a "crime" to obtain a civil protection order. Despite being civil orders designed to protect, not to punish, these state law systems inevitably will be required to impose new barriers to orders of protection if petitioner's view of the First Amendment prevails, frustrating state efforts to protect at—risk domestic violence victims. (Brief in Support of Respondent, 2014)

This organization was predicting the long-term outcome of a ruling supportive of Elonis, so now time will tell the result of the Supreme Court decision.

Stalking

The third crime to be examined in this chapter is online stalking, which, when done between intimate partners, is a form of domestic violence. "Cyber stalking" or "online stalking" has been defined as using electronic communication to repeatedly harass another (Goodno, 2007). The traditional difference between threatening and stalking is that the latter generally targets conduct and therefore requires a pattern in order to prosecute while the former only requires one threat to prosecute successfully (Cal. Penal Code §§ 422, 646.9).

The term "Facebook Stalker" has garnered a sort of benign humorous connotation in popular culture (Dubow, 2007). However, online stalking is a growing problem, and individuals have been successfully prosecuted for using electronic means to include social media to repeatedly stalk or contact others. Like with issuing threats, cyber stalkers attempt to exert control over victims by placing them in fear through online monitoring (Dubow, 2007). The harm caused by cyber stalking ranges from fear to depression to post-traumatic stress disorder (Dubow, 2007).

Examples of using the Internet to stalk another include a case from the Washington, D.C. area where a fourteen-year-old girl posed as a boy and started a relationship with another local girl (White, 2010). After the victim's father discovered the relationship, he prohibited the fourteen-year-old girl from having any future contact with his daughter. However, the young girl continued to contact the victim via social media going so far as to create bogus Facebook profiles and pretending to be different boys. Eventually, the police were called, and the young girl was charged with stalking.

The federal government and all states have some type of stalking statute, but not all states have laws specifically targeting cyber stalking (Brenner, 2012). This is not to say, however, that cyber stalking goes unpunished. In most instances, cyber stalkers, like traditional stalkers, can be prosecuted under a number of different criminal statutes.

Massachusetts is one state that has a law specifically addressing cyber stalking. The Massachusetts statute reads as follows:

> [w]illfully and maliciously engaging in conduct that seriously alarms or annoys a specific person and would cause reasonable person to suffer substantial emotional distress and makes a threat with the intent to place person in fear of death or bodily injury. Such conduct, acts or threats include, but are not limited to, conduct, acts or threats conducted by mail or by use of a telephonic or telecommunication device including, but not limited to, electronic mail, Internet communications and facsimile communications. Stalking is a felony that is punishable by imprisonment in the state prison for up to five years or by a fine of not more than $1000, or imprisonment in the house of correction for not more than two and one-half years or both. (Mass. Gen. Laws Ann. 265 §43 (West 2014))

The cyber stalking law on the national level is the Federal Interstate Stalking Punishment and Prevention Act (FISPPA). As originally written, FISPPA prohibited a person, who had crossed state lines, from using the mail or commerce to put another in reasonable fear of death or serious injury. In 2000, the jurisdictional hook of the statute was changed from "travel across a State line" to "travel[] in interstate commerce." This modification turned FISPPA into a statute that targeted both traditional and online stalking. The statute was again expanded in 2006 to criminalize causing "substantial emotional distress" to another person using an "interactive computer service" (18 U.S.C. §2261(1)–(2) (2006)). FISPPA now reads as follows:

Whoever ... with the intent ... to kill, injure, harass, or place under surveillance with the intent to kill, injure, harass, or intimidate, or cause substantial emotional distress to a person in another State or tribal jurisdiction or within the special maritime and territorial jurisdiction of the United States ... uses the mail, any interactive computer service, or any facility of interstate or foreign commerce to engage in a course of conduct that causes substantial emotional distress to that person or places that person in reasonable fear of death of, or serious bodily injury to [that person, a member of the immediate family ... or a spouse or intimate partner of that person] ... shall be punished.... (18 U.S.C. §2261(1)–(2) (2006))

Revenge Porn

Revenge porn is the final crime to be examined. Generally speaking, revenge porn involves the sharing, without consent, of another's private sexual images. These images are taken by either the victim or a former intimate partner and then shared through electronic means with others. These images may or may not include identifying personal information about the victim to include full name and social media profiles. A study completed by McAfee reported that about 10 percent of ex-partners have threatened to reveal risqué photos of their former partner online. Of that 10 percent, approximately 60 percent carried out their threats (Smith, 2013).

Victims of revenge porn suffer shame, embarrassment, and fear. In addition, some victims have lost friendships and employment opportunities because of the images posted about them on the Internet. The following case study involving Holly Jacobs offers a real-world example of the type of harm suffered by revenge porn victims and the challenges in preventing revenge porn from occurring.

Case Study 9.2

On January 1, 2009, Holly Jacobs received a frantic call from a friend who informed her that she needed to look at her Facebook profile because it had a nude photo of her (Roy, 2013). By the time Jacobs was able to get online, the photo was gone. Jacobs suspected that her Facebook page had been hacked by a former long-distance boyfriend with whom she had previously swapped sexual photos and videos (Miller, 2014). He denied any involvement and claimed that his Facebook page had also been hacked (Miller, 2014). From that point on, Jacobs made it a habit to regularly Google herself (Roy, 2013).

Several months after the Facebook incident, Jacobs discovered a large number of nude photos of herself on the website of amihotornotnude.com. Accompanied with the photos was Jacobs' full name (Roy, 2013). Upon first seeing the images, Jacobs said her stomach dropped and she felt ill.

In 2011, nude images of Jacobs went viral and were on 200 websites within three days (White, 2013). These photos had her full name, email address and a screenshot of her Facebook profile. Nude photos of Jacobs were also sent via email to her co-workers and supervisor at Florida International University, which subsequently caused her to quit her job.

Jacobs did everything possible to both disassociate herself from the images and to get them removed from the Internet. In one year, she switched her address eight times. She also legally changed her name from Holli Thometz to Holly Jacobs. However, these preventive steps did not stop random strangers from reaching out and informing her that "they saw the picture and they loved it, and they used it for their own personal pleasure" (White, 2013).

To get the images removed from the Internet, Jacobs hired both an attorney and an Internet specialist. In addition, she regularly filed Digital Millenium Copyright Act (DMCA) takedown requests with sites that hosted the images. However, as quickly as she was able to get the images removed from one website, they would appear on another. Jacobs also tried to counter the nude images by placing positive information about herself on the Internet (Roy, 2013). Her hope was that when someone researched her online they would find more than just the nude images.

Jacobs' pleas to the police for assistance were initially rebuffed as she was repeatedly told that since she was over 18 and the photos were consensually taken there was nothing they could do. Eventually, Jacobs's ex-boyfriend was criminally charged with stalking, harassment, and unlawful publication. This marked one of the few times that a victim has actually filed a criminal charge against a former intimate partner for revenge porn (Roy, 2013). Unfortunately for Jacobs, the prosecution ultimately dropped the charges because of a lack of evidence (Miller, 2013).

Jacobs has also filed a civil lawsuit, which is still pending, against her former boyfriend (Corbin, 2013). In the lawsuit, Jacobs alleges that her ex-boyfriend through his distribution of videos and photos invaded her privacy, publicly disclosed private facts, and caused intentional infliction of emotional distress. Jacobs has also included the websites and servers who host her nude images in the lawsuit.

In 2012, prior to filing the lawsuit, Jacobs decided that rather than hide in the shadows she would go public and share her experience with others. This in turn led her to create her own website entitled endrevengeporn.com which provides support and advocacy for victims of revenge porn (Roy, 2013). She also formed the organization Cyber Civil Rights Initiative (CCRI). Currently, Jacobs, who has gone on to earn her Ph.D., spends a large portion of her time publicly advocating on behalf of revenge porn victims and urging for the passage of tougher criminal penalties against those who disseminate revenge porn. In deciding to come forward and share her story, Jacobs stated,

> [e]verybody is going to see me naked, and everybody's going to see me do things I never wanted anybody to see except the person I was with. But if it's in the name of the cause and to change the laws about this, then I'm happy to do it. We're all naked underneath our clothes. (Roy, 2013)

In most instances, the revenge porn victim is a young woman like Holly Jacobs, but this is not always the case; sometimes the victims of revenge porn are men. In Cincinnati, Ohio a middle-aged male doctor began an affair with one of his married middle-aged female patients (Perry, 2013). During the relationship, the doctor sent the patient lewd videos and pictures of himself. The patient eventually ended the affair and reported the doctor to the State Medical Board. This ultimately led the doctor to surrender his medical license. The patient then alleges that the doctor called her place of employment and had her terminated.

Shortly after her termination, the patient posted the lewd videos and photos of the doctor on Facebook and YouTube. The information was taken down by the patient but not before the doctor and others learned about them. The doctor then brought legal action against the patient for invasion of privacy and to prevent her from ever posting the videos and photos again online. The patient has also brought her own legal action against the doctor claiming that he used his status to take advantage of her.

Other examples of men as victims of revenge porn include two recent high-profile cases. In the first instance, the Chief of Staff to a Republican Congressman resigned after a woman with whom he had a prior relationship tweeted a picture of the staffer's genitalia to his boss's account (Valenti, 2014). In the second instance, a married conservative pundit was placed on leave from his professorship at the Naval War College after a picture of his genitalia was posted on Twitter by his online paramour who later apologized for her actions (Crocker, 2014).

At present, thirteen states have criminal laws directly targeting revenge porn. Of these thirteen, most treat revenge porn as a misdemeanor but some like Arizona categorize it as a felony (Ariz. Rev. Stat. § 13-1425, 2014). Also, some revenge porn laws require the criminal defendant upon conviction to register as a sex offender.

Of the states that don't have specific laws on revenge porn, many target the activity through other criminal statutes such as harassment, extortion, and stalking. Also, some states are in the process of and/or considering enacting their own revenge porn laws. For example, state legislatures in Hawaii, Wisconsin, Maryland, and New York have introduced revenge porn specific legislation in their respective states (Brill, 2014).

California is one of the thirteen states that have passed a law directly targeting revenge porn. A brief review of the California statute will illustrate some of the challenges with creating and enforcing such laws. At the outset it should be noted that the California law as first passed did not include "selfies." The law has since been amended to include selfies. The law now reads as follows:

> (4) (A) Any person who intentionally distributes the image of the intimate body part or parts of another identifiable person, or an image of the person depicted engaged in an act of sexual intercourse, sodomy, oral copulation, sexual penetration, or an image of masturbation by the person depicted or in which the person depicted participates, under circumstances in which the persons agree or understand that the image shall remain private, the person distributing the image knows or should know that distribution of the image will cause serious emotional distress, and the person depicted suffers that distress.
>
> (B) A person intentionally distributes an image described in subparagraph (A) when he or she personally distributes the image, or arranges, specifically requests, or intentionally causes another person to distribute that image.
>
> (C) As used in this paragraph, "intimate body part" means any portion of the genitals, the anus, and in the case of a female, also includes any portion of the breasts below the top of the areola, that is either uncovered or clearly visible through clothing. (Cal. Pen. Code §647, 2014)

As written, the California law does not apply to redistributors, only the person who makes the initial distribution or posting. Also, the law is inapplicable to instances where the sexual images were obtained through hacking. In addition, the law only applies to "circumstances in which the persons agree or understand that the image shall remain private."

To be successfully convicted under the California law, the government must prove that the victim suffered serious emotional distress. This generally requires the victim to testify, which is not always a straightforward proposition.

Of all the laws targeting online harassment, revenge porn has come under the greatest amount of criticism. This is due to a variety of reasons. First, some believe that the government should not be involved in the activities of two consenting adults. They see revenge porn, like defamation and invasion of privacy, as a civil matter not a criminal one. Thus, they argue that the recourse for a revenge porn victim, like someone who has been defamed or had their privacy invaded, is to bring a civil action and sue, similar to what the doctor did in Cincinnati.

The proponents of criminalization argue that civil lawsuits don't work because many of the criminal defendants are judgment-proof, i.e., they don't have the economic resources to pay money damages. They also point to the time and expense associated with bringing a civil lawsuit.

Another criticism against criminalization is that the injuries suffered by the victims are self-inflicted. These opponents claim that, unlike all other forms of harassment, victims of revenge porn are not true "victims" because they either photographed or recorded themselves or willingly allowed it to happen. Opponents argue that the real problem with revenge porn lies with the victims themselves and thus rather than punish those who reveal or distribute the information more effort should be made at educating people about the long-term consequences of allowing or sending risqué images of themselves online.

In contrast, revenge porn law proponents claim that this line of thinking blames the victim for being a victim and ignores today's new reality in which people in relationships regularly exchange risqué photos. They also point to the fact that sexting has become quite common among both Digital Immigrants and Digital Natives. In a recent Pew study, 20 percent of smartphone users reported receiving a nude photograph (McKalin, 2014).

Revenge porn law opponents also argue that these laws are unnecessary because victims have other remedies available to them to include Digital Millennium Copyright Act (DMCA) takedown notices. For example, if the victim finds a risqué photo of herself online that she took, she can inform the hosting site that pursuant to the DMCA it is violating her copyright by displaying the image.

Of course, this remedy only works if the victim took the image. Plus, it does not stop the image from showing up on another site. Thus, the victim ends up spending a significant amount of her time, like Holly Jacobs, tracking down the image wherever it might pop up. Also, if the host site is located outside of the United States, it might not be as concerned about violating the DMCA.

The strongest argument against criminalizing revenge porn concerns the First Amendment. In a nutshell, opponents claim that revenge porn laws criminalize the publication of speech in the form of images. First Amendment advocates point out that we don't criminalize gossip or other truthful but embarrassing information about people that is revealed in public. Thus, they wonder why should embarrassing photos be treated differently?

Another concern with respect to the First Amendment centers on the unintended consequences of criminalization. For example, some wonder whether a person could be criminally charged for sharing or republishing images of nude celebrities that have been leaked online. Others wonder if a person could be charged for sharing an image of a woman breastfeeding or the pyramid stacking of the half-naked prisoners at Abu Ghraib.

Proponents of criminalization say that this parade of horribles would not occur so long as the law targeting revenge porn is narrowly tailored. For example, they point to the guidance put out by the ACLU which has a long track record of defending First Amendment rights. According to the ACLU, a revenge porn law can pass constitutional scrutiny if

> "[i]t ... designate[s] that the perpetrator had malicious intent, that his or her action caused actual harm, that he or she acted knowingly without consent, and that the victim had an expectation of privacy." (Halloran, 2014)

Those who favor criminalizing revenge porn also note that not all speech is subject to First Amendment protections, e.g., obscenity, fraud, defamation, true threats (as illustrated by *Elonis v. United States*), incitement, or speech integral to criminal conduct (United States v. Cassidy, 2011). Finally, proponents of criminalization argue that criminal laws are needed because revenge porn when combined with online impersonation has the potential for physical harm to the victim as illustrated by *U.S. v. Sayer*.

In addition to the new and proposed laws targeting revenge porn, there are several groups that have been created to help victims of revenge porn to include the previously mentioned CCRI and Without My Consent. Among other things, these organizations provide victims step-by-step instructions on how to remove revenge porn images from the Internet. These groups also attempt to bring attention to the problems raised by revenge porn and look for long-term solutions to prevent it from reoccurring.

References

18 U.S.C. § 2261(1)–(2) (2006).
18 U.S.C. § 875(c).
Ariz. Rev. Stat. § 13-1425 (2014).

Bahr, J. (2012, March 28). *No Jail Time for Woman Accused in ID Theft*. Retrieved Nov. 30, 2014 from The Observer Online: http://www.theobserver.com/?p=6981.

Brady, E., & George, R. (2013, January 18). *Manti Te'o's 'Catfish' Story is a Common One*. Retrieved Nov. 30, 2014 from USA Today: http://www.usatoday.com/story/sports/ncaaf/2013/01/17/manti-teos-catfish-story-common/1566438/.

Brenner, S. (2012). *Cybercrime, Criminal Threats from Cyberspace* (First Indian Edition ed.). New Delhi: Pentagon Press.

Brenner, S. W. (2010). *Cybercrime: Criminal Threats from Cyberspace*. Secaucus, New Jersey: Praeger.

Brief of the Domestic Violence Legal Empowerment and Appeals Project and Professor Margaret Drew as Amici Curiae in Support of Respondent, at 1, Elonis v. United States, 2014 WL 5035111 ((2014) (No. 13-983)).

Brill, S. (2014, Feb. 25). *The Growing Trend of 'Revenge Porn' and the Criminal Laws that May Follow*. Retrieved Nov. 23, 2014, from Huffington Post: http://www.huffingtonpost.com/steven-brill/the-growing-trend-of-revenge-porn_b_4849990.html.

Cal. Pen. Code §647 (2014).

Cal. Pen. Code, §528.5(a) (West 2014).

Cal. Penal Code §§422, 646.9. (n.d.).

Corbin, C. (2013, Sep. 12). *'Revenge Porn' Victim Devotes, Life to Fighting to Change Nation's Laws*, Retrieved Nov. 30, 2014 from Fox News: http://www.foxnews.com/us/2013/09/12/florida-woman-victimized-by-nude-photos-fights-against-cyber-rape/.

Crocker, L. (2014, Jun. 28). *Too Late to 'Pologize for NSA Revenge Porn Leak*. Retrieved Nov. 25, 2014 from The Daily Beast: http://www.thedailybeast.com/articles/2014/06/28/too-late-to-pologize-for-nsa-revenge-porn-leak.html.

Drake, B. (2014, Dec. 1). *The Darkest Side of Online Harassment: Menacing Behavior*. Retrieved Dec. 1, 2014 from Pew Research Center: http://www.pewresearch.org/fact-tank/2014/12/01/the-darkest-side-of-online-harassment-menacing-behavior/.

Dubow, B. (2007, Mar. 8). *Confessions of "Facebook Stalkers."* Retrieved Nov. 20, 2014 from USA TODAY: http://usatoday30.usatoday.com/tech/webguide/internetlife/2007-03-07-facebook-stalking_n.htm.

Goodno, N. H. (2007). Cyberstalking, a New Crime: Evaluating the Effectiveness of Current State and Federal Laws. *Mo. L. Rev., 72* (125).

Halloran, L. (2014, Mar. 6). *Race to Stop 'Revenge Porn' Raises Free Speech Worries*. Retrieved Nov. 23, 2014 from NPR: http://www.npr.org/blogs/

itsallpolitics/2014/03/06/286388840/race-to-stop-revenge-porn-raises-free-speech-worries.

Hoffmeister, T. A. (2012). Investigating Jurors in the Digital Age: One Click at a Time. *University of Kansas Law Review, 60*, 611–648.

Lipton, J. (2011). Combating Cyber-Victimization. *Berkeley Tech. L. J.,* (26) 1104. Mass. Gen. Laws Ann. 265 § 43 (West 2014).

McIntyre v. Ohio Elections Comm'n, 514 U.S. 334 (1995).

McKalin, V. (2014, Feb. 16). *Sexting Not Just Popular Among Teens, New Study Suggests*. Retrieved Nov. 23, 2014 from Tech Times: http://www.techtimes.com/articles/3434/20140216/sexting-not-just-popular-among-teens-new-study-suggests.htm.

Miller, M. (2013, Oct. 17). *Revenge Porn Victim Holly Jacobs "Ruined My Life," Ex Says*. Retrieved Dec. 1 2014 from Miami New Times: http://www.miaminewtimes.com/2013-10-17/news/revenge-porn-holly-jacobs-ryan-seay/.

Perry, K. (2013, Dec. 9). *"Revenge Porn" Case Involves Doctor, Patient*. Retrieved Nov. 22, 2014 from Enquirer: http://archive.cincinnati.com/article/20131209/NEWS/312090018/-Revenge-porn-case-involves-doctor-patient.

Smith, N. (2013, Feb. 5). *Security of Risque Photos Overestimated*. Retrieved Nov. 22, 2014 from Business News Daily: http://www.businessnewsdaily.com/3887-scorned-partners-may-expose-data.html.

Stark, E. (2013). Coercive Control. In N. Lombard, & L. McMillan, *Violence Against Women: Current Theory & Practice in Domestic Abuse* (pp. 17–33). Jessica Kingsley.

Tex. Penal Code, § 33.07(a) (West 2013).

United States v. Cassidy, 814 F. Supp. 2d 574 (D. Md. 2011).

United States v. Elonis, CRIM. A. 11-13, 2011 WL 5024284 (E.D. Pa. Oct. 20, 2011).

United States v. Sayer, Nos. 2:11-CR-113-DBH, 2:11-CR-47-DBH (D. Me. May 15, 2012).

United States v. Wheeler, 12-CR-0138-WJM, 2013 WL 1942213 (D. Colo. May 10, 2013).

Valenti, J. (2014, June 26). *It's Still Revenge Porn When the Victim is a Man and the Picture is of his Penis*. Retrieved Nov. 25, 2014 from The Guardian:http://www.theguardian.com/commentisfree/2014/jun/26/revenge-porn-victim-conservative-man-penis

Watts v. United States, 394 U.S. 705 (1969).

White, J. (2010, May 12). *Girl Who Posed as Boy on Facebook Arrested for Stalking*. Retrieved Nov. 20, 2014 from Wash. Post: http://voices.washingtonpost.com/crime-scene/josh-white/a-14-year-old-prince-william-c.html.

White, M. (2012, Oct 7). *Revenge Porn: Caught in a Web of Spite.* Retrieved November 26, 2014 from Sydney Morning Herald: http://www.smh.com.au/digital-life/digital-life-news/revenge-porn-caught-in-a-web-of-spite-20131007-2v21q.html.

Windsor, E. (2014, Aug. 14). Retrieved November 15, 2014 from Twitter: https://twitter.com/Queen_UK.

Chapter Ten

Future Directions

Shelly Clevenger

The preceding chapters have presented an overview of a gamut of offenses committed online and/or with the use of technology. In moving forward into the future, it is imperative that there be more attention paid to the connection between technology and crime, particularly in regards to intimate partner abuse (IPA), crimes against children, and sex crimes. This chapter will present a discussion about what is needed in the future in terms of prevention, ways to assist the victims as well as the offender, and also how to expand upon current practices or programs. The need for legislation will also be presented.

Prevention

Cybercrime or crime committed using technology is in need of greater preventative measures. As many of these crimes are new, people working in the field, or in society in general, may be unfamiliar with the ways that they are committed and also how to protect themselves. In order to work to prevent these types of crimes, awareness and education are important. This section will provide suggestions for the future in terms of prevention for law enforcement, individuals, youth, and corporate efforts.

Law Enforcement

One of the key agenda items for many law enforcement agencies, as well as educational institutions is prevention of crime. While crimes using technology are new and the investigative initiatives a work in progress, there is hope for the future through programs that show promise. Collaboration among law enforcement agencies to fight and prevent online offenses is a key component going forward. As many local law enforcement agencies struggle with apprehending, charging and prosecuting Internet crimes, there is the need for training, guidance and/or a partnership from a federal agency in order for there to be improvement in the future.

There are some current partnerships of this nature which provide encouragement and could serve as model for other programs and/or warrant expansion. One such program that shows promise is *The Internet Crimes against Children* (ICAC) *Task Force Program*. It was created in 1998 to assist federal, state, and local law enforcement to produce and implement programs regarding crimes committed against children online and it continues to expand. The ICAC currently works to train individuals to investigate and prevent Internet crimes. In 2013, the ICAC trained over 30,000 law enforcement personnel, more than 3,500 prosecutors and 5,300 other professionals working in the field (Office of Juvenile Justice and Delinquency Prevention, 2014). Research has indicated by investing resources in departments and the training of officers to investigate these types of crimes, it has led to greater success in the overall investigation (Marcum, Higgins, Freiburger and Ricketts, 2010; Marcum and Higgins, 2011), which is why providing more agencies and individuals with training and resources would likely mean more success in prevention of such crimes in the future.

Another promising program is U.S. Immigration and Customs Enforcement (ICE) and Homeland Security Investigations (HSI) *Operation Predator*. This is an international project that seeks to identify, investigate and apprehend offenders who produce, possess and exchange child pornography, travel abroad for sex with minors and participate in sex trafficking with children. In order to accomplish this goal, *Operation Predator* works with local and state law enforcement across the United States and also participates in 61 Internet Crimes Against Children (ICAC) Task Forces. The HSI also works with other federal agencies, such as the National Center for Missing & Exploited Children, to maximize effectiveness and resources.

One of the unique aspects of *Operation Predator* is that the program is worldwide and has formed a partnership with Interpol, and HSI special agents have been placed in foreign countries to investigate crimes. In addition, HSI helped found the *Virtual Global Taskforce* which joins law enforcement, nongovernmental agencies and also private partners to combat child exploitation and pornography on a global scale. *Operation Predator* has also targeted individual citizens to become involved in the fight against these types of online crimes. The program developed an app that individuals may download to their phones or notebooks. The app provides alerts about predators that may be shared with others through social media and email. It also lets the user submit information online and provides a toll free number that one could call. The app gives the user updates about arrests and prosecutions of offenders and supplies other resources available for them to access regarding ICE and global initiatives.

The Internet Crimes against Children (ICAC) *Task Force Program* and *Operation Predator* are a good starting point for future initiatives. In moving forward, one of the pertinent items for prevention of Internet crimes is increasing training for those individuals working in the criminal justice system. As many personnel currently working in law enforcement or in prosecution of such crimes may not have the knowledge of how Internet and technology-based crimes are committed or how to go about investigating them, training is essential. Through training and education, these individuals can become better prepared in the future to identify, investigate and prosecute the offense. This training may come at the hands of a partnership between local and state or federal law enforcement agencies. An expansion of the ICAC to even more individuals across the country is needed so that everyone nationwide is equipped to handle these types of crimes. The nature of Internet crimes differs from other types of crime and as such requires collaboration between agencies. Also, working with others on a global scale through *Operation Predator* is another step in the right direction for the future. Due to the fact that the Internet connects individuals, including offenders, worldwide, an initiative to work to fight these crimes on a global scale is important. The future of law enforcement in preventing online crimes hinges upon the fact that they become trained and properly educated on the basics of these crimes.

Individuals

One of the key issues for individuals is how to protect themselves from victimization online. This will continue to be a growing concern for the future as the world continues to become more technologically advanced and reliant upon technology. There are currently programs that a person could utilize to protect themselves from certain online crimes. However, the issue becomes how many people are aware of these programs or would have access to them. There is also the issue of a lack of training of individuals in the field to assist individuals with these programs or software. For the future of prevention, the proper expansion of these programs, increased awareness for consumers, and education of individuals who work in the field with victims would allow more individuals to benefit from these services. There are a few programs that, if expanded, show promise.

The first promising program is through *Tor*, which was originally created and implemented as a project for the U.S. Navy to guard communication. It is currently used today by civilians to stop a person from tracking another's transmission location, see who they are talking to online or what sites they are visiting, as it protects against "traffic analysis." *Tor* offers the *Tor Browser Bun-*

dle, which is free software that is similar to ordinary browsers, but it comes configured to make it harder for individuals to be tracked online. The Browser Bundle works to delete a person's browser's history, location, and IP address from the website the person is browsing. It also erases traces from the computer the browser is hosted on. This software is available online through *Tor's* website and there are online instructions to assist users.

Tor has also been working with domestic violence programs in the hopes of counteracting cyberstalking. *Tor* provides an incognito operating system that allows victims to be anonymous online with an onion router that hides their identity so as not to allow their stalker or abuser to know that they are online and/ or what they are doing online (Tor, 2014). This allows for the prevention of cyberstalking as the offender would not be able to trace where the individual is and/or what they are doing online. However, while the services offered by *Tor* are a step in the right direction for assisting victims and preventing crime, many social workers and employees in domestic violence shelters do not have the technological skills needed to assist interested individuals with installation or operation of these types of programs. In aims to improve that, *Tor* has partnered with *Emerge*, the *National Network to End Domestic Violence* (NNEDV) and *Transition House*, a domestic violence shelter in Cambridge, Massachusetts, to educate personnel about the technology that could assist victims (Neal, 2014).

In order for a greater number of victims to benefit, these services and education need to be expanded to more employees in a greater number of locations in the future as many victims struggle with issues of cyberstalking and harassment and often face a limited amount of resources available to help them. The use of software by *Tor*, or ones like it, could enable victims to keep themselves and their information safe and prevent cyberstalking and also allow them to reach out for help online in a safe way (Tor, 2014).

There has also been another promising initiative, *The Technology Safety Project* of the Washington State Coalition against Domestic Violence. This is a pilot project working to assist victims and prevent future incidents of abuse, both online and off and has been working to increase safe computer and Internet access for victims of domestic violence. This is being done through education about safety and privacy online, as well as how to use technology to help find resources for victims, such as jobs and housing. At each domestic violence shelter or service agency, there is one employee at the site who receives technology training and they then become the "Tech Advocate" who is responsible for training other staff, volunteers, and victims. In addition to the technology training, another unique component about this program is that it examines whether the victims receiving services have experienced any kind of abuse from the offender online or through the use of technology. Most domestic violence shelters or agencies do not ask in their intake interviews or evaluations if there was a cyber or technology component to the abuse, but this project has incorporated that into its protocol (Washington State Coalition Against Domestic Violence, 2014).

A review of this program found that the majority of the 384 respondents were very satisfied with the training, with 86.2 percent reporting high satisfaction (Finn & Atkinson, 2009). In the future, components of *The Technology Safety Project* could be incorporated to other states domestic violence shelters or service agencies. Training individuals working in domestic violence shelters on ways to help victims protect themselves online could improve the quality of the services offered. In addition, asking victims who receive services about abuse through technology and the Internet would allow for more information to be collected and known about an emerging topic and assist agencies in helping victims.

In addition, *The National Center for Victims of Crime* has created a Stalking Resource Center that provides a plethora of information for individuals on their website about stalking, both in-person and cyberstalking. One such item that is available online is a printable document that is a stalking log. It allows the victim to keep track of information pertaining to incidents of stalking. The document has a place for the victim to enter the date, time, and location of the incident, as well as a witness name, address and phone number (if there was a witness). There is also a place to record the police report number, officer's name who took the incident and their badge number (The National Center for Victims of Crime, 2014). This form is geared toward in-person stalking. However, this form could be modified for cyberstalking victims. For the "location," the form could include "Type of stalking" or "Mode of stalking" and a place to add a description of what type of cyberstalking incident occurred. For example, the victim could enter if the incident involved email or Facebook or a cell phone and provide the specific details. The use of this form would be beneficial for victims of stalking to use, as well as for law enforcement and domestic violence agencies as it could assist in more success in the arrest and prosecution of offenders. In addition, recording such information on a regular basis may assist in more information being known about the nature of cyberstalking and ways victim can protect themselves.

Overall, there are some promising programs that currently exist that can help individuals protect themselves online. Moving into the future, the expansion of programs, as well as promotion of the services available, is necessary to help people. For many, the idea of cyber victimization is still a new phenomenon in which they may not be familiar or aware of until they find themselves being victimized. The use of *Tor* software can assist individuals in protecting their online privacy and also help victims to seek out help. The initiatives that are being seen with *The Technology Safety Project* and *The National Center for Victims of Crime* Stalking Resource Center are both promising and provide hope for the future. However, it will only be through the other domestic violence shelters offering technology assistance and asking about abuse online that more victims can be helped and more information known about that aspect of abuse, as well as the incorporation of the cyberstalking log for use by victims and also disseminated for use by law enforcement and domestic violence shelters/agencies.

Youth

One of the key demographics for prevention of online crimes is young people, and prevention programs are often held in schools. Programs of this nature, often referred to as Internet Safety Education (ISE) programs, are a recent initiative in which schools are trying to prevent the victimization of children online. Some of the leading programs in the nation are *IKeepSafe*, *I-SAFE*, *Netsmartz,* and *Web Wise Kids.* All of these programs incorporate safety tips and information about prevention in their materials that are passed out to schools or disseminated online. However, Jones, Mitchell and Walsh (2013) discovered that in their evaluation of these four programs that the current approach is not effective. They point to the lack of research-based information on topics such as online predators and harassment, as well a failure to provide skill-based learning objectives. The researchers also note that there is a lack of opportunities for youth to practice new skills and there is insufficient time for learning. Part of the issue with these current programs is that law enforcement is not trained in pedagogy and curriculum development, and they are often the ones administering the education to children in schools. Jones, Mitchell and Walsh (2013) suggest that they also may not have the best attitude in regards to the subject matter as officers have the tendency to focus on crime, danger, and punishment. It is also often difficult for law enforcement with the many demands on their time to commit to teach these sessions on a regular basis. The solution may be to have law enforcement personnel present laws relating to topics in the sessions and have someone else, such as a school resource officer or teacher, teach the other information (Jones, Mitchell and Walsh, 2013). However, if the programs were to be taught by an officer, it could be beneficial to have one officer assigned to teaching the sessions and perhaps receive training in teaching and curriculum development before implementing the ISE. Jones, Mitchell and Walsh (2013) suggest that changes in the overall curriculum of the ISE programs are in order for success to be seen. For example, they suggest that a one-time 45-minute program that instructs youth not to cyber bully or not to share sexual pictures is not an effective intervention as most youth know that this behavior is wrong and/or risky, and a one-time program is not enough. Multiple intervention programs of adequate length that provide an enhanced utilization of research about online behaviors/crimes, more active learning strategies, and skill building that allow youth to absorb the information as well as practice the skills they learn are essential.

In addition, ISE programs need to eliminate or rely less upon the use of scare tactics as part of the information provided. Most youth do not participate in the behaviors in which the ISE are trying to scare them out of. Most ISE programs combine topics and strategies. This is problematic as the tools that a young person would need to avoid cyber bullying are different than those needed to recognize being groomed by a predator online or to be able to identify if they are being cyberstalked. The topics may be in need of an overhaul as subjects such as Internet predators, in which it is often assumed and presented that the predator uses deceit and lures the child to meet with them. But in reality, this type of situation typically involves a teen who knows how old the offender is and agrees to meet for the sexual encounter as they believe that they are in love with this person. Sexting is another topic that has many facets within youth culture that is not yet fully understood and may require a delicate hand in presentation. Warning youth that if they sext they may face prosecution, sex offender status and harsh punishments may not be the best way to deter them from such behavior.

Corporate Efforts

As Internet use continues to expand, the involvement of corporations to assist in the prevention and prosecution of cybercrime may become necessary. The largest and most widely used search engine, Google, has taken steps to combat Internet crimes, such as identity theft, cyberstalking, cyberbullying, child pornography and exploitation of children. Users of Google can access all of the items though the Google Safety Center. This provides how-to guides for users to take steps to protect themselves and their families. For example, part of the Safety Center includes the use the *Safe Search* function to block pornographic images from appearing in search results (Google Safety Center, 2014).

Google has also partnered with local law enforcement, as well federal agencies, to assist with investigations pertaining to online crime. Google has partnered with the National Center for Missing and Exploited Children to promote an online campaign which educates Internet users, promotes safety and provides resources. They have also supported the program of *Wired Safety*, which provides training to youth. Google has a team within the company devoted to assisting with efforts to combat child exploitation and child pornography.

Google prohibits any type of advertising that promotes illegal material and consistently reviews the site. If any child pornography is discovered, it is reported to the *National Center for Missing and Exploited Children*. The company encourages individuals using Google to report illegal ads and, once found, Google removes it immediately. In the future, other corporate efforts and partnerships with law enforcement could assist in the fight against online victimization (GetNetWise, 2014).

In addition to Google, Verizon Wireless has also taken part in the effort to assist with prevention of cybercrimes, as well as help victims of domestic violence. In 2001, the company launched *HopeLine*. This is a program that provides phones that have been refurbished and provide the user with talk, text, voicemail and caller ID functions (Verizon Wireless, 2014). This program is useful for all victims of intimate partner abuse, but it can be especially helpful to those who have had issues with cyberstalking or tracking of their phones by their partner. Having a new phone that the abuser is unaware of can allow for victims to start over and prevent future victimization.

Offenders

Online offenders may have different treatment needs than those who commit offenses offline. Going forward, addressing the needs of this specific group of offenders could reduce crime. In terms of existing treatment programs specifically aimed at online offenders, it is rather limited. However, as Internet and technology-based crimes continue to increase, there will be more a need for programs aimed at treating these offenders. There are two programs that show promise. One is based in the United Kingdom and targets online sexual offenses, and the other is a pilot program in the United States that targets online behaviors of domestic abusers.

The Internet Sex Offender Treatment Program (i-SOTP), operated in the United Kingdom, could serve as a model for programs in the United States. This program was implemented in 2006 and is aimed at treating male offenders who have been convicted of non-contact Internet offenses. The offenders who take part in this program are assessed and placed into a low, medium or high risk category using a risk matrix. If the offender falls into a high risk category, or they used the Internet to commit contact offenses, they will be treated in a longer term, more general sex offender treatment program (Middleton, Mandeville-Norden, & Hayes, 2009). The program consists of a group therapy format with 35 two-hour sessions that are delivered twice a week. The program covers issues such as the motivation behind offending and what needs it met for the offender, awareness of the victim, building emotional and relationship skills, as well as a plan for a new life and ways to prevent relapses into offending (National Sex Offender Management Service, 2014). Middleton, Mandeville-Norden & Hayes (2009), in their assessment of the i-SOTP, found that over time the offenders who participated in the program were more apt to take responsibility for their actions, had a reduction in attitudes which were supportive of child sexual abuse and a reduction in the over-identification they had with children.

Another example of a promising program that could be a model for implementing future programs is currently in its early stages and is being operated by *Emerge*. The organization was founded in 1977 with the goal of treating domestic violence offenders. Recently, the program is working to address the online component of intimate partner abuse, as well as the physical. This is being done through incorporating the treatment of online offenders into traditional offender treatment programs that in the past only targeted other types of domestic abuse. This is being done as it is being recognized that intimate partner abuse can occur through technology and the Internet as well as in person (Emerge, 2014).

The fact that the i-SOTP program targeted online sexual offenders and *Emerge* is working to address the online component of domestic violence with a specific treatment plan provides groundwork for future programs. However, in the creation of such programs, there should also be enhancements made that set up an offender for success. Even if an offender who committed an online offense received a specialized treatment program, the skills that they acquire in treatment may not be able to be transferred to the online environment. One reason for this is that when the offender is receiving treatment, they may not be online, as part of the punishment for online offenses typically is no Internet access. If the offender cannot legally access the Internet while being treated, the offender is not able to aptly apply the skills that are being learned in treatment. This poses a problem as the offender will inevitably go back to Internet use eventually and there may be quite a gap from the time they receive the treatment to their return to the use of the Internet (De Almeida Neto, Eylanda, Wareb, Galouzisa, & Kevin, 2013). Part of an offender's treatment needs to include a transition into proper online use. This could be done through treatment as well as through computerized brief interventions. The computerized intervention would consist of questions asked to the offender to assess the risk for reoffending and how closely their therapy goals are being met with their current online behavior. This can serve to reinforce good decisions and behavior and rectify poor ones. Also, if this questionnaire to gauge progress is conducted online, this could be beneficial as this is the environment in which the crime was committed. It can help the offender reacquaint him/herself with positive online behaviors. Also, if it is done while the offender is in therapy, it can be addressed. This technique has been utilized in the past with treatment of Internet addiction (Young, 2006). The use of the online routine questionnaires, having the offender reintegrate to online use while in therapy, with the intervention could potentially benefit offenders and help to reduce crime.

Legislation

While there has been headway made in criminalizing cybercrimes, there are still behaviors that need to be addressed with the passage of legislation in order to help victims and prevent crime. One area that is still lacking legislation is revenge pornography. Revenge pornography (also referred to as non-consensual pornography or cyber rape) occurs when a person posts and/or distributes naked or sexual photographs or videos of an individual without their consent online (even if the picture was initially taken with consent of the individual). In addition to posting the photo or video online, the offender can also provide personal information about the individual. This can include their name, address, telephone number, email address, as well as place of employment. Offender can also provide links to the social media pages of the victim so that the person viewing the photo or video can have direct access to the person online. This can be publicly and emotionally damaging to victims. It can also put the victim in physical danger when the offender attaches the victim's personal information along with the image.

Offenders who commit revenge pornography are often protected as not all states have a law criminalizing this act. In 2013 and 2014, legislation against revenge pornography was enacted in 15 states (Arizona, California, Colorado, Delaware, Georgia, Hawaii, Idaho, Maryland, New York, New Jersey, Pennsylvania, Texas, Utah, Virginia, and Wisconsin). In 2014, bills were introduced or pending in 28 states. However, in some states the laws have failed to be enacted (Alabama, Connecticut, Florida, Kentucky, Missouri, South Carolina, Tennessee, and Washington) (National Conference of State Legislatures, 2014). There have been arguments made that laws against revenge pornography violate the First Amendment and the freedom of speech, that individuals should be able to freely express themselves by posting pictures and/or videos online, especially when these items are their personal property.

The Cyber Civil Rights Initiative (CCRI) has created a campaign, *End Revenge Porn*, with the goal of educating the public, raising awareness and also lobbying for the passage of state and federal laws criminalizing revenge pornography, without imposing on the First Amendment. The CCRI is currently working with legislators to pass these laws and seeks to have a federal law against revenge porn. The passage of a federal law would prompt states to enact their own legislation, as well as have law enforcement investigate and prosecute these crimes. Legislation criminalizing revenge porn is necessary as many victims find themselves without options. Many victims who report incidents to the police find that since the photo or video was legally obtained by the offender with the victim's consent that it legally belongs to the offender and is their property and the offender cannot be prosecuted under criminal harassment laws. Another problem that victims face is that when an offender posts pictures to a revenge porn site, one must pay in order to the have the pictures removed. Without any legal remedies or rights provided to the victims under the law, they often find themselves feeling powerless.

Revenge porn legislation is not just a domestic issue, but international as well. Currently, there is a law proposed as part of a more general Criminal Justice and Courts Bill in the United Kingdom that is working its way through Parliament. If this passes, the law would include revenge porn photos that are shared through social networks, email, text message and paper. Guilty offenders could face up to two years' incarceration (BBC News, 2014). Also, sexual images used to threaten and coerce an individual into sexual activity could be prosecuted under the Sexual Offences Act 2003, which carries a maximum sentence of 14 years' incarceration. The passage of this revenge porn legislation is the United Kingdom's way of making a statement about the wrongness of revenge porn and attempting to fight back against those that commit such acts (Ross, 2014).

While the legality of revenge porn still hangs in the balance, there remains the issue of the revenge porn sites that offenders can post pictures and information on. In the past, operators of revenge sites also have come under fire for allowing these types of images and information to be posted. Hunter Moore's *Is Anyone Up?*, a website which published photos of young girls, as well as revenge porn, in addition to including an image had the name, addresses and employers of the women in the photo or video, was shut down in 2012 after a variety of law suits and campaigns which attacked the website.

However, there are other sites to take its place. Myex.com is still a functioning site in which individuals can post pictures or videos directly to the web. It is an international site and contains postings from all over the world. In order to post on this site, the required information one must have about the person in the image is their name, country they live in, gender and age. There is also a place for the person to enter the Facebook or Twitter information for the victim. Myex.com also requires the person submitting the photo or video to write up a title and an explanation about the person featured. In this area, a person can include whatever other information that they want, such as home address, phone number or employer information. Additionally, you can search this site for a person by name in the search box (Myex.com).

The site claims that if a victim wants to find out who posts the pictures that Myex.com does not keep records of who posts, such as emails, or IP addresses, that images are untraceable. This site does offer a button next to the picture or video that says "Remove my name." However, the site does not provide much guidance about what this exact process is. An individual must fill out information on a link on the site and either provide documentation that the images are copyrighted and owned by them or provide a photo ID. That is all the information given for the removal process other than this statement "As a general rule if you don't want photos of you ending up on the internet be more careful who you send them too or better yet don't send them at all." Myex.com does state that law enforcement will be given top priority with requests submitted for removal of images (Myex.com, 2014). Without legislation against revenge pornography, this site and its contents are totally legal. Myex.com was only one example of a revenge porn site; there are others just like it up and operating. In moving forward, legislation needs to be passed to criminalize revenge porn and also websites that propagate it.

References

BBS News. (2014 13, October) *'Revenge porn' illegal under new UK law.* http://www.bbc.com/news/29596583.

The Cyber Civil Rights Initiative. (2014). *End revenge porn.* http://www.cybercivilrights.org/erp_campaign.

De Almeida Neto, A. C., Eylanda, S., Wareb, J., Galouzisa, J., & Kevin, A. (2013). Brief Interventions: Solving the 'Internet Sex Offender Paradox'. *Psychiatry, Psychology and Law, 20,* (2): 182–187.

Emerge. (2014). http://www.emergedv.com/.

Finn, K., & Atkinson, T. (2009). Promoting the Safe and Strategic Use of Technology for Victims of Intimate Partner Violence: Evaluation of the Technology Safety Project. *Journal of Family Violence, 24,* 53–9.

Getnetwise (2014). Google Online Initiatives for Internet Safety. http://www.getnetwise.org/about/supporters/google.

Google Safety Center. (2014). https://www.google.com/safetycenter/.

Jones, L. M., Mitchell, K. J., & Walsh, W.A. (2013) *Evaluation of Internet Child Safety Materials Used by ICAC Task Forces in School and Community Settings, Final Report.* U.S. Department of Justice. https://www.ncjrs.gov/pdffiles1/nij/grants/242016.pdf.

Marcum, C. D., & Higgins, G. E. (2011). Combating Child Exploitation Online: Predictors of Successful ICAC Task Forces. *Policing,* 5 (4): 310–316.

Marcum, C. D., Higgins, G. E., Freiburger, T. L., and Ricketts, M. L. (2010). 'Policing Possession of Child Pornography Online: Investigating the Training and Resources Dedicated to the Investigation of Cyber Crime.' *International Journal of Police Science and Management* 12(4): 516–525.

Middleton, D., Mandeville-Norden, R., & Hayes, E. (2009). Does treatment work with internet sex offenders? Emerging findings from the Internet Sex Offender Treatment Programme (i-SOTP). *Journal of Sexual Aggression,* 15, 5–19.

Myex.com. (2014). *Submit your ex.* http://www.myex.com/.

National Center for Victims of Crime. (2014). *Stalking Resource Center.* http://www.victimsofcrime.org/our-programs/stalking-resource-center.

National Conference of State Legislatures. (2014). *State revenge porn legislation.* http://www.ncsl.org/research/telecommunications-and-information-technology/state-revenge-pornlegislation.aspx.

National Sex Offender Management Service. (2014). *Internet Sex Offender Treatment Programme* (i-sotp). http://cppt.org.uk/what-we-do/accredited-programmes/sexual-offender-treatment-programme/i-sotp/.

Neal, M. (2014, May 9). *Tor Is Being Used as a Safe Haven for Victims of Cyberstalking.* Motherboard. http://motherboard.vice.com/read/tor-is-being-used-as-a-safe-haven-for-victims-of-cyberstalking.

Office of Juvenile Justice and Delinquency Prevention. (2014). The Internet Crimes against Children (ICAC) Task Force Program. http://www.ojjdp.gov/programs/progsummary.asp?pi=3.

Ross, T. (2014, October 12). *U.K. to make 'revenge porn' illegal: Ex-partners will face up to two years in jail for sharing intimate images.* The Telegraph. http://news.nationalpost.com/2014/10/12/u-k-to-make-revenge-porn-illegal-ex-partners-will-face-up-to-two-years-in-jail-for-sharing-intimate-images/.

Tor (2014). *Tor Project: Anonymity Online.* https://www.torproject.org/.

U.S. Immigration and Customs Enforcement (ICE). (2014). Homeland Security Investigations (HSI). Operation Predator. http://www.ice.gov/predator/.

Verizon Wireless. (2014). *HopeLine.* http://www.verizonwireless.com/aboutus/hopeline/.

Washington State Coalition Against Domestic Violence (2014). *Technology Safety Pilot Project.* http://wscadv2.org/projects.cfm?aid=3920a1b9-c298-58f6-0ff4c59527bafe6d.

Working to Halt Online Abuse (2014). http://www.haltabuse.org/.

Young, K. (2006). *Internet Addiction Test (IAT).* Retrieved October 1, 2013, from http://www.netaddiction.com/resources/internet_addiction_test.htm.

Conclusion

This edited volume presented information on the intersection between technology and intimate partner violence (IPV). As technology has developed within the past decades, it has given way to new types of victimization. Offenders have utilized cell phones, computers and the Internet to harm their intimate partners and commit crime. Crimes such as cyberstalking, sexting, sextortion and revenge pornography are all a result of the current digital era in which technology dominates. Offenders are now able to terrorize their partners through acts of violence and aggression in person, as well as through technology. In response to the changing face of crime in the cyber era, law enforcement and legislators have had to change their approach and tactics. Law enforcement agencies at the local and federal level have increased efforts to prevent and combat these crimes with specialized training and task forces. In addition, legislation has been passed in many states (and is currently under consideration in others) to ensure that offenders are properly charged and victims receive justice.

Another important component of the impact of technology on IPV is the growth of academic research in the area. Research has revealed the characteristics, modus operandi and motives of offenders, the suffering of the victims and the response of the criminal justice system. The chapters within this volume discussed existing research and relevant topics, as well as presented theoretical tenets that represent the current state of IPV and cybercrime.

Index

Backchanneling, 61
Battered Husband Syndrome, 23, 38
Battered Wife Syndrome (Wife battery, 17, 25, 26, 32) (wife beating, 22, 25)
British Journal of Criminology, 179
Capable guardian, 144, 162
Catfishing, 141, 155, 156
Centers for Disease Control and Prevention (CDC), 14, 27, 28, 32, 33, 37, 39, 98, 108, 117, 137
Centre for Cyber Victim Counselling (CCVC), 169, 174, 175, 178, 179, 184
Cisgender, 32
Coercive Control, 15, 20, 36, 38, 96, 99, 100, 103, 116, 122, 123, 125, 126, 129, 136, 139, 203
Coercive Controlling Violence, 99
Common Couple Violence, 25, 36, 103, 119, 138
Conflict Tactics Scale, 22, 37, 39, 117
Content Related Crimes, 171, 173
Copresence, 48, 49, 51, 62, 63, 64, 74
Criminology, 75, 76, 78, 92, 93, 94, 119, 137, 161, 162, 163, 167, 184, 185

Cyber Obsessional Pursuit (COP), 106
Cyber dating abuse, 126, 130
Cyber romances, 6, 157
Cyberabuse, 96, 102, 103, 104, 105, 111, 113, 114, 115, 116, 125, 126, 127, 128, 129, 130, 131, 133, 135, 136
Cyberbullying, 75, 78, 84, 85, 91, 93, 94, 115, 126, 129, 130, 136, 138, 147, 158, 160, 161, 166, 173, 177, 184, 211
Cybercrime, 8, 9, 11, 80, 84, 90, 93, 94, 96, 102, 115, 125, 150, 152, 156, 164, 165, 167, 168, 169, 170, 171, 172, 173, 174, 175, 176, 177, 178, 179, 180, 181, 182, 183, 184, 185, 202, 205, 211, 212, 214, 219
Cyberharassment, 9, 95, 111, 115, 126, 129, 130, 131, 132, 133
Cyberspace, 7, 10, 11, 12, 66, 67, 68, 70, 71, 73, 114, 137, 138, 167, 168, 169, 170, 171, 172, 177, 181, 183, 185, 202
Cyberstalking, 9, 78, 82, 85, 94, 95, 101, 102, 104, 106, 111, 113–118, 121–128, 133–139, 183, 202, 208–212, 217, 219

Digital Millennium Copyright Act (DMCA), 197, 200
Digital piracy, 8
Domestic Abuse Intervention Project, 97, 116
Downward distribution, 142
Economic abuse, 20, 33
Elias, Ian Martin, 107
Elias, Nicollette Naomi, 107
Emerge, 32, 155, 208, 213, 216
Emotional abuse, 19, 20, 126
EndRevengePorn.org, 149
Exclusively Internet-Based Relationships, 43
Fake Avatar, 168, 169, 171, 172, 173, 177
Family violence researchers, 21, 25
Federal Interstate Stalking Punishment and Prevention Act (FISPPA), 195
Female vs. Male Sexting, 144
Feminist theorists, 21
Gay, 13, 29, 30, 31, 35, 36, 37
Gender symmetry, 21, 24, 25, 26, 28, 29, 34, 119, 123, 138
Google Safety Center, 211, 216
Global Positioning System (GPS), 100, 108, 109, 119, 122, 127, 128, 130, 132, 139
Gunn, Christopher, 151
Hacking, 8, 11, 77, 79, 94, 148, 150, 152, 162, 168, 169, 171, 176, 179, 199
Heterosexism, 30
Heterosexual, 13, 22, 29, 30, 31, 33, 34, 37, 117, 149, 154 (heterosexual intimate relationships, 24) (heterosexual IPA rates, 29)
High tech methods, 128
Homophobia, 30, 31, 33
Homosexual, 33, 37, 54, 154
Hyperpersonal communication, 6
Hyperpersonal interactions, 53, 54
Identity Support, 46, 48
IKeepSafe, I-SAFE, Netsmartz, and Web Wise Kids, 210
iknowthatgirl.com, 148
Illegal exploitation of mainframe computers and operating systems, 8
Information and Communication Technologies (ICT), 95, 100, 105, 111, 114, 115, 119, 134, 138, 170
Interlocutors, 43, 45, 46, 62
Internet, 3–12, 41–43, 50, 51, 53, 62, 65–74, 78, 85, 91, 93–95, 97, 100, 101, 105, 117, 118, 121, 122, 127, 130, 133, 134, 135, 137, 141, 143, 144, 147–158, 161, 162, 164, 167, 168, 170, 172–174, 176–185, 187, 188, 190, 191, 192, 195, 196, 197, 201, 202, 205–214, 216, 217, 219
Internet Crime Complaint Center (IC3), 176
Internet Safety Education (ISE) programs, 210
Interstate Communication Act (ICA), 192
IPA, 14, 15, 16, 17, 18, 19, 20, 21, 22, 25, 26, 27, 28, 29, 30, 31, 32, 125, 126, 127, 128, 129, 130, 131, 132, 136, 205
Intimate partner abuse, 8, 9, 13, 16, 19, 22, 23, 28, 96, 97, 98, 99,

100, 101, 103, 105, (intimate partner abusers, 112), 114, 116, 125, 137, 188, 205, 212, 213
Intimate partner terrorism, 96, 103, 105, 114
Intimate Partner Violence (IPV), 13, 30, 34, 35, 36, 37, 38, 39, 83, 84, 91, 98, 103, 117, 118, 119, 121, 122, 123, 139, 216, 219
Interpersonal cybercrimes, 167, 168, 169, 170, 171, 172, 173, 174, 175, 176, 177, 178, 179, 180, 181, 182
IsAnyoneup.com, 148
Jacobs, Holly, 112, 119, 149, 196, 197, 198, 200, 203
Keyloggers, 127, 128
Lesbian, 13, 29, 30, 31, 33, 35, 36, 37, 38, 39
LGBT, 18, 29, 30, 31, 32, 36
Lifestyle-Routine Activities Theory, 76, 77, 94
Logan, Jessica, 147, 165
Low tech methods, 127, 128
MacKinnon, Catharine, 104, 120
Male Gaze, 104
Malware attacks, 8
Martel, Jennifer, 14
Massively Multiplayer Online Role-Playing Games (MMORPGs), 49, 51, 52, 53, 54, 74
Moderation Hypothesis, 82, 83, 85
Motivated offender, 77, 81, 82, 144
Multiplexing, 43, 50, 62
Mulvey, Laura, 104
Mutual Violent Control, 26, 103, 131, 132
Myex.com, 215, 216, 216

Nonconsensual Pornography, 110, 112
Non-Governmental Organization (NGO), 175, 178, 180, 181, 182, 206
Obsessive Relational Intrusion (ORI), 106
Offline-to-online Relationships, 50, 62
Online dating/romance scams, 152–155
Online Harassment, 77, 84, 85, 91, 123, 124, 137, 183, 187, 192, 200, 202
Online Impersonation, 188–192
Online relationships, 5, 6, 7, 10, 12, 50–54, 62, 66, 69, 71, 73, 138
Online-to-offline Relationships, 54, 60
Operation Predator, 206, 207, 217
Opportunity Perspective, 75, 76, 79, 83
Patriarchy, 22, 25, 34, 118
Patriarchal Terrorism, 25, 26, 36 103, 119, 138
People v. Liberta, 17, 37
Physical abuse, 98, 100, 126
Primarily Internet-Based Relationships, 43, 73
Privacy Related Crimes, 171
realexgirlfriends.com, 148
Relational Identity, 45, 48, 62, 64, 65
Relationship Maintenance, 47, 48, 52, 63, 64, 66
Remy, Jared, 14, 34, 37
Revenge porn, 86, 110–112, 117, 118, 121, 141, 147–149, 156–159, 161–165, 168, 169,

171–173, 177, 178, 182, 184, 187–189, 196–204, 214–217, 219
Revenge porn legislation, 162, 215, 217
Romantic Relationship, 5, 7, 9, 41, 42, 43, 45, 46, 47, 48, 50, 52, 59, 62, 63, 64, 65, 66, 67, 70, 72, 73, 101, 106, 154
Rule of Thumb, 16
Safe Search, 211
Schulman, Nev, 54, 155, 164
Screenloggers, 127, 128
Seay, Ryan, 149, 203
Self, 44, 46, 48, 51, 53, 57, 58, 66, 68, 69, 71, 72, 73, 74, 155, 164
Self-presentation, 44, 46, 47, 54, 56, 57, 58, 59, 61, 63, 64, 65, 66, 65, 69, 72
Sexting, 79, 80, 86, 94, 110, 111, 118, 141, 142, 143, 144, 145, 146, 147, 156, 157, 158, 159, 160, 161, 162, 163, 164, 165, 200, 203, 211, 219
Sextortion, 141, 150, 151, 152, 156, 157, 158, 159, 160, 161, 162, 163, 219
Sexual abuse, 19, 20, 98, 114, 120, 126, 152, 213
Sexual solicitation of minors (in regards to minors) 6, 7, 172
Situational couple violence, 21, 26, 36, 103, 117, 119, 120, 131
Snail Mail, 42
Social guardianship, 168
Social Networking Sites (SNS), 41, 42, 43, 54, 61, 64, 67, 95, 100, 105, 132, 141, 152, 153, 155, 170, 172, 173, 174

Spiritual abuse, 15
Spyware, 100, 108, 109, 128, 135
Stalking Resource Center, 209, 210, 217
Suitable targets, 77
Symbolic Pictorial Attack, 171, 174
Technological abuse, 15
Telecopresence, 48, 49, 50
Texting, 112, 113, 132
The Cyber Civil Rights Initiative (CCRI), 111, 112, 148, 150, 198, 201, 214, 216
The General Theory of Crime, 75, 78, 80, 82, 92, 93, 144
The Internet Crimes against Children (ICAC), 206, 207, 216, 217
The Internet Crimes against Children (ICAC) Task Force Program, 151
The Internet Sex Offender Treatment Program (i-SOTP), 212, 217
The Laws of Chastisement, 16
The National Center for Victims of Crime, 209, 210
The Protection of Children against Sexual Exploitation Act, 145
The Technology Safety Project, 118, 208, 209, 210, 216
Threats, 15, 20, 21, 25, 27, 79, 82, 98, 100, 106, 107, 108, 111, 115–117, 121, 126, 128, 129, 132, 149–152, 169, 170, 172, 174, 187, 192–196, 201, 202
Tor, 207, 208, 209, 217
Tor Browser Bundle, 207
Transgender, 13, 29, 32, 36, 37, 39
Triple-A-Engine, 127

Trolling, 169, 171, 173, 174, 177
Unauthorized Access, 8, 171, 172
U.S. v. Elonis, 192
U.S. v. Sayer, 189, 201
Verbal abuse, 19, 113
Verizon Wireless Hopeline, 212, 217
Violence Against Women Act, 18, 21, 33, 97, 112, 123
Violent resistance, 26 36, 103, 119, 131, 132

Virtual Communities, 54, 60, 61
Youth Internet Safety Survey, 7
Warranting, 59, 65, 73
Webb, Amy, 57, 58
Working to Halt Online Abuse (WHOA) 101, 123, 169, 175, 178, 179, 217
XTube, 148